BEAUVOIR AND POLITICS

Approaching Simone de Beauvoir's feminism and social commentary as a resource to understand our current crises, *Beauvoir and Politics: A Toolkit* brings together established and emerging scholars to apply her insights to gender studies, political philosophy, decolonisation, intellectual history, age theory, and critical phenomenology. This collection starts from key concepts in Beauvoir's oeuvre and relates them to contemporary debates, asking how her notion of ambiguity speaks to lived experiences that have been highly politicized in recent years. The volume offers an important critical appraisal of Beauvoir's legacy, demonstrating the contemporary relevance of her thought as it diagnoses the present and looks toward change for a better future.

Liesbeth Schoonheim is a post-doctoral researcher (*Wissenschaftliche Mitarbeiterin*) in political theory at Humboldt University in Berlin, Germany. Recent publications include "Resistance: An Arendtian Reading of Solidarity and Friendship in Foucault" (2021, *Foucault Studies*) and "Beauvoir and Writing as the Creation of the Self: Memoirs, Diaries, Biography" (2020, *Sartre Studies International*).

Karen Vintges is an associate researcher at the Amsterdam Institute for Humanities Research of the University of Amsterdam. Her publications include *Feminism and the Final Foucault* (co-edited with Dianna Taylor, 2004) and *A New Dawn for the Second Sex: Women's Freedom Practices in World Perspective* (2017), and other books in Dutch.

BEAUVOIR AND POLITICS

A Toolkit

Edited by Liesbeth Schoonheim and Karen Vintges

Designed cover image: © Alba Martínez Feito

First published 2024
by Routledge
605 Third Avenue, New York, NY 10158

and by Routledge
4 Park Square, Milton Park, Abingdon, Oxon OX14 4RN

Routledge is an imprint of the Taylor & Francis Group, an Informa business

© 2024 selection and editorial matter, Liesbeth Schoonheim and Karen Vintges; individual chapters, the contributors

The right of Liesbeth Schoonheim and Karen Vintges to be identified as the authors of the editorial material, and of the authors for their individual chapters, has been asserted in accordance with sections 77 and 78 of the Copyright, Designs and Patents Act 1988.

All rights reserved. No part of this book may be reprinted or reproduced or utilized in any form or by any electronic, mechanical, or other means, now known or hereafter invented, including photocopying and recording, or in any information storage or retrieval system, without permission in writing from the publishers.

Trademark notice: Product or corporate names may be trademarks or registered trademarks, and are used only for identification and explanation without intent to infringe.

Library of Congress Cataloging-in-Publication Data
Names: Schoonheim, Liesbeth, editor. | Vintges, Karen, editor.
Title: Beauvoir and Politics: A Toolkit / edited by Liesbeth Schoonheim and Karen Vintges.
Description: New York, NY : Routledge, 2023. | Includes bibliographical references and index. |
Identifiers: LCCN 2023014827 (print) | LCCN 2023014828 (ebook) | ISBN 9781032431925 (hardback) | ISBN 9781032431918 (paperback) | ISBN 9781003366089 (ebook)
Subjects: LCSH: Beauvoir, Simone de, 1908-1986--Influence. | Feminism. | Political science--Philosophy. | Women--Social conditions.
Classification: LCC B2430.B344 S564 2023 (print) | LCC B2430.B344 (ebook) | DDC 848/.91409--dc23/eng/20230608
LC record available at https://lccn.loc.gov/2023014827
LC ebook record available at https://lccn.loc.gov/2023014828

ISBN: 978-1-032-43192-5 (hbk)
ISBN: 978-1-032-43191-8 (pbk)
ISBN: 978-1-003-36608-9 (ebk)

DOI: 10.4324/9781003366089

Typeset in Times New Roman
by Taylor & Francis Books

CONTENTS

List of figures vii
List of contributors viii

Introduction 1
Liesbeth Schoonheim and Karen Vintges

1 Situating Simone de Beauvoir in Contemporary
Political Theory 13
Liesbeth Schoonheim

PART I
Changing Myths **29**

2 Incel Violence and Beauvoirian Otherness 31
Filipa Melo Lopes

3 Must We Eliminate All Myths? Simone de Beauvoir and
the Myth-Affirmative Feminist Tradition 48
Adam Kjellgren

4 Beauvoir, Bardot, and *Burqinis*: Making Sense of Modern
France 67
Catherine Raissiguier

PART II
Lived Ambiguities 89

5 Uses of Ambiguity as Tool: A Black Feminist Phenomenologist Reflects on the Year 2020 (and Ambiguous Futures) 91
Qrescent Mali Mason

6 Beauvoir, the Philosophy of Freedom, and the Rights of Black Women during French Colonial Times 111
Nathalie Nya

PART III
Situated Experiences 125

7 Old Age and the Question of Authenticity 127
Sonia Kruks

8 Expectant Anxiety in *The Second Sex* 147
Kate Kirkpatrick

PART IV
Fighting Back 165

9 'Muscular Revolt': Resisting Gender Oppression through Counter-Violence 167
Dianna Taylor

10 "I Didn't Ask for It": Balkan Women vs. the Invisibility of Rape 186
Ana Maskalan

11 Why Thoughtfulness Matters: Black Lives Matter and Elsewhere 211
Elaine Stavro

Index *229*

FIGURES

5.1 Screenshot of ambiguities suggested by participants at the conference "Simone de Beauvoir: New Perspectives for the 21st Century" (June 2020)   105
8.1 Jizō statues at Zōjō-ji Temple, Japan   154

CONTRIBUTORS

Kate Kirkpatrick is a Fellow in Philosophy and Christian Ethics at Regent's Park College, University of Oxford. Her research focuses on intersections between philosophy, religion, and culture, especially in twentieth-century French phenomenology, existentialism, and feminism. She is the author of several books and articles on French existentialism, including *Sartre on Sin* (Oxford University Press, 2017), *Sartre and Theology* (Bloomsbury, 2017), *The Mystical Sources of Existentialist Thought* (with George Pattison, Routledge, 2018), and *Becoming Beauvoir: A Life* (Bloomsbury, 2019). Her current project is a philosophical commentary on Simone de Beauvoir's *The Second Sex*.

Adam Kjellgren is a PhD student in the History of Ideas at Stockholm University, Sweden. His dissertation deals with conceptualizations of myth within feminist theory, focusing on the works of Simone de Beauvoir, Mary Daly, and Donna Haraway. His most recent publications are "Myth-Making As a Feminist Strategy: Rosi Braidotti's Political Myth" (*Feminist Theory*, 2021) and "The Myth of Woman: Simone de Beauvoir and the Anthropological Discourse on Myth" (*History of European Ideas*, 2023).

Sonia Kruks is the Robert S. Danforth Professor of Politics Emerita at Oberlin College, USA. Her research interests lie at the intersections of phenomenology, existentialism, and feminist theory. Her most recent book is *Simone de Beauvoir and the Politics of Ambiguity* (2012). Prior books include *Retrieving Experience: Subjectivity and Recognition in Feminist Politics* (2001); *Situation and Human Existence: Freedom, Subjectivity and Society* (1990), and *The Political Philosophy of Merleau-Ponty* (1987). She presently serves on the editorial board of *Sartre Studies International* and the advisory board of *Simone de Beauvoir Studies*.

Ana Maskalan is a Senior Research Associate in the Centre for Youth and Gender Studies at the Institute for Social Research in Zagreb, Croatia. She received her PhD from the Department of Philosophy at the Faculty of Humanities and Social Sciences, University of Zagreb. Her areas of research interest (besides gender and utopian studies) are theories of body identity, transhumanism, pop culture, cyberculture, culture of fear, and political and social issues of social justice and discrimination. She is the author of *Woman's Future: The Philosophical Discussion on Utopia and Feminism* (ISRZ/Plejada: Zagreb, 2015) and co-author (with Mladen Labus, Lino Veljak, and Mirjana Adamovic) of *Identity and Culture* (ISRZ: Zagreb, 2014).

Qrescent Mali Mason is an Assistant Professor of Philosophy at Haverford College, USA, a Co-Associate Editor of *Hypatia: Journal of Feminist Philosophy*, and served as President of the International Simone de Beauvoir Society from 2020 to 2022. In 2021, she won a Leeway Foundation Grant for Art and Social Change for her multimedia art installation *The Self-Translation Cycle*. Her most recent writing includes "#BlackGirlMagic as Resistant Imaginary" and "We Feel Grateful and Alive to Be Doing This Work Together: Phenomenological Reflections on a 2020 Summer of Feminist Research across Difference." She is currently working on a book manuscript titled *On Ambiguity*.

Filipa Melo Lopes is a Lecturer in Social and Political Philosophy at the University of Edinburgh, specializing in social theory and ontology, feminist politics, and sexual ethics. She is particularly interested in using Beauvoir's work to offer new feminist analyses of contemporary popular culture. Her publications include "Perpetuating the Patriarchy: Misogyny and Post-(Feminist) Backlash" (2019, *Philosophical Studies*) and "'Half Victim, Half Accomplice': Cat Person and Narcissism" (2021, *Ergo*).

Nathalie Nya's areas of expertise are political theory, ethics, post-colonial philosophy, philosophy of race, feminism, and womanism. She teaches at Case Western Reserve University, USA. She is the author of *Simone de Beauvoir and the Colonial Experience: Freedom, Violence, and Identity* (2019). She is working on a second manuscript that puts in dialogue political theory, ethics, and post-colonial philosophy.

Catherine Raissiguier completed her undergraduate education in France, and holds an MA in Women's Studies/American Studies and a PhD in Comparative and International Education from the State University of New York at Buffalo, USA. She is currently Chair and Professor of Women and

Gender Studies at Hunter College/City University of New York. The author of *Becoming Women/Becoming Workers: Identity Formation in a French High School* (1994) and *Reinventing the Republic: Gender, Migration and Citizenship in France* (2010), Raissiguier is currently working on a book project examining the formation of France as a modern nation, tentatively titled *Bombs, Beaches, and Burqinis: Making Sense of Modern France*.

Liesbeth Schoonheim is a postdoctoral researcher in Political Theory at Humboldt University in Berlin, Germany. Previously, she was a junior postdoctoral research fellow of the Research Foundation Flanders (FWO) at KU Leuven, Belgium. She has published on questions regarding resistance, political violence, historiography and literature, and corporeality including in *Foucault Studies, History of European Ideas*, and *Philosophy Today*.

Elaine Stavro has taught in the departments of Political Studies, Women's Studies, and Philosophy at Trent University, Canada, since 1991. She has written numerous articles on Simone de Beauvoir and most recently published *Emancipatory Thinking: The Political Thought of Simone De Beauvoir* (2018). Her research focuses on feminist thinking and radical democratic theory, specifically the intersection of deliberation and affect. This is reflected in such articles as "SARS and Alterity: The Toronto–China Binary" (*New Political Science*, 2014); "The Museum as a Site of Democratic Pedagogy" (*World of Science and Technology*, 2017); and her forthcoming book *Democracy and Event: The Promise and Perils of Catastrophe* (Routledge, 2023).

Dianna Taylor is Professor of Philosophy at John Carroll University in Cleveland, Ohio. She is the author of *Sexual Violence and Humiliation: A Foucauldian-Feminist Perspective* (Routledge, 2020), editor of *Michel Foucault: Key Concepts* (Acumen, 2010), and co-editor of *Feminist Politics: Identity, Difference, Agency* (Rowman & Littlefield, 2007) and *Feminism and the Final Foucault* (University of Illinois Press, 2004). Her current research analyzes rage and counter-violence as feminist resources for resisting and preventing sexual violence, and the sexual humiliation such violence produces.

Karen Vintges is Associate Researcher at the Amsterdam Institute for Humanities Research of the University of Amsterdam, Netherlands. Her published works include *Philosophy as Passion: The Thinking of Simone de Beauvoir* (Indiana University Press, 1996 [originally in Dutch, 1992]); *Feminism and the Final Foucault*, co-edited with Dianna Taylor (Illinois University Press, 2004); and *A New Dawn for the Second Sex* (Amsterdam University Press, 2017), as well as several other books in Dutch.

INTRODUCTION

Liesbeth Schoonheim and Karen Vintges

Simone de Beauvoir is mostly remembered for her groundbreaking work on feminism and existentialist ethics, as well as for her autobiographies in which she describes her life as a woman intellectual. This collection links these concerns with her profound contributions to political thinking. Our contention that Beauvoir provides important conceptual tools for understanding contemporary politics starts from her social and political engagement:[1] she acted in solidarity with the important struggles of her lifetime, such as the Algerian war of independence, the anti-Vietnam war movement, the student protests of 1968, and the feminist movement; and she opposed fascism and right-wing politics in both domestic and foreign affairs.[2] The essays brought together in this collection share the conviction that Beauvoir's life and work provide a 'toolkit' that offers the philosophical means to problematize the political present. As 'tools,' her concepts are sharpened and adjusted for contemporary applications by bringing in new perspectives and approaches that are prefigured in the 'kit' Beauvoir herself provided. Written from a plethora of geographical locations—from Martinique and the U.S. to France and the former Yugoslavia—the next 11 essays show different ways in which this conceptual sharpening takes place, and draw on fields such as Black feminism, political theory, and phenomenology.

This collection builds on but also extends the insights gained by the current revival in Beauvoir scholarship.[3] While this revival is heterogeneous, we can distinguish two main approaches: firstly, a historical approach that leans towards French and Francophone studies.[4] Under this approach, we could also place those studies focusing on Beauvoir's literary works, including her autobiographies.[5] This approach typically searches for the various personal, literary, intellectual, and political relationships that Beauvoir engaged in besides Sartre, building on previous work that debunked the image of Beauvoir as *la grande Sartreuse*.[6] A central question that thus emerges is how Beauvoir shaped herself through these various relationships as well as through her highly diverse oeuvre. This process of becoming is primarily understood as ethico-political self-creation, i.e. the construction through writing and other exercises in an art of existence. Beauvoir thus cultivated a specific *ethos* as a woman intellectual in an engagement with others.[7]

Secondly, philosophical approaches stress the ongoing relevance of Beauvoir, especially regarding feminist debates on subjectivity and experience.[8] Feminist and critical phenomenologists in particular have drawn on Beauvoir,[9] while her work is also interrogated from a Black feminist tradition.[10] Key to these contributions is how the various axes of oppression shape lived experience and determine the possibilities of resistance, where these conditions are considered to be historically contingent. It is in particular the latter approach to which the current collection is indebted, with most contributions in this book having a more overtly political goal by starting from questions of political mobilization and stressing the collective dimension of political action.

In this introduction we elaborate on our 'toolkit' approach to Beauvoir, and provide a chapter overview. The next chapter sketches the various debates that form the background for the essays in this collection.

A 'Toolkit' Approach against Totalizing Theory

Why approach Beauvoir's oeuvre as a toolkit?[11] Is it merely a nice catchphrase to dodge the painstaking work of reconstructing her thought? Or is it a symptom of neoliberal academia, where the worth of research lies in its 'valorization,' and the inflationary language of an author's 'unique contribution' abounds?[12] We believe that more is at stake. The non-systematic and instrumental approach that we propose here is indebted to philosopher Michel Foucault, who on various occasions refers to his own work as a toolbox.[13] On a practical level, it indicates the priority of political action over theory: concrete, local struggles and their use of concepts are more important than the integrity and consistency of a theory that claims to be all-encompassing. This also means that the theorist is not in a position to prescribe the goals and strategies of political agents. Criticizing the general intellectual whose theoretical claims supposedly comprehend the totality of social relations, Foucault writes: "I would like my books to be a kind of tool-box which others can rummage through to find a tool with which they can do whatever seems good to them, in their area. […] I write for users, not readers."[14] Foucault objects that grand theories such as Marxism and psychoanalysis claim a total view of social relations and have inhibiting effects, putting the brakes on discontinuous, particular, and local critiques.[15]

Despite his objection, however, he argues that these grand theories provide tools that are useful locally, that is, in specific fields of inquiry as well as particular fights. Very importantly, such a recuperation of useful concepts requires the suspension of "the theoretical unity of their discourse."[16] In line with Foucault's comments, we argue that Beauvoir's thought is flawed insofar as she provides a grand theory; yet, it also offers concepts for specific, local uses.

To approach Beauvoir's oeuvre as a toolkit is to suspend any claim to a unifying, systematic account of politics and society. Such unifying claims can be found, for instance, in her works of social critique, *The Second Sex* [1949] and *Old Age* [1970]. *The Second Sex* develops a grand historical narrative of patriarchy that is based on Hegelian mechanisms of othering, positing that "a fundamental hostility to any other consciousness is found in consciousness itself."[17] Beauvoir would later take issue with her overly idealistic framework, arguing that she should have based her analysis "not on an idealistic and *a priori* struggle of consciences, but on the facts of supply and demand."[18] This is indeed the approach she takes in *The Long March* [1957] and *Old Age*, as a result of which she at times seems to reduce the social status of women and the elderly to their—weak—economic position.[19] In these and similar moments, Beauvoir seems to be arrogating for herself a privileged and abstract perspective from which to survey all of society and to dictate which groups are in a position to initiate change.

Yet, notwithstanding these problematic totalizations in Beauvoir's theory of patriarchy and social oppression, we believe it can be used locally—a use which is supported by Beauvoir's situational approach. Indeed, Hegelian and Marxist dialectics are in her writing—to use Foucault's words—often "cut up, ripped up, torn to shreds, turned inside out, displaced, caricatured, dramatized, theatricalized, and so on."[20] Hers is an attempt to understand marginalized experiences and the possibility for collective action. As a consequence, she foregrounds particularity and inconsistency, to which she usually subordinates theoretical systematicity. For example, she does not define the struggle for recognition by a dialectic movement towards reconciliation, but tweaks it to allow for different modes of othering and modes of resistance. Furthermore, as we discuss at more length below, she is committed to a perspectivism in which subjects can have very different experiences even if they are in the same situation, and she is equally committed to a notion of the self that is marked by ambiguity and tension.

The essays in this collection share a non-totalizing reading of Beauvoir, and are firmly rooted in the present. They illustrate that "thought itself," as Hannah Arendt writes, "arises out of incidents of living experience and must remain bound to them as the only guidepost by which to take its bearings."[21]

Structure of the Book

The essays in this collection are grouped together in four sections, namely 1) changing myths; 2) lived ambiguities; 3) situated experiences; and 4) fighting back. Preceding these four parts, the first chapter by Liesbeth Schoonheim provides an overview of the debates in contemporary political theory that form the background of the essays in this collection. She distinguishes three topics with regard to which Beauvoir is relevant: political mobilization, and in particular the rehabilitation by theorists of radical democracy of affect and of myth; political strategy, and the critique of counter-violence as well as institutional reform; and, finally, feminist debates on the status of experience. On each of these topics, Schoonheim argues, Beauvoir has valuable insights to offer.

The first part of this volume deals with Beauvoir's view on myths and the way it opens up a debate on the deconstruction of myths and their operation in contemporary politics. In Chapter 2, Filipa Melo Lopes looks at incel violence, and argues that the two most common feminist analyses of incels' actions, which focus on their objectification of women or their sense of entitlement to women's attention, are insufficient. They fail to account for incels' distinctive ambivalence towards women, namely their oscillation between obsessive desire and violent hatred. Melo Lopes proposes instead that what incels want is a Beauvoirian 'Other'—discussed by Beauvoir in her chapter on myths in terms of the 'Eternal Feminine'. For Beauvoir, when men conceive of women as Other, women function as *sui generis* entities through which men can experience themselves as praiseworthy heroes, but also endanger men's self-described exceptionality. Melo Lopes then goes on to give an illustrative analysis of Elliot Rodger's autobiographical manifesto, "My Twisted World," showing how Beauvoir's analysis of the myth of woman sheds light on Rodger's racist and classist attitudes and gives us a better understanding of his ambivalence towards women. Beauvoir, according to Melo Lopes, therefore constitutes a powerful and overlooked theoretical alternative to accounts centered on objectification and entitlement.

In Chapter 3, Adam Kjellgren argues that Simone de Beauvoir's feminist classic, *The Second Sex*, is a valuable resource in assessing the role of myth in contemporary politics, and particularly in feminism. Starting from recent feminist and political theoretical reappraisals of myth, Kjellgren challenges the popular assumptions that myth belongs to irrational and so-called non-civilized societies—an assumption that also echoes in contemporary political theory when only populism and the alt-right movement are associated with myth. In fact, however, Beauvoir's chapter on the 'Eternal Feminine' suggests, according to Kjellgren, that myth constitutes a troublesome but well-integrated aspect of life in all modern, patriarchal societies. Beauvoir has often been wrongly accused of trying to discard myth, but she never states that all myths must be eliminated. Kjellgren assesses what, according to Beauvoir, distinguishes harmful from non-harmful myths, arguing that Beauvoir develops an ethically (rather than ontologically) grounded critique of myth. Harmful myths are those that have negative consequences, in that they circumscribe human freedom. Kjellgren concludes by suggesting that the success of Beauvoir's argument follows in part from her capacity as a myth-maker.

Catherine Raissiguier draws in Chapter 4 on a short piece by Beauvoir titled *Brigitte Bardot and the Lolita Syndrome* [1959]. This short text sets out to unpack the Bardot myth and to analyze the new model of women's sexuality that it embodies. Unlike the few critical commentaries that debate whether Beauvoir is right in championing Bardot's subversive representation of women's sexual agency in post-war France, Raissiguier investigates what Beauvoir's text might tell us about BB as a representative, albeit contradictory, piece of the collective construction of modern France. Raissiguier thus traces how BB ultimately could become a symbol of modern France, as Bardot turned into an animal rights activist who deploys anti-immigrant and anti-Muslim rhetoric. Beauvoir's text enables us, according to Raissiguier, to reflect on the recent 'burqini' controversy in France, when Marine Le Pen reminded French people that "the French beaches are those of Bardot and Vadim" and not spaces where women go to cover up.

The second part of this volume deals with two key concepts of Beauvoir's existentialist ethics, namely freedom and ambiguity, and explores their limitations for understanding Black feminist resistance. In Chapter 5, Qrescent Mali Mason looks back at the ambiguous dimensions of the year 2020. Writing from the standpoint of a Black American feminist philosopher, Mason maps the ambiguities in Beauvoir's work and life, and draws on the work of other feminist thinkers who are also complex and brilliant. These ambiguities pertain for instance to Beauvoir's love life and anti-racist politics, and are narrated in Mason's auto-theoretical essay as a source of both inspiration and ambivalence. Mason's essay, and the conference presentation on which it is based, offer a pause to think about the ubiquity of the ambiguities that emerged in 2020 and thereafter. In both the essay and the lecture, the audience is explicitly invited to contribute their own ambiguities, thus enacting philosophy as a collective practice. Ambiguity, then, is an existential concept, but it also describes an ethical attitude, one that helped Mason navigate a year that was itself full of ambiguities.

Nathalie Nya inquires in Chapter 6 whether and how Beauvoir's concept of situated freedom gives pride of place to the struggles of colonized, Black women. Comparing Beauvoir to Paulette Nardal, the Martinican writer, politician, and suffragist, Nya shows how the latter would have taken issue with Beauvoir's assertions that women's freedom is limited. Nardal, who established feminist organizations in Martinique and who was educated in the French system, was adamant that it was important for Martinican women to vote, regardless of their education and political leaning. Although Nardal never met Beauvoir or Sartre, according to Nya she would have been much more in agreement with Sartre's radical and ontological concept of freedom than with Beauvoir's situated notion. Yet Nya concludes by arguing that both Nardal and Beauvoir opened up the conversation on the freedom of the oppressed, contributing in different ways to discussions of freedom in feminism and post-colonial philosophy; and both analyses of Beauvoir and Nardal contribute to a philosophy of freedom, offering starting points from which the situation of white women and non-white women can be further defined.

In the next part, we focus on the critical-phenomenological recuperation of marginalized experiences, namely aging and pregnancy. In Chapter 7, Sonia Kruks starts with an apparent shift between *The Second Sex* and *Old Age*: whereas the former values the authentic pursuit of freedom even in situations of alterity, the latter describes sympathetically many kinds of behavior that Beauvoir would previously have condemned as bad faith. This change raises the question of whether Beauvoir has abandoned her prior ethical framework entirely—a question that Kruks answers with a firm no. Rather, for those whose prior lives have been impoverished materially as well as culturally and existentially, the authentic pursuit of freedom is effectively blocked by the conditions of old age, and Beauvoir does not condemn their resignation as bad faith. For those, on the other hand, who have lived prior lives of creativity and material abundance, authentic freedom remains possible in old age—and yet, Beauvoir does not condemn them when they fall into resigned passivity due to failing health and other losses. Kruks concludes by arguing that free, authentic action might be exercised in apparently trivial acts that can nevertheless be very significant to the person performing them, such as crossing the street, walking up a staircase, or preparing one's own food.

Kate Kirkpatrick argues in Chapter 8 against the framing of 'choice,' on which both the reputedly too-positive account of pregnancy by Iris Marion Young and the overwhelmingly negative, 'marginalized' cases of pregnancy highlighted by Caroline Lundquist rely. Instead, turning to Beauvoir's discussion of pregnancy in *The Second Sex*, Kirkpatrick argues it describes but does not name a dimension of the subjective experience of pregnant persons that she calls 'expectant anxiety.' This concept problematizes the polarizing rhetoric of 'choice' by attending to the subjective experience of pregnancy, in particular the facing of a range of radically different (unknown and, in many cases, unknowable) concrete possibilities for one's own life and a possible human other. Kirkpatrick draws on contemporary cultural and literary representations of pregnancy, abortion, and miscarriage to illustrate this concept, including the Japanese Buddhist practice of *mizuko kuyō* and two novelistic depictions of infertility and abortion—Ayobami Adebayo's *Stay With Me* [2017] and Britt Bennett's *The Mothers* [2016].

Finally, referring back to many of the themes first broached in the second part of the volume, the collection turns to accounts of 'fighting back,' whether through acts of counter-violence or other forms of political organization. Dianna Taylor argues in Chapter 9 that, from a Beauvoirian perspective, counter-violence is a necessary and ethical response to sexual violence. Starting from the argument that fascism and colonialism are, like normative gender, oppressive political systems, and that Beauvoir encourages the use of violence against the former, Taylor concludes that she would also approve the use of counter-violence against the sexual violence that undergirds the normative gender order. Yet this very same gender order also instills an ambivalence in women regarding their capacity to violence. Taylor draws on radical feminism as well as an analysis of the recent film *Promising Young Woman* [2020] to show how women can overcome this ambivalence through muscular revolt, which combats their oppression and allows for their self-transformation.

In Chapter 10, Ana Maskalan investigates the online initiative "I Didn't Ask for It" (#nisamtrazila) that was started in 2021 by a Serbian actress, and which rocked the five former Yugoslavian countries as thousands of women reported the various forms of sexual abuse to which they were exposed during their childhood, education, and employment, oftentimes by person(s) they knew and looked up to. Maskalan situates the initiative in its social and political context, namely the complex permeation of the socialist attitude towards women's rights and sexual violence, the unresolved traumas of mass wartime rapes, and the resurgence of nationalism and the concomitant experience of Balkan masculinity as being under threat. Maskalan first shows how the sexual violence suffered by the women is part of processes of othering as described by Beauvoir. Furthermore, following Beauvoir's argument that communist reform is insufficient to improve women's situation, Maskalan argues that the proclaimed gender equality under Tito obscured the enduring oppression of women. After analysing the women's testimonies and their dismissal in terms of epistemic injustice, Maskalan concludes with the backlash against "I Didn't Ask for It." The ambivalence that is expressed towards women who are in the public eye—such as actresses—is, according to her, described by Beauvoir's myth of the eternal feminine.

In the eleventh and final chapter, Elaine Stavro turns to Beauvoir's theory of the individual as free and situated in relations with others to argue for an account of political action that involves reflection and organization. Criticizing vital materialists such as Rosi Braidotti, Jodi Dean and Stefan Jonsson for their focus on indeterminacy and spontaneity, Stavro suggests that their turn to things, amorphous affects, and human and non-human assemblages minimizes the significance of human ingenuity, organization, and strategy. The latter, according to Stavro, are required for radical democratic projects and coalitions. By extending Beauvoir's thinking around sensation and perception—and by drawing on her activism, such as her engagement in the defense of Djamila Boupacha—Stavro focuses on embodied and situated affect rather than autonomous affects, which is a central concept of the vital materialists.

Acknowledgements

Many of the papers collected in this volume were initially presented at the international conference *De Beauvoir: New Perspectives for the 21st Century*, which was hosted and funded by the Institute of Philosophy, KU Leuven (Belgium). We thank our co-organizers of that event, Ashika Singh and Julia Jansen, as well as the participants, for their generous contributions. The cover illustration is designed by Alba Martínez Feito. We are very grateful to Meryl Altman for reading and commenting on the manuscript.

Chapter 2 by Filipa Melo Lopes is a revised and shortened version of "What Do Incels Want? Explaining Incel Violence Using Beauvoirian Otherness," *Hypatia* 38(1), 2023, 134-156. Copyright by Filipa Melo Lopes, 2023. Published by Cambridge University Press on behalf of Hypatia, a Nonprofit Corporation.

Notes

1. For recent work on the political philosophy of Beauvoir, see Lori Jo Marso, *Politics with Beauvoir: Freedom in the Encounter* (Durham, NC: Duke University Press, 2017) and Elaine Stavro, *Emancipatory Thinking: Simone de Beauvoir and Contemporary Political Thought* (Montreal: McGill-Queen's University Press, 2018). See also Simone de Beauvoir, *Political Writings*, ed. Margaret Simons and Marybeth Timmermann (Urbana: University of Illinois Press, 2012).
2. 'Politics' should not be limited to a narrow set of institutions and juridico-political concepts; it also includes concrete, anti-colonial, anti-racist, Marxist, and feminist fights, and operations of oppression that often involve violent processes of othering as well as socio-economic inequality. For arguments in favor of such an extensive account of politics and political theory, see Wendy Brown, "At the Edge," in *What Is Political Theory?*, ed. Stephen K. White and J. Donald Moon (London/Thousand Oaks/New Delhi: SAGE, 2004).
3. Over the last years, the critical edition of Beauvoir's less well-known works in English has been published: her collected memoires appeared in 2018 in the prestigious *Pléiade* series; and *Simone de Beauvoir Studies*, the journal dedicated to her work, has been very successfully relaunched.
4. Meryl Altman, *Beauvoir in Time* (Leiden: Brill Rodopi, 2020); Judith G. Coffin, *Sex, Love, and Letters: Writing Simone de Beauvoir* (Ithaca: Cornell University Press, 2020); Marine Rouch, "'Vous êtes descendue d'un piédestal': une appropriation collective des Mémoires de Simone de Beauvoir par ses lectrices (1958–

1964)," *Littérature* 191, no. 3 (October 9, 2018): 68–82; Kate Kirkpatrick, *Becoming Beauvoir: A Life* (London: Bloomsbury, 2019).

5 Elizabeth Fallaize, *The Novels of Simone de Beauvoir* (London/New York: Routledge, 1990); Ursula Tidd, *Simone de Beauvoir, Gender and Testimony* (Cambridge: Cambridge University Press, 1999), https://doi.org/10.1017/CBO9780511485893; Shannon M. Mussett, "The Failure of Female Identity in Simone de Beauvoir's Fiction," in *A Companion to Simone de Beauvoir*, ed. Laura Hengehold and Nancy Bauer (Oxford: Wiley Blackwell, 2017), 367–378; Eric Levéel, "Simone de Beauvoir: s'écrire, se dire, se promener: le triptyque de 1946," *Simone de Beauvoir Studies* 31, no. 1 (December 14, 2020): 68–85, https://doi.org/10.1163/25897616-bja10022.

6 The argument that Beauvoir was a philosopher in her own right was initially formulated by feminist philosophers over the course of the 1990s. See Eva Lundgren-Gothlin, *Sex and Existence: Simone de Beauvoir's The Second Sex* (London: Athlone, 1996); Karen Vintges, *Philosophy as Passion: The Thinking of Simone de Beauvoir* (Bloomington: Indiana University Press, 1996); Debra Bergoffen, *The Philosophy of Simone de Beauvoir: Gendered Phenomenologies, Erotic Generosities* (Albany: State University of New York Press, 1997); Margaret A. Simons, *Beauvoir and the Second Sex: Feminism, Race, and the Origins of Existentialism* (Lanham, MD: Rowman & Littlefield, 1999); Nancy Bauer, *Simone de Beauvoir, Philosophy, and Feminism* (New York: Columbia University Press, 2001). In a more philological vein, and based on the posthumously published diaries and letters, the argument can be found in Edward Fullbrook and Kate Fullbrook, *Sex and Philosophy: Rethinking de Beauvoir and Sartre* (London: Bloomsbury, 2008); and Simons' Introduction to Simone de Beauvoir, *Diary of a Philosophy Student: Volume 1, 1926–27*, ed. Barbara Klaw, Sylvie Le Bon de Beauvoir, and Margaret A. Simons (Urbana/Chicago: University of Illinois Press, 2006).

7 Toril Moi, *Simone de Beauvoir: The Making of an Intellectual Woman* (Oxford/Cambridge, MA: Blackwell, 1994); Vintges, *Philosophy as Passion*; Liesbeth Schoonheim, "Beauvoir and Writing as the Creation of the Self: Memoirs, Diaries, Biography," *Sartre Studies International* 26, no. 1 (June 1, 2020): 77–88, https://doi.org/10.3167/ssi.2020.260107.

8 Sonia Kruks, *Retrieving Experience: Subjectivity and Recognition in Feminist Politics* (Ithaca, NY: Cornell University Press, 2018); Sonia Kruks, *Simone de Beauvoir and the Politics of Ambiguity* (Oxford/New York: Oxford University Press, 2012).

9 Sara Heinämaa, *Toward a Phenomenology of Sexual Difference: Husserl, Merleau-Ponty, Beauvoir* (Lanham, MD: Rowman & Littlefield, 2004); Sara Ahmed, *Queer Phenomenology: Orientations, Objects, Others* (Durham, NC: Duke University Press, 2006); Alia Al-Saji, "Material Life: Bergsonian Tendencies in Simone de Beauvoir's Philosophy," in *Differences: Rereading Beauvoir and Irigaray*, ed. Emily Parker and Anne Van Leeuwen (New York: Oxford University Press, 2018).

10 bell hooks, "True Philosophers: Beauvoir and bell," in *Beauvoir and Western Thought from Plato to Butler*, ed. Shannon M. Mussett and William S. Wilkerson (Albany: State University of New York Press, 2012), 227–236; Kathryn T. Gines, "Comparative and Competing Frameworks of Oppression in Simone de Beauvoir's The Second Sex," *Graduate Faculty Philosophy Journal* 35, no. 1/2 (July 1, 2014): 251–273, https://doi.org/10.5840/gfpj2014351/212; Patricia Hill Collins, "Simone de Beauvoir, Women's Oppression and Existential Freedom," in *A Companion to Simone de Beauvoir*, ed. Laura Hengehold and Nancy Bauer (Oxford: Wiley Blackwell, 2017), 325–338.

11 Karen Vintges, *A New Dawn for the Second Sex: Women's Freedom Practices in World Perspective* (Amsterdam: Amsterdam University Press, 2017), 18.

12 'Valorization' is a term used in the Netherlands and Flanders (Belgium) to refer to the societal impact of scientific research; it initially pertained to strategic research in the life sciences and STEM and the marketization of their research results by for-profits, and is now also deployed in evaluating research projects in the humanities and social sciences.
13 Michel Foucault, "Prisons et asiles dans le mécanisme du pouvoir," in *Dits et écrits 1954–1988: I, 1954–1975*, ed. Daniel Defert and François Ewald, trans. A. Ghizzardi (Paris: Gallimard, 1994), 1391. Foucault analyzes disciplinary power in terms of its 'tools,' but also applies this strategic approach to his own work, including his genealogies. See, for instance, Michel Foucault, "On the Genealogy of Ethics: An Overview of Work in Progress," in *Ethics: Subjectivity and Truth*, ed. Paul Rabinow, vol. 1, The Essential Works of Michel Foucault 1954–1984 (New York: New Press, 1997), 261; Michel Foucault, *Society Must Be Defended: Lectures at the Collège de France, 1975–76*, ed. David Macey (London: Penguin, 2004), 6–7, 14; Michel Foucault, "From Torture to Cellblock," in *Foucault Live: (Interviews, 1961–1984)*, ed. Sylvère Lotringer, trans. John Johnston (New York: Zone Books, 1996), 149. Gilles Deleuze, in an interview with Foucault, also expounds on their take on Marxism as a tool-box; see "Intellectuals and Power," in *Foucault Live*, trans. Donald Bouchard and Sherry Simon, 76.
14 Foucault, "Prisons et asiles," 1391–1392 (translation ours; 'tool-box' is used in English in the original French text).
15 Cf. Foucault, *Society Must Be Defended*, 6.
16 Ibid. Situated theory-formation has become commonplace, especially in feminist political philosophy. See, for instance María Lugones, "Playfulness, 'World'-Travelling, and Loving Perception," *Hypatia* 2, no. 2 (1987): 3–19, https://doi.org/10.1111/j.1527-2001.1987.tb01062.x; Sandra G. Harding, *Feminism and Methodology: Social Science Issues* (Bloomington: Indiana University Press, 1987); Nancy C.M. Hartsock, *Money, Sex, and Power: Toward a Feminist Historical Materialism* (Boston, MA: Northeastern University Press, 1985); Patricia Hill Collins, *Black Feminist Thought: Knowledge, Consciousness, and the Politics of Empowerment* (London/New York: Routledge, 2002); Iris Marion Young, *Justice and the Politics of Difference* (Princeton, NJ: Princeton University Press, 2011).
17 Simone de Beauvoir, *The Second Sex*, trans. Constance Borde and Sheila Malovany-Chevallier (New York: Vintage, 2011), 7.
18 Simone de Beauvoir, *Force of Circumstance*, trans. Richard Howard (Harmondsworth, UK: Penguin, 1968), 202.
19 Simone de Beauvoir, *Old Age* (London: Penguin, 1977), 97–100; Simone de Beauvoir, *The Long March: An Account of Modern China*, trans. Austryn Wainhouse (London: Phoenix, 2001), chap. 3, "The Family."
20 Foucault, *Society Must Be Defended*, 6.
21 Hannah Arendt, *Between Past and Future: Eight Exercises in Political Thought*, ed. Jerome Kohn (London: Penguin, 2006), 14.

References

Ahmed, Sara. *Queer Phenomenology: Orientations, Objects, Others*. Durham, NC: Duke University Press, 2006.

Al-Saji, Alia. "Material Life. Bergsonian Tendencies in Simone de Beauvoir's Philosophy." In *Differences: Rereading Beauvoir and Irigaray*, edited by Emily Parker and Anne Van Leeuwen. New York: Oxford University Press, 2018.

Altman, Meryl. *Beauvoir in Time*. Leiden: Brill Rodopi, 2020.

Arendt, Hannah. *Between Past and Future: Eight Exercises in Political Thought.* Edited by Jerome Kohn. London: Penguin, 2006.
Bauer, Nancy. *Simone de Beauvoir, Philosophy, & Feminism.* New York: Columbia University Press, 2001.
Beauvoir, Simone de. *Diary of a Philosophy Student: Volume 1, 1926–27.* Edited by Barbara Klaw, Sylvie Le Bon de Beauvoir, and Margaret A. Simons. Urbana/Chicago: University of Illinois Press, 2006.
Beauvoir, Simone de. *Force of Circumstance.* Translated by Richard Howard. Harmondsworth: Penguin, 1968.
Beauvoir, Simone de. *Old Age.* London: Penguin, 1977.
Beauvoir, Simone de. *Political Writings.* Edited by Margaret A. Simons and Marybeth Timmermann. Urbana: University of Illinois Press, 2012.
Beauvoir, Simone de. *The Long March: An Account of Modern China.* Translated by Austryn Wainhouse. London: Phoenix, 2001.
Beauvoir, Simone de. *The Second Sex.* Translated by Constance Borde and Sheila Malovany-Chevallier. New York: Vintage, 2011.
Bergoffen, Debra. *The Philosophy of Simone de Beauvoir: Gendered Phenomenologies, Erotic Generosities.* Albany: State University of New York Press, 1997.
Brown, Wendy. "At the Edge." In *What Is Political Theory?*, edited by Stephen K. White and J. Donald Moon. London/Thousand Oaks/New Delhi: SAGE, 2004.
Coffin, Judith G. *Sex, Love, and Letters: Writing Simone de Beauvoir.* Ithaca: Cornell University Press, 2020.
Collins, Patricia Hill. *Black Feminist Thought: Knowledge, Consciousness, and the Politics of Empowerment.* London/New York: Routledge, 2002.
Collins, Patricia Hill. "Simone de Beauvoir, Women's Oppression and Existential Freedom." In *A Companion to Simone de Beauvoir*, edited by Laura Hengehold and Nancy Bauer, 325–338. Oxford: Wiley Blackwell, 2017.
Fallaize, Elizabeth. *The Novels of Simone de Beauvoir.* London/New York: Routledge, 1990.
Foucault, Michel. "From Torture to Cellblock." In *Foucault Live (Interviews, 1961–1984)*, edited by Sylvère Lotringer, translated by John Johnston, 146–149. New York: Zone Books, 1996.
Foucault, Michel. "On the Genealogy of Ethics: An Overview of Work in Progress." In *Ethics: Subjectivity and Truth*, edited by Paul Rabinow: 253–280. Vol. I of The Essential Works of Michel Foucault 1954–1984. New York: New Press, 1997.
Foucault, Michel. *Society Must Be Defended: Lectures at the Collège de France, 1975–76.* Edited by David Macey. London: Penguin, 2004.
Foucault, Michel. "Prisons et asiles dans le mécanisme du pouvoir." In *Dits et écrits: 1954–1988: I*, edited by Daniel Defert and François Ewald, translated by A. Ghizzardi, Vol, I, 1954–1970: 1389–1393. Paris: Gallimard, 1994.
Foucault, Michel, and Gilles Deleuze. "Intellectuals and Power." In *Foucault Live: (Interviews, 1961–1984)*, translated by Donald Bouchard and Sherry Simon, 74–82. New York: Zone Books, 1996.
Fullbrook, Edward, and Kate Fullbrook. *Sex and Philosophy: Rethinking de Beauvoir and Sartre.* London: Bloomsbury, 2008.
Gines, Kathryn T. "Comparative and Competing Frameworks of Oppression in Simone de Beauvoir's *The Second Sex.*" *Graduate Faculty Philosophy Journal* 35, no. 1/2 (July 1, 2014): 251–273. https://doi.org/10.5840/gfpj2014351/212.

Harding, Sandra G. *Feminism and Methodology: Social Science Issues*. Bloomington: Indiana University Press, 1987.

Hartsock, Nancy C.M. *Money, Sex, and Power: Toward a Feminist Historical Materialism*. Boston, MA: Northeastern University Press, 1985.

Heinämaa, Sara. *Toward a Phenomenology of Sexual Difference: Husserl, Merleau-Ponty, Beauvoir*. Lanham, MD: Rowman & Littlefield, 2004.

hooks, bell. "True Philosophers: Beauvoir and bell." In *Beauvoir and Western Thought from Plato to Butler*, edited by Shannon M. Mussett and William S. Wilkerson, 227–236. Albany: State University of New York Press, 2012.

Kirkpatrick, Kate. *Becoming Beauvoir: A Life*. London: Bloomsbury, 2019.

Kruks, Sonia. *Simone de Beauvoir and the Politics of Ambiguity*. Oxford/New York: Oxford University Press, 2012.

Kruks, Sonia. *Retrieving Experience: Subjectivity and Recognition in Feminist Politics*. Ithaca: Cornell University Press, 2018.

Levéel, Eric. "Simone de Beauvoir: s'écrire, se dire, se promener: le triptyque de 1946." *Simone de Beauvoir Studies* 31, no. 1 (December 14, 2020): 68–85. https://doi.org/10.1163/25897616-bja10022.

Lugones, María. "Playfulness, 'World'-Travelling, and Loving Perception." *Hypatia* 2, no. 2 (1987): 3–19. https://doi.org/10.1111/j.1527-2001.1987.tb01062.x.

Lundgren-Gothlin, Eva. *Sex and Existence: Simone de Beauvoir's The Second Sex*. London: Athlone, 1996.

Marso, Lori Jo. *Politics with Beauvoir: Freedom in the Encounter*. Durham, NC: Duke University Press, 2017.

Moi, Toril. *Simone de Beauvoir: The Making of an Intellectual Woman*. Oxford/Cambridge, MA: Blackwell, 1994.

Mussett, Shannon M. "The Failure of Female Identity in Simone de Beauvoir's Fiction." In *A Companion to Simone de Beauvoir*, edited by Laura Hengehold and Nancy Bauer, 367–378. Oxford: Wiley Blackwell, 2017.

Rouch, Marine. "'Vous êtes descendue d'un piédestal': une appropriation collective des Mémoires de Simone de Beauvoir par ses lectrices (1958–1964)." *Littérature* 191, no. 3 (October 9, 2018): 68–82.

Schoonheim, Liesbeth. "Beauvoir and Writing as the Creation of the Self: Memoirs, Diaries, Biography." *Sartre Studies International* 26, no. 1 (June 1, 2020): 77–88. https://doi.org/10.3167/ssi.2020.260107.

Simons, Margaret A. *Beauvoir and the Second Sex: Feminism, Race, and the Origins of Existentialism*. Lanham, MD: Rowman & Littlefield, 1999.

Stavro, Elaine. *Emancipatory Thinking: Simone de Beauvoir and Contemporary Political Thought*. Montreal: McGill-Queen's University Press, 2018.

Tidd, Ursula. *Simone de Beauvoir, Gender and Testimony*. Cambridge: Cambridge University Press, 1999. https://doi.org/10.1017/CBO9780511485893.

Vintges, Karen. *Philosophy as Passion: The Thinking of Simone de Beauvoir*. Bloomington: Indiana University Press, 1996.

Vintges, Karen. *A New Dawn for the Second Sex: Women's Freedom Practices in World Perspective*. Amsterdam: Amsterdam University Press, 2017.

Young, Iris Marion. *Justice and the Politics of Difference*. Princeton: Princeton University Press, 2011.

1

SITUATING SIMONE DE BEAUVOIR IN CONTEMPORARY POLITICAL THEORY

Liesbeth Schoonheim

The four parts of this volume address questions such as: How can we deconstruct the emotionally charged, mythic images of femininity and masculinity that pervade right-wing movements while acknowledging the role that alternative myths and altered affects can play in political mobilization against these movements? How do concepts that were framed in the binary terms of gender allow for a more intersectional understanding of anti-racist, feminist resistance? How can we elucidate the lived experiences of those who belong to marginalized groups, without reifying those groups? How can we support the emancipatory struggle to end oppression and inequality while taking seriously how these struggles might require actions—violent or otherwise morally troublesome—that potentially reproduce oppression and inequality? These questions are raised against the background of various debates in political theory, which I discuss in this chapter. I focus on three topics, which do not strictly correspond to different parts of the volume but recur throughout the collection. While some of the approaches to these topics are indebted to Beauvoir's ideas, they mostly developed independently of her thought but would—so I argue—benefit from the resources of her oeuvre.

Political Mobilization: Affect and Myth

The first topic, which I discuss in this section, pertains to *political mobilization*, which should be regarded in light of the demise of Marxist analyses of class consciousness. More in particular, we have witnessed in the last three decades a revaluation of elements that have routinely been dismissed by normative political philosophy: affect and myths. If these elements were named by normative political philosophers (whether deliberative, Rawlsian, or otherwise), it was often in a derogatory manner as irrational, and in order to diagnose (and, some would say, pathologize) right-wing politics. Yet, as support for socialist and liberal politics drops and right-wing politics is on the rise, many on the left have argued that these elements should be recuperated and enlisted in left-wing politics. This recuperation is also motivated by a criticism of models of social progress in which myth and affect are elements that a modern society can and should leave behind. Effective mobilization requires not so much "the unforced force of the better argument," to use Jürgen Habermas's famous expression,[1] but the strategic use of affects and myths.

While most agree on the importance of affect as motivation, they disagree on its particular status. New vitalists, who have been influenced by Deleuze and Spinoza, argue that affects are autonomous: they originate in our biological wiring and are independent of deliberate, mental processes. As a consequence, they are not intentional: even if they might have triggers, they do not have an intentional object.[2] Very importantly, by stressing the bodily dimensions, these theorists aim to sketch a motivational force that decenters the subject. Others would sympathize with the link between corporeality and affect but take issue with the absence of an intentional object, either because they follow a more psychoanalytic account of the drives or adopt a phenomenological approach.[3] Yet others are not interested in questions of the body, and link the passions to discursive formations.[4]

Whereas the debate on affect draws heavily on neuroscience and biology, the one on myth draws on literary analysis. Not surprisingly, then, the underlying anthropological stakes differ: the argument that humans and animals are similar can be found in debates on affect but is lacking in those on myths. Indeed, contemporary takes on myth typically deploy humanist categories of meaning and significance, and draw on psychoanalysis. This applies to those who, like Chiara Bottici, investigate political myth—that is, the stories that are constitutive of the identity of political collectives and their institutions. Importantly, political myths are not transhistorical, but subject to change as social and political conditions change. In addition to substantiating this point with émigré thinkers (predominantly Blumenberg), Bottici also derives a critique from it on Freud and Jung, who, in her view, do not sufficiently acknowledge historical variation. Both propose that the elements of myth are provided by the unconscious, either as an individual structure (Freud) or a collective repository of archetypes (Jung). Feminist approaches to myth generally share Bottici's critical interrogation of psychoanalysis. Focusing on mythical representations of women and femininity, scholars such as Irigaray and Cixous deconstruct these representations while holding on to some tenets of the unconscious, while others like Cavarero carry out a similar deconstruction but flat out reject the unconsciousness.[5]

It is fair to say that Beauvoir has enabled these feminist approaches to myth even if she is not always explicitly named. Her chapters on myth in

The Second Sex analyze depictions of femininity in high and low culture to show how these mystify and 'other' concrete women. Furthermore, these images are the product of historically contingent conditions: the woman-goddess, for instance, issues from the frustrations in early agricultural societies at the unpredictability of nature, while the rise of the market economy in bourgeois society gave rise to the woman as the angel of the house and the one who provides shelter against the competitive outside world. Beauvoir's great contribution lies in highlighting the institutional and interpersonal context of these myths, and their changes throughout history.[6] The essays in this collection, such as those by Kjellgren, Melo Lopes, Raissiguier, and Maskalan, are unique in that they take up the feminist critique entailed in Beauvoir's approach while also showing the relevancy for recent work on political myth. Furthermore, by sidestepping the methodological questions raised by the psychoanalytic approaches listed above, their essays suspend, to paraphrase Foucault, the unifying aspects of Beauvoir's theory. To summarize, these papers go beyond the opposition between constructivist appraisals and liberal dismissals of myth, highlighting the gendered and racialized dimension of their contemporary operation.

What about affect? Beauvoir, as the essays by Stavro, Kruks, and Kirkpatrick illustrate, takes up a fruitful yet underappreciated position in this debate. For starters, while Beauvoir allows for the autonomy of the body and bodily responses, and while the passions (Beauvoir's preferred term) are embodied, she does not reduce them to the body. Indeed, insofar as existence is, for Beauvoir, both embodied and conscious, she is more interested in how the passions function in our processes of *becoming* than whether they are mental or physical phenomena. Furthermore, passions usually emerge in our relationships with others: in a relevant passage, Beauvoir discusses a child who cried because the concierge's son had died, and who was chastised by his parents for doing so. "But that," Beauvoir comments ironically, "was a dangerous thing to teach. Useless to cry over a little boy who is a stranger: so be it. But why cry over one's brother?"[7] Cited to mark the difference with Sartre, who would dismiss emotions and hence suggest that we can exert a certain control over them,[8] the quote illustrates that, for Beauvoir, our emotional responses escape us, setting up relations that we had not anticipated and that defy social expectations as to who should matter to us. On the other hand, the denial of our finitude—which we understand here as the "incapacity to be in charge of other people"[9]—is also accompanied by a range of passions, such as anger, frustration, fatigue, pleasure, and so on.[10] The passions, in other words, emerge in our practical engagement with others, and are malleable insofar as we can adapt our attunement to others. Insofar as emancipatory politics is the collective struggle against oppression and for the freedom of others, it is also always 'passionate'—just as reactionary politics draws on the feelings corresponding to the denial of openness and uncontrollability.

Strategies of Resistance: Counter-Violence and Institutional Reform

The above two issues concern the mobilization of opposition. Another topic that is intensely debated concerns strategy: what are the aims of this opposition, and what means can be used for it? The most pressing issue here is the use of counter-violence. In radical democracy, we should start by noting a deep-seated suspicion of instrumental approaches to violence. This suspicion is often closely linked to a rejection of a teleological conception of history. As history is no longer taken to develop towards revolution, we can no longer evaluate acts of counter-violence by assessing whether they will further or impede this progress.[11] Similarly, and as Walter Benjamin powerfully reminds us, a critique of violence should not be confused with reviewing its justifications, which are typically provided in instrumental terms. Means-end reasoning implies, in this approach, that acts of violence are evaluated as being proportional or disproportional. These justifications operate within a liberal framework in which the use of violence can be delimited but not truly critiqued.[12]

Finally, the notion of violence itself has been widened in recent years: from a more narrow notion that refers to the use of physical force by one person against the body of another (or against one's possessions), it is now taken to exceed a face-to-face encounter and also to consist in such diverse aspects as the exclusionary dimensions of language, the differential impact of natural disasters, and economic exploitation.[13] Indeed, what counts as violence is itself the object of politics, and the epithet 'violence' seems to be often used to discredit opposition to the state and to capitalist modes of production.

While the literature on counter-violence and nonviolence is vast, it might be worthwhile to point to some recent contributions that can be brought into a fruitful dialogue with Beauvoir. Highly influential, Butler's recent work argues for nonviolent resistance, an argument that is based on a relational ontology in which each of us is exposed and vulnerable to others.[14] Even if these arguments are articulated in a distinctively contemporary Levinasian vocabulary, its concerns can be traced back to second wave feminism, such as care ethics and women's peace camps. The arguments in favor of nonviolence have often been criticized for providing an ethical rather than a political response: in emphasizing the appeal by the other, it fails to address, so the objection runs, the kind of collective action that is required for changing institutional and socio-economic conditions.[15] Furthermore, this contestation might involve acts of violence; and, from a feminist perspective, this would also entail denaturalizing women's so-called innate inclination to refrain from violence. At the same time, outside of the more strictly academic debates, the issue of counter-violence is also hotly debated among activists. Nonviolence is often associated with movements for civil disobedience, such as the Indian independence struggle and the

Civil Rights Movement. The arguments for nonviolence by Gandhi and Martin Luther King presuppose a human existence that is good, and that is harmed by suffering as well as committing violence.[16] On the other hand, there are those who argue that the fight against fascism has historically required a large repertoire of acts of physical resistance, which can range from fistfights and disturbing right-wing events to armed attacks.[17]

On a different note, political strategy can also be thematized in relation to institutional reform and the endowment of rights. Again, the literature here is vast; but what matters for our discussion is the opposition between critical legal studies and those approaches that try to recuperate and extend rights. The former might start from a Marxist critique of rights as dissimulating social relations of inequality and exploitation as relationships of reciprocity in which individuals can supposedly freely enter into a contractual relationship with one another; or it might start from a post-structuralist position, in which individual rights are part of subjectivation and individualization processes such that they produce the individual that is supposedly the bearer of these rights.[18] On the other hand, we might find those who, arguing from a feminist or intersectional perspective, reject a liberal-individualist conception of rights but hold on to the importance of a relational account of rights, as well as the great emancipatory potential of subjectivation as a right-bearing subject.[19]

How does Beauvoir help us in re-orienting these debates? We might want to start marking her distance from, for instance, Merleau-Ponty and Sartre as she provides us, especially in her fiction, with a tentative criticism of the instrumental approach to counter-violence.[20] Admittedly, she did not do so with the same ardor as, say, Hannah Arendt.[21] A comparison with Arendt helpfully underscores how Beauvoir overcomes the opposition between ethics and politics that haunts the contemporary debates on nonviolence: like Arendt, Beauvoir considers counter-violence in relation to the concrete conditions of oppression which it seeks to alter—her approach is, to use Arendtian terms, political insofar as it is world-oriented. At the same time, and in contradistinction from Arendt, Beauvoir couples this world-orientation to the lived ambiguities of using violence. Beauvoir highlights the tension inherent to acts of counter-violence: they are aimed at the liberation from oppression and against the violence that is yielded against those who are othered, such as women and colonized peoples. Yet these acts involve the objectification of the perpetrators of oppression, and oftentimes also of oneself and one's collaborators. The tension that thus arises cannot be resolved but only endured. Beauvoir has explored this tension in her fiction, such as *The Blood of Others*, as well in her moral essays, especially *The Ethics of Ambiguity*.

The historical backdrops of Beauvoir's reflections on counter-violence are the French struggle against fascism during the Second World War and the Algerian resistance against the French occupation—situations in which counter-violence has a relatively clear goal, namely liberation from a foreign military power. Dianna Taylor argues in her contribution to this collection that Beauvoir's analysis can also be extended to gender-based oppression. In what might be read as an important difference from the proponents of nonviolence and civil disobedience, Beauvoir would not argue that the use of violence is necessarily harmful. She at times even appears to suggest it might restore a primordial reciprocity that has been violated.[22] She also, however, contends that it constitutes a rupture between people, in which case she would disagree with Sartre when he is stating that violence "is man re-creating himself."[23]

What about other, nonviolent strategies? While Beauvoir was involved in various campaigns, she often refrains from theoretically elaborating on them. Hence, we mostly read in an almost anecdotal manner about her involvement with the various forms of campaigning and consciousness-raising.[24] The essays in this collection by Stavro, Maskalan, and Nya amend that by thinking with Beauvoir about social movements fighting against race- and gender-based violence as well as the suffragist struggle in Martinique. The latter issue brings us to the issue of women's rights, a topic on which Beauvoir has not written extensively. Her position can only be reconstructed indirectly, for instance by calling to mind her ironic assertion, in the opening pages of *The Second Sex*, that the Woman Question is annoying and that "it is now almost over" as women have been granted the right to vote.[25] Her irony should not be confused, however, with a Marxist critique of rights, and her aim is not to debunk rights as a liberal fiction that hides and enables the underlying structures of exploitation. Rights and other institutional issues are, for Beauvoir, part of one's 'situation.' This implies firstly that the formal rights and entitlements of women have an impact on their agency; and, secondly, that women's liberation requires more than transforming the relationships of production—indeed it requires overhauling all social, interpersonal, and institutional conditions.[26] Arguing against Beauvoir's notion of situated freedom, Nya compares Beauvoir's position with that of Martinican suffragette Paulette Nardal to show how the latter proposes a more radical notion of freedom that motivates the struggle for women's voting rights. In a different vein, Ana Maskalan shows in her contribution that, notwithstanding the massive mobilization of women in the former Yugoslavia, institutional change is hindered by firmly entrenched patriarchal patterns.

The Question of Lived Experience

Lived experience is a key term in the phenomenological method. It has also been put to political uses by Beauvoir, Fanon, and many others to call attention to those experiences that have often been dismissed from theory-production because, in Foucault's formulation, they "have been disqualified as nonconceptual knowledges, as insufficiently elaborated knowledges: naive knowledges, hierarchically inferior knowledges, knowledges that are below the required level of erudition or scientificity."[27] Yet, the status of lived experience has also been much debated, in particular in the wake of post-structuralist feminist critiques of a naïve empiricism that pervaded, in their view, second wave feminism. Joan Scott, in her landmark 1991 essay "The Evidence of Experience," argues against the idea that we can recuperate women's experience.[28] The post-structuralist critique of lived experience starts from the discursive construction of experience to highlight how the elucidation of lived experience fails to expose its own historically contingent conditions of possibility. As a consequence, so the argument runs, the phenomenological method reifies these experiences as well as the groups to which these are attributed.

Responses to this argument on the social construction of experience have typically stressed the embodied dimension of experience. Embodiment, the phenomenological response holds, exceeds discourse and allows for constructing feminist solidarity, if not group-identity. Furthermore, attention to embodiment is compatible with historical surveys of the depersonal conditions under which one experiences one's body. In one of the most significant contributions to this debate, Sonia Kruks argues for a methodological pluralism in which one pole explores experience from an impersonal or "third-person" stance, its project being explanatory; the other pole explores it from a "first-person" stance, in terms of its personal meaning, as an experience to be grasped or understood rather than explained.

While the status of experience is still a crucial topic in feminist debates, this debate has somewhat abated in recent years: phenomenology has embraced the historically contingent conditioning of experience (as evidenced in critical phenomenology[29]), while Foucauldian social-constructivism has been increasingly interpreted through a phenomenological lens.[30] This shift has also enabled a rewriting of Beauvoir's position in this debate. During the eighties and the nineties, Beauvoir had been important for post-structuralists who praised her for posing the question of how sexual difference or gender is constituted while faulting her for her 'Cartesian' moments in which she posits a subject that precedes this difference.[31] Less ambivalently, she was invoked in the same period by feminist phenomenologists to stress the embodied dimension of women's existence.[32] More recently, she is embraced as a critical phenomenologist *avant la lettre*. The first part of *The Second Sex* describes the historical conditions (discursive as well as socio-economic and juridico-political) of lived experiences that are elaborated on in the second part—a method repeated by *Old Age*. Crucially, while the question of experience has mostly been raised in regard to gender and race, it is also a helpful concept in thinking about old age and pregnancy, as Kruks and Kirkpatrick show in their contributions to this collection.

A major factor in the critique of experience was the argument put forward by feminists of color who argued that most white women writers claimed a so-called universal feminine perspective that in fact was limited to their own social position, and that abnegated the perspectives of women of color and their privileged insight in patriarchy and its imbrication with white supremacy.[33] This intersectional critique does not reject experience as, in fact, it centers the experiences of marginalized women; but it does problematize the assumption of a shared experiential basis for 'woman' and for the feminist movement. This critique is also leveled against Beauvoir. The question is not so much whether and how Beauvoir included theorizing by racialized women (she barely did), but whether her theoretical framework allows for this inclusion. A key question in this regard is how different forms of oppression relate to one another. More specifically, should they be considered as analogous or as intersecting? Kathryn Belle writes that Beauvoir opts for the former and, as a consequence, erases the experience of those who are located at the intersection of race and gender, and hence fails to include the experiences of racialized women.[34] Other Black feminists, such as Patricia Hill Collins, have largely agreed with Belle,[35] while yet others, such as bell hooks, have approached Beauvoir with an eye to what can be recuperated from her thought for an intersectional feminism.[36]

Along the lines of the latter, Qrescent Mali Mason's contribution proposes an ethical attitude of 'ambiguity' that acknowledges our contemporary ambivalences regarding Beauvoir's political and personal actions, such as her affairs with female students and her position on racism, refraining from resolving the contradictory meaning these actions might have. Furthermore, the intersectional critique has historical-methodological implications: rather than comparing Beauvoir with well-established systematic thinkers such as Sartre and Merleau-Ponty, maybe we should instead set up dialogues with those thinkers whose knowledge has been dismissed as too local and as barely passing the threshold of knowledge—in particular, thinkers whose experiences have been relegated to the margins because they are located at the intersection of various axes of oppression. The question, then, is with which other authors can we compare Beauvoir?[37] Nathalie Nya takes up this question in her chapter, which introduces us to the important work of Paulette Nardal.

Finally, the issue of lived experience also raises a methodological question: if lived experience, especially by those who have historically been oppressed, is crucial to theory-formation, which genres facilitate this best? What genres, on the other hand, are open to those who argue that theory-formation requires decentering lived experience? The first question has been extensively engaged with by Black and Latin and Chicana feminists, even if not exactly in these terms. Many of them have written auto-theoretical works, of which Mason's contribution to this collection is an example.[38] They also advance a notion of theorizing as a practical, non-scholarly activity that starts from socially determinate positions.[39] The second question has been affirmatively answered by post-structuralists who turn to storytelling to expose the structural conditions of experience and their historical permutations.[40] While this approach does not imply a wholesale rejection of the genre of (auto-)biography, it problematizes it insofar as post-structuralism mostly starts from the death of the author and the suspension of the subject as a unifying principle that precedes the text.[41]

Beauvoir's reflections on genre and on philosophical activity resonate particularly strongly with the first set of authors while to a certain extent supplementing the latter. This is particularly clear with regard to her autobiographies. She is interested, on the one hand, in exploring how certain absolutes of the human condition, such as mortality or the uncontrollability of action, are lived individually. At the same time, she wants to expose the historically contingent conditions under which she—and those of her generation, class, and gender—lived. In her autobiographies, Beauvoir writes, "it is a question of starting from the singularity of my life in order to find a generality, that of my era, that of the milieu in which I live."[42] More generally, she expresses ambivalence regarding moral treatises and systematic works of philosophy, and prefers autobiographies, novels, and works of social critique that allow the descriptions of concrete and unique lived experiences. These experiences are conditioned by the subject's social position but not reducible to it, and Beauvoir's works of fiction and non-fiction show how one and the same situation can be experienced in contrary ways by different individuals. At its best, this perspectivism abstains from claims to a privileged epistemic vantage point and starts from the very local knowledges of subjects.[43]

Conclusion

This cursory overview cannot do justice to the many uses of Beauvoir for contemporary political theory. It is not unique in wanting to show the political and philosophical insights that her oeuvre harbors: this has often and very productively been done by stressing her proximity and originality vis-à-vis her contemporaries who had been firmly anchored in the philosophical canon, such as Sartre, Merleau-Ponty, and Heidegger.[44] The aim of this chapter, however, is oriented toward current debates and, as a consequence, is more selective and splintered in its revaluation of Beauvoir. Rather than a shortcoming, I believe this fragmentation is a strength of the 'tool-box' approach outlined in the Introduction to this volume. This approach also entails that future research on Beauvoir follows from the exigencies forced on us by understanding and acting upon the major crises of our times, such as the environmental catastrophe that is currently unfolding, the increasing disparity in wealth in a globalized world, and the persistence of racialized and gendered hierarchies throughout their different mutations. These crises solicit a "hyper- and pessimistic activism"[45] in which the tools provided by Beauvoir's work and life may serve as guideposts for change.

Notes

1 Jürgen Habermas, *Inclusion of the Other: Studies in Political Theory*, ed. Ciaran Cronin and Pablo De Greiff (Boston: MIT Press, 1998), 37.
2 Brian Massumi, "The Autonomy of Affect," *Cultural Critique*, no. 31 (1995): 83–109, https://doi.org/10.2307/1354446; Brian Massumi, *Politics of Affect* (New York: Wiley, 2015). For a critique of non-intentionality, see Ruth Leys, "The Turn to Affect: A Critique," *Critical Inquiry* 37, no. 3 (March 2011): 434–72, https://doi.org/10.1086/659353; for a response to Leys' charge, see William E. Connolly, "The Complexity of Intention," *Critical Inquiry* 37, no. 4 (June 2011): 791–98, https://doi.org/10.1086/660993.
3 Sara Ahmed, *The Cultural Politics of Emotion* (New York: Routledge, 2013).
4 Chantal Mouffe, *On the Political* (London/New York: Routledge, 2005).
5 Hélène Cixous, "The Laugh of the Medusa," trans. Keith Cohen and Paula Cohen, *Signs: Journal of Women in Culture and Society* 1, no. 4 (1976): 875–893, https://doi.org/10.1086/493306; Adriana Cavarero, *In Spite of Plato: A Feminist Rewriting of Ancient Philosophy* (New York: Routledge, 1995).
6 See also Fanon, who writes: "Jung locates the collective unconscious in the inherited cerebral matter. But there is no need to resort to the genes; the collective unconscious is quite simply the repository of prejudices, myths, and collective attitudes of a particular group." Frantz Fanon, *Black Skin, White Masks*, trans. Richard Philcox (New York: Grove, 2008), 165.
7 Simone de Beauvoir, "Pyrrhus and Cineas," in *Philosophical Writings*, ed. Margaret Simons, Marybeth Timmermann, and Mary Beth Mader, trans. Marybeth Timmermann (Urbana: University of Illinois Press, 2004), 92.
8 Karen Vintges, *Philosophy as Passion: The Thinking of Simone de Beauvoir* (Bloomington: Indiana University Press, 1996), 53, Ch.4 passim.
9 Janell Watson, "Feminism as Agonistic Sorority: An Interview with Bonnie Honig," *Minnesota Review* 2013, no. 81 (November 2013): 109, https://doi.org/10.1215/00265667-2332165.
10 Beauvoir categorizes these responses in the various character types in *The Ethics of Ambiguity*, such as the adventurer and the sub-man, and she describes them in a less systematic manner in her fiction and works of social critique. Simone de Beauvoir, *The Ethics of Ambiguity* (New York: Open Road Integrated Media, 2011), 44ff.
11 Hannah Arendt, *On Violence* (New York: Houghton Mifflin Harcourt, 1970).
12 Walter Benjamin, "Critique of Violence," in *Reflections: Essays, Aphorisms, Autobiographical Writings*, ed. Peter Demetz, trans. Edmund Jephcott (New York: Schocken, 1986), 277–300.
13 In the vast literature, see for instance Pierre Bourdieu and Loïc J.D. Wacquant, *An Invitation to Reflexive Sociology* (Chicago: University of Chicago Press, 1992); Étienne Balibar, *Violence and Civility: On the Limits of Political Philosophy* (New York: Columbia University Press, 2015); Elizabeth Frazer and Kimberly Hutchings, *Violence and Political Theory* (Cambridge: Polity, 2020).
14 Judith Butler, *The Force of Nonviolence: The Ethical in the Political* (London: Verso, 2020); Adriana Cavarero, Judith Butler, and Bonnie Honig, *Toward a Feminist Ethics of Nonviolence* (New York: Fordham University Press, 2021).
15 Jacques Rancière, "The Ethical Turn of Aesthetics and Politics," *Critical Horizons* 7, no. 1 (2006): 1–20; Bonnie Honig, *Antigone, Interrupted* (Cambridge: Cambridge University Press, 2013).
16 Mahatma Gandhi, *The Moral and Political Thought of Mahatma Gandhi*, ed. Raghavan N. Iyer, vol. 3 (Oxford: Clarendon, 1987); Martin Luther King Jr., "Letter from Birmingham Jail," 1963, King Institute, Stanford University, https://kinginstitute.stanford.edu/sites/mlk/files/letterfrombirmingham_wwcw_0.pdf.

17 Peter Gelderloos, *How Nonviolence Protects the State* (Donji Budački, Croatia/ Olympia, WA: Active Distribution/Detritus Books, 2021); Dave Hann, *Physical Resistance: Or, A Hundred Years of Anti-Fascism*, ed. Louise Purbrick (Winchester, UK: Zero Books, 2013).
18 Wendy Brown, "Suffering Rights as Paradoxes," *Constellations* 7, no. 2 (2000): 208–29, https://doi.org/10.1111/1467-8675.00183.
19 Iris Marion Young, *Justice and the Politics of Difference* (Princeton, NJ: Princeton University Press, 2011); Patricia J. Williams, *The Alchemy of Race and Rights* (Cambridge, MA: Harvard University Press, 1991).
20 Simone de Beauvoir, *The Mandarins* (London: 4th Estate, 2018); Simone de Beauvoir, *The Blood of Others* (London: Penguin, 1964); Maurice Merleau-Ponty, *Humanism and Terror: An Essay on the Communist Problem*, trans. John O'Neill (Boston, MA: Beacon, 1969); Jean-Paul Sartre, "Preface," in *The Wretched of the Earth*, by Frantz Fanon, trans. Constance Farrington (London: Penguin, 2001), 7–26.
21 Hannah Arendt, "The Eggs Speak Up," in *Essays in Understanding, 1930–1954: Formation, Exile, and Totalitarianism*, ed. Jerome Kohn (New York: Schocken, 1994), 270–84; Arendt, *On Violence*.
22 Beauvoir, *The Ethics of Ambiguity*.
23 Sartre, "Preface," 18. Beauvoir is cautious on the effect of violence on the self; as such, she can be read as agreeing with Arendt and Fanon, who, notwithstanding his approval of decolonial violence, implicitly warns against it through his case studies. See Frantz Fanon, *The Wretched of the Earth*, trans. Constance Farrington (London: Penguin, 2001), 200–250.
24 See in particular her autobiographies: Simone de Beauvoir, *Force of Circumstance*, trans. Richard Howard (Harmondsworth: Penguin, 1968); Simone de Beauvoir, *All Said and Done*, trans. Patrick O'Brian (London: Penguin, 1977).
25 Simone de Beauvoir, *The Second Sex*, trans. Constance Borde and Sheila Malovany-Chevallier (New York: Vintage, 2011), 3.
26 See, for instance Beauvoir, *The Second Sex*, 760–61.
27 Michel Foucault, *Society Must Be Defended: Lectures at the Collège de France, 1975–76*, ed. David Macey (London: Penguin, 2004), 7.
28 Joan Scott, "The Evidence of Experience," *Critical Inquiry* 17, no. 4 (Summer 1991): 773–97; Judith Butler, *Gender Trouble: Feminism and the Subversion of Identity* (New York: Routledge, 2011); Lois McNay, "Agency and Experience: Gender as a Lived Relation," *Sociological Review* 52, no. 2 suppl. (October 2004): 175–90, https://doi.org/10.1111/j.1467-954X.2005.00530.x.
29 Gail Weiss, Gayle Salamon, and Ann V. Murphy, *50 Concepts for a Critical Phenomenology* (Evanston, IL: Northwestern University Press, 2019); Gayle Salamon, "What's Critical about Critical Phenomenology?," *Puncta: Journal of Critical Phenomenology* 1, no. 1 (November 2018): 8–17; Lisa Guenther, "Six Senses of Critique for Critical Phenomenology," *Puncta: Journal of Critical Phenomenology* 4, no. 2 (2021): 5–23.
30 Johanna Oksala, *Feminist Experiences: Foucauldian and Phenomenological Investigations* (Evanston, IL: Northwestern University Press, 2016); Sara Ahmed, *Living a Feminist Life* (Durham, NC: Duke University Press, 2016).
31 Judith Butler, "Sex and Gender in Simone de Beauvoir's Second Sex," *Yale French Studies*, no. 72 (1986): 35–49, https://doi.org/10.2307/2930225; Judith Butler, "Performative Acts and Gender Constitution: An Essay in Phenomenology and Feminist Theory," *Theatre Journal* 40, no. 4 (December 1988): 519–31.
32 Sandra Lee Bartky, *Femininity and Domination: Studies in the Phenomenology of Oppression* (New York: Routledge, 1990); Iris Marion Young, *Throwing Like a Girl and Other Essays in Feminist Philosophy and Social Theory* (Bloomington:

Indiana University Press, 1990); Sara Heinämaa, *Toward a Phenomenology of Sexual Difference: Husserl, Merleau-Ponty, Beauvoir* (Lanham, MD: Rowman & Littlefield, 2004).
33 Cherríe Moraga and Gloria Anzaldúa (eds.), *This Bridge Called My Back: Writings by Radical Women of Color* (Watertown, MA: Persephone, 1981); bell hooks, *Ain't I a Woman: Black Women and Feminism* (Boston, MA: South End Press, 1981); Audre Lorde, *Sister Outsider* (London: Penguin, 2019); Kimberlé Crenshaw, "Mapping the Margins: Intersectionality, Identity Politics, and Violence against Women of Color," *Stanford Law Review* 43, no. 6 (July 1991): 1241–99, https://doi.org/10.2307/1229039.
34 Kathryn T. Gines [now Belle], "Comparative and Competing Frameworks of Oppression in Simone de Beauvoir's The Second Sex," *Graduate Faculty Philosophy Journal* 35, no. 1/2 (July 2014): 251–73, https://doi.org/10.5840/gfpj2014351/212; Kathryn T. Gines, "Simone de Beauvoir and the Race/Gender Analogy in *The Second Sex* Revisited," in *A Companion to Simone de Beauvoir*, ed. Laura Hengehold and Nancy Bauer (Hoboken, NJ: Wiley Blackwell, 2017), 47–58, https://doi.org/10.1002/9781118795996.ch4.
35 Patricia Hill Collins, "Simone de Beauvoir, Women's Oppression and Existential Freedom," in *A Companion to Simone de Beauvoir*, ed. Laura Hengehold and Nancy Bauer (Hoboken, NJ: Wiley Blackwell, 2017), 325–38.
36 bell hooks, "True Philosophers: Beauvoir and Bell," in *Beauvoir and Western Thought from Plato to Butler*, ed. Shannon M. Mussett and William S. Wilkerson (Albany: State University of New York Press, 2012), 227–36.
37 See also Meryl Altman, *Beauvoir in Time* (Leiden: Brill Rodopi, 2020), 153.
38 Audre Lorde, *Zami: A New Spelling of My Name* (London: Penguin, 2018); Patricia Hill Collins, *Black Feminist Thought: Knowledge, Consciousness, and the Politics of Empowerment* (New York: Routledge, 2002); María Lugones, *Pilgrimages/Peregrinajes: Theorizing Coalition against Multiple Oppressions* (Lanham, MD: Rowman & Littlefield, 2003); Gloria Anzaldúa, *Borderlands/La Frontera: The New Mestiza*, 4th ed. (San Francisco: Aunt Lute Books, 2007).
39 Patricia Hill Collins, *Intersectionality as Critical Social Theory* (Durham, NC: Duke University Press, 2019); Kristie Dotson, "How Is This Paper Philosophy?," *Comparative Philosophy* 3, no. 1 (December 2012): 121, https://doi.org/10.31979/2151-6014(2012).030105.
40 Joan Scott, "Storytelling," *History and Theory* 50, no. 2 (May 2011): 203–9; see also Hannah Arendt, *Men in Dark Times* (San Diego: Harcourt Brace Jovanovich, 1968).
41 Examples abound, but worthy of mention here might be: Michel Foucault, *Herculine Barbin: Being the Recently Discovered Memoirs of a Nineteenth-Century French Hermaphrodite* (New York: Knopf Doubleday, 2013); David M. Halperin, *Saint Foucault: Towards a Gay Hagiography* (Oxford: Oxford University Press, 1997).
42 Simone de Beauvoir, "My Experience as a Writer," in *"The Useless Mouths" and Other Literary Writings*, ed. Margaret Simons and Marybeth Timmermann (Urbana/Chicago: University of Illinois Press, 2011), 291.
43 See also the Introduction on our Foucauldian 'tool-box' approach.
44 For literature on Sartre, see n. 6 in the Introduction; for Heidegger, see Nancy Bauer, "Being-with as Being-against: Heidegger Meets Hegel in *The Second Sex*," *Continental Philosophy Review* 34, no. 2 (June 2001): 129–49, https://doi.org/10.1023/A:1017968905153; Eva Gothlin, "Reading Simone de Beauvoir with Martin Heidegger," in *The Cambridge Companion to Simone de Beauvoir*, ed. Claudia Card (Cambridge: Cambridge University Press, 2003), 45–65; for Merleau-Ponty, see Gail Weiss, "Beauvoir and Merleau-Ponty: Philosophers of

Ambiguity," in *Beauvoir and Western Thought from Plato to Butler*, ed. Shannon M. Mussett and William S. Wilkerson (Albany: State University of New York Press, 2012), 171–90; Suzanne Laba Cataldi, "The Body as a Basis for Being: Simone de Beauvoir and Maurice Merleau-Ponty," in *The Existential Phenomenology of Simone de Beauvoir*, ed. Wendy O'Brien and Lester Embree (Dordrecht: Springer, 2013), 85–106; for Arendt, see Andrea Veltman, "Simone de Beauvoir and Hannah Arendt on Labor," *Hypatia* 25, no. 1 (2010): 55–78; Liesbeth Schoonheim, "Arendt and Beauvoir on Romantic Love," in *Hannah Arendt and the History of Thought*, ed. Marguerite La Caze and Daniel Brennan (Lanham, MD: Lexington, 2022), 97–116.
45 Michel Foucault, "On the Genealogy of Ethics: An Overview of Work in Progress," in *Ethics: Subjectivity and Truth*, ed. Paul Rabinow (New York: New Press, 1997), 256.

References

Ahmed, Sara. *Living a Feminist Life*. Durham, NC: Duke University Press, 2016.
Ahmed, Sara. *The Cultural Politics of Emotion*. New York: Routledge, 2013.
Altman, Meryl. *Beauvoir in Time*. Leiden: Brill Rodopi, 2020.
Anzaldúa, Gloria. *Borderlands/La Frontera. The New Mestiza*. 4th ed. San Francisco: Aunt Lute Books, 2007.
Arendt, Hannah. *Men in Dark Times*. San Diego: Harcourt Brace Jovanovich, 1968.
Arendt, Hannah. *On Violence*. New York: Houghton Mifflin Harcourt, 1970.
Arendt, Hannah. "The Eggs Speak Up." In *Essays in Understanding, 1930–1954: Formation, Exile, and Totalitarianism*, edited by Jerome Kohn, 270–284. New York: Schocken, 1994.
Balibar, Étienne. *Violence and Civility: On the Limits of Political Philosophy*. New York: Columbia University Press, 2015.
Bartky, Sandra Lee. *Femininity and Domination: Studies in the Phenomenology of Oppression*. New York: Routledge, 1990.
Bauer, Nancy. "Being-with as Being-against: Heidegger Meets Hegel in The Second Sex." *Continental Philosophy Review* 34, no. 2 (June 2001): 129–149. https://doi.org/10.1023/A:1017968905153.
Beauvoir, Simone de. *All Said and Done*. Translated by Patrick O'Brian. London: Penguin, 1977.
Beauvoir, Simone de. *Force of Circumstance*. Translated by Richard Howard. Harmondsworth: Penguin, 1968.
Beauvoir, Simone de. "My Experience as a Writer." In *"The Useless Mouths" and Other Literary Writings*, edited by Margaret Simons and Marybeth Timmermann, 275–301. The Beauvoir Series. Urbana/Chicago: University of Illinois Press, 2011.
Beauvoir, Simone de. "Pyrrhus and Cineas." In *Philosophical Writings*, edited by Margaret Simons, Marybeth Timmermann, and Mary Beth Mader, translated by Marybeth Timmermann. Urbana: University of Illinois Press, 2004.
Beauvoir, Simone de. *The Blood of Others*. London: Penguin, 1964.
Beauvoir, Simone de. *The Ethics of Ambiguity*. New York: Open Road Integrated Media, 2011.
Beauvoir, Simone de. *The Mandarins*. London: 4th Estate, 2018.
Beauvoir, Simone de. *The Second Sex*. Translated by Constance Borde and Sheila Malovany-Chevallier. New York: Vintage, 2011.

Benjamin, Walter. "Critique of Violence." In *Reflections: Essays, Aphorisms, Autobiographical Writings*, edited by Peter Demetz, translated by Edmund Jephcott, 277–300. New York: Schocken, 1986.

Bourdieu, Pierre, and Loïc J.D. Wacquant. *An Invitation to Reflexive Sociology*. Chicago: University of Chicago Press, 1992.

Brown, Wendy. "Suffering Rights as Paradoxes." *Constellations* 7, no. 2 (2000): 208–229. https://doi.org/10.1111/1467-8675.00183.

Butler, Judith. *Gender Trouble: Feminism and the Subversion of Identity*. New York: Routledge, 2011.

Butler, Judith. "Performative Acts and Gender Constitution: An Essay in Phenomenology and Feminist Theory." *Theatre Journal* 40, no. 4 (December 1988): 519–531.

Butler, Judith. "Sex and Gender in Simone de Beauvoir's Second Sex." *Yale French Studies*, no. 72 (1986): 35–49. https://doi.org/10.2307/2930225.

Butler, Judith. *The Force of Nonviolence: The Ethical in the Political*. London: Verso, 2020.

Cavarero, Adriana. *In Spite of Plato: A Feminist Rewriting of Ancient Philosophy*. New York: Routledge, 1995.

Cavarero, Adriana, Judith Butler, and Bonnie Honig. *Toward a Feminist Ethics of Nonviolence*. New York: Fordham University Press, 2021.

Cixous, Hélène. "The Laugh of the Medusa." Translated by Keith Cohen and Paula Cohen. *Signs: Journal of Women in Culture and Society* 1, no. 4 (July 1976), 875–893. https://doi.org/10.1086/493306.

Collins, Patricia Hill. *Black Feminist Thought: Knowledge, Consciousness, and the Politics of Empowerment*. New York: Routledge, 2002.

Collins, Patricia Hill. "Simone de Beauvoir, Women's Oppression and Existential Freedom." In *A Companion to Simone de Beauvoir*, edited by Laura Hengehold and Nancy Bauer, 325–328. Hoboken, NJ: Wiley Blackwell, 2017.

Collins, Patricia Hill. *Intersectionality as Critical Social Theory*. Durham, NC: Duke University Press, 2019.

Connolly, William E. "The Complexity of Intention." *Critical Inquiry* 37, no. 4 (June 2011): 791–798. https://doi.org/10.1086/660993.

Crenshaw, Kimberlé. "Mapping the Margins: Intersectionality, Identity Politics, and Violence against Women of Color." *Stanford Law Review* 43, no. 6 (July 1991): 1241–1299. https://doi.org/10.2307/1229039.

Dotson, Kristie. "How Is This Paper Philosophy?" *Comparative Philosophy* 3, no. 1 (December 2012): 121. https://doi.org/10.31979/2151-6014(2012).030105.

Fanon, Frantz. *Black Skin, White Masks*. Translated by Richard Philcox. New York: Grove, 2008.

Fanon, Frantz. *The Wretched of the Earth*. Translated by Constance Farrington. London: Penguin, 2001.

Foucault, Michel. *Herculine Barbin: Being the Recently Discovered Memoirs of a Nineteenth-Century French Hermaphrodite*. New York: Knopf Doubleday, 2013.

Foucault, Michel. "On the Genealogy of Ethics: An Overview of Work in Progress." In *Ethics: Subjectivity and Truth*, edited by Paul Rabinow, 1: 253–280. The Essential Works of Michel Foucault 1954–1984. New York: New Press, 1997.

Foucault, Michel. *Society Must Be Defended: Lectures at the Collège de France, 1975–76*. Edited by David Macey. London: Penguin, 2004.

Frazer, Elizabeth, and Kimberly Hutchings. *Violence and Political Theory*. Cambridge: Polity, 2020.

Gandhi, Mahatma. *The Moral and Political Thought of Mahatma Gandhi.* Edited by Raghavan N. Iyer. Vol. 3. Oxford: Clarendon, 1987.
Gelderloos, Peter. *How Nonviolence Protects the State.* Donji Budački, Croatia/ Olympia, WA: Active Distribution/Detritus Books, 2021.
Gines, Kathryn T. "Comparative and Competing Frameworks of Oppression in Simone de Beauvoir's *The Second Sex.*" *Graduate Faculty Philosophy Journal* 35, no. 1/2 (July 2014): 251–273. https://doi.org/10.5840/gfpj2014351/212.
Gines, Kathryn T. "Simone de Beauvoir and the Race/Gender Analogy in The Second Sex Revisited." In *A Companion to Simone de Beauvoir*, edited by Laura Hengehold and Nancy Bauer, 47–58. Hoboken, NJ: Wiley, 2017. https://doi.org/10.1002/9781118795996.ch4.
Gothlin, Eva. "Reading Simone de Beauvoir with Martin Heidegger." In *The Cambridge Companion to Simone de Beauvoir*, edited by Claudia Card, 45–65. Cambridge: Cambridge University Press, 2003.
Guenther, Lisa. "Six Senses of Critique for Critical Phenomenology." *Puncta: Journal of Critical Phenomenology* 4, no. 2 (2021): 5–23.
Habermas, Jürgen. *Inclusion of the Other: Studies in Political Theory.* Edited by Ciaran Cronin and Pablo De Greiff. Boston: MIT Press, 1998.
Halperin, David M. *Saint Foucault: Towards a Gay Hagiography.* Oxford: Oxford University Press, 1997.
Hann, Dave. *Physical Resistance: Or, A Hundred Years of Anti-Fascism.* Edited by Louise Purbrick. Winchester: Zero Books, 2013.
Heinämaa, Sara. *Toward a Phenomenology of Sexual Difference: Husserl, Merleau-Ponty, Beauvoir.* Lanham, MD: Rowman & Littlefield, 2004.
Honig, Bonnie. *Antigone, Interrupted.* Cambridge: Cambridge University Press, 2013.
hooks, bell. *Ain't I a Woman: Black Women and Feminism.* Boston, MA: South End Press, 1981.
hooks, bell. "True Philosophers: Beauvoir and Bell." In *Beauvoir and Western Thought from Plato to Butler*, edited by Shannon M. Mussett and William S. Wilkerson, 227–236. Albany: State University of New York Press, 2012.
King Jr., Martin Luther. "*Letter from Birmingham Jail*," 1963. King Institute, Stanford University. https://kinginstitute.stanford.edu/sites/mlk/files/letterfrombirmingham_wwcw_0.pdf.
Laba Cataldi, Suzanne. "The Body as a Basis for Being: Simone de Beauvoir and Maurice Merleau-Ponty." In *The Existential Phenomenology of Simone de Beauvoir*, edited by Wendy O'Brien and Lester Embree, 85–106. Dordrecht: Springer, 2013.
Leys, Ruth. "The Turn to Affect: A Critique." *Critical Inquiry* 37, no. 3 (March 2011): 434–472. https://doi.org/10.1086/659353.
Lorde, Audre. *Sister Outsider.* London: Penguin, 2019.
Lorde, Audre. *Zami: A New Spelling of My Name.* London: Penguin, 2018.
Lugones, María. *Pilgrimages/Peregrinajes: Theorizing Coalition against Multiple Oppressions.* Lanham, MD: Rowman & Littlefield, 2003.
Massumi, Brian. *Politics of Affect.* New York: Wiley, 2015.
Massumi, Brian. "The Autonomy of Affect." *Cultural Critique*, no. 31 (1995): 83–109. https://doi.org/10.2307/1354446.
McNay, Lois. "Agency and Experience: Gender as a Lived Relation." *Sociological Review* 52, no. 2 suppl (October 2004): 175–190. https://doi.org/10.1111/j.1467-954X.2005.00530.x.

Merleau-Ponty, Maurice. *Humanism and Terror: An Essay on the Communist Problem*. Translated by John O'Neill. Boston, MA: Beacon, 1969.
Moraga, Cherríe, and Gloria Anzaldúa (eds.). *This Bridge Called My Back: Writings by Radical Women of Color*. Watertown, MA: Persephone, 1981.
Mouffe, Chantal. *On the Political*. London/New York: Routledge, 2005.
Oksala, Johanna. *Feminist Experiences: Foucauldian and Phenomenological Investigations*. Evanston, IL: Northwestern University Press, 2016.
Rancière, Jacques. "The Ethical Turn of Aesthetics and Politics." *Critical Horizons* 7, no. 1 (2006): 1–20.
Salamon, Gayle. "What's Critical about Critical Phenomenology?" *Puncta: Journal of Critical Phenomenology* 1, no. 1 (November 2018): 8–17.
Sartre, Jean-Paul. "Preface." In *The Wretched of the Earth*, by Frantz Fanon, 7–26. Translated by Constance Farrington. London: Penguin, 2001.
Schoonheim, Liesbeth. "Arendt and Beauvoir on Romantic Love." In *Hannah Arendt and the History of Thought*, edited by Marguerite La Caze and Daniel Brennan, 97–116. Lanham, MD: Lexington, 2022.
Scott, Joan. "Storytelling." *History and Theory* 50, no. 2 (May 2011): 203–209.
Scott, Joan. "The Evidence of Experience." *Critical Inquiry* 17, no. 4 (Summer 1991): 773–797.
Veltman, Andrea. "Simone de Beauvoir and Hannah Arendt on Labor." *Hypatia* 25, no. 1 (2010): 55–78.
Vintges, Karen. *Philosophy as Passion: The Thinking of Simone de Beauvoir*. Bloomington: Indiana University Press, 1996.
Watson, Janell. "Feminism as Agonistic Sorority: An Interview with Bonnie Honig." *Minnesota Review* 2013, no. 81 (November 2013): 102–125. https://doi.org/10.1215/00265667-2332165.
Weiss, Gail. "Beauvoir and Merleau-Ponty: Philosophers of Ambiguity." In *Beauvoir and Western Thought from Plato to Butler*, edited by Shannon M. Mussett and William S. Wilkerson, 171–190. Albany: State University of New York Press, 2012.
Weiss, Gail, Gayle Salamon, and Ann V. Murphy. *50 Concepts for a Critical Phenomenology*. Evanston, IL: Northwestern University Press, 2019.
Williams, Patricia J. *The Alchemy of Race and Rights*. Cambridge, MA: Harvard University Press, 1991.
Young, Iris Marion. *Justice and the Politics of Difference*. Princeton, NJ: Princeton University Press, 2011.
Young, Iris Marion. *Throwing like a Girl and Other Essays in Feminist Philosophy and Social Theory*. Bloomington: Indiana University Press, 1990.

PART I
Changing Myths

2
INCEL VIOLENCE AND BEAUVOIRIAN OTHERNESS

Filipa Melo Lopes

In recent years, incel violence has moved from obscure corners of the internet into mainstream news. The label—short for 'involuntary celibate'—is associated mainly with online communities of men who take themselves to be systematically romantically and sexually rejected by women.[1] In 2014, 22-year-old Elliot Rodger became the poster child for the phenomenon, shooting down seven people and killing himself in a "Day of Retribution" for his loneliness. Since then, other attackers have cited similar motives, often linking themselves directly to Rodger.[2] From "pathetic, sad, ridiculous, [and] laughable," incels have become routinely discussed as a serious threat to public safety and as domestic terrorists.[3]

But what has really captured the public imagination is the seemingly "incongruous mindset" of these violent attackers.[4] Their disarming insistence on their own unattractiveness and inferiority is a far cry from strongman machismo. But their misogynistic vitriol can rival the most hateful rhetoric ever produced about women. They seem obsessed with hyperfeminine women whom they both desire and decry. To explain this paradoxical set of attitudes, mainstream commentators have often invoked individual factors, such as mental illness. However, feminists have pushed back and argued that incel violence is actually a *systemic* and *gendered* phenomenon linked to patriarchal attitudes in the broader culture. They have offered two explanations along these lines. One depicts incel attacks as a byproduct of the dehumanizing *objectification* of women. Another highlights a sense of *entitlement* to sex and love on the part of these men.

In this chapter, I will take on board the feminist idea that incel attackers are not just troubled individuals, and that they crystalize gender dynamics present in their wider social environment. However, I will argue that both

DOI: 10.4324/9781003366089-4

models presented by feminists are explanatorily insufficient because they fail to account for incels' distinctive ambivalence towards women. I will offer a different explanation, drawing on Simone de Beauvoir's notion of woman as 'Other'. According to Beauvoir, when men view women as Others, they represent them as *sui generis* beings: at once human subjects and embodiments of the natural world. As Others, women function as unique entities through which men can shore up a vain sense of themselves as pure agency in the world—as what Beauvoir calls 'sovereign subjects'. Incels' incoherent projection of their hopes and fears onto a feminine Other is what takes them from obsessive eroticization to lethal hatred. I will show that this Beauvoirian account yields a better explanation of incel violence by using it to analyze Elliot Rodger's 137-page autobiographical manifesto, *My Twisted World*. Rodger has been invoked directly by several other incel murderers, and has become revered as a 'saint' and 'martyr' in incel circles, where other attackers are often described as 'going ER' (i.e. Elliot Rodger).[5] This widespread identification with Rodger's self-narrative thus warrants an analysis of *My Twisted World* as significantly representative of the mindset behind incel violence.

The Problem of Incel Ambivalence

One of the most baffling things about incels is the way they direct violent hatred towards the same people they obsessively desire. Beautiful women are so important to them that their rejection is a life-ending tragedy. But these "goddesses" are also "evil, slutty bitches" and disgusting "whores."[6] Incels seem to both put women on pedestals of desirability and throw them down to the depths of repulsion. Elliot Rodger famously articulated this ambivalence: "I will attack the very girls who represent *everything I hate* in the female gender: the *hottest* sorority of UCSB [University of California, Santa Barbara's Alpha Phi]" (*MTW*, 132; emphasis mine).

How do we explain this apparent contradiction? One initially appealing strategy is to deem it an acute case of sour grapes and to say that the ambivalence is only superficial: incels' disdain and anger are ways of coping with loneliness. However, feminists have pointed out that this is an inadequate explanation. Many other women and men face systematic and prolonged sexual rejection and struggle with a lack of intimacy. The contingents of female incels (or 'femcels') online are a vivid testament to this.[7] But they do not all respond by declaring war on the people they desire or by going on killing sprees. Feminists have maintained that this swing from love to hate cannot be explained by appealing to an individual, gender-neutral psychology.[8] Incels turn from attraction to violence because they see women in a particular way. What is this representation that fuels incel desire and incel hate? Two answers have emerged. The first is that incels desire women as objects without the capacity for choice. Call this *objectification*. The second is that incels see women as servants that owe them sex and love. Call this *entitlement*.

The core idea of objectification is that incels are driven by a patriarchal conviction that "women are decorative sexual objects, and that male worth is measured by how good-looking a woman they acquire."[9] They dehumanize women in that they regard them as lacking characteristically human capacities, such as the capacity to choose, to have a subjective point of view, or to have complex emotions.[10] In this way, incels expect women to be like dolls. And social norms, economic dependency, and other constraints meant that, until relatively recently, the world matched these expectations: men could just pick women off the shelf, so to speak. However, over the last century, women have gained substantial "economic and cultural power."[11] They now have independent incomes, their social status is not determined by marriage, and, in the era of 'dating apps', they too can swipe right or left. These supposed objects are now choosing, expressing feelings and preferences. Incels are then men taken aback by this new reality.

However, as Kate Manne has pointed out, the attitudes and actions of someone like Elliot Rodger "not only presuppose but seem to *hinge* on women's presumed humanity."[12] The point here is twofold. First, objectification misses what is attractive about women for incels. Rodger wants women to notice him, to admire him, "to check him out" (*MTW*, 98, 122). And a mere simulation of this attention will not do. For example, when his parents hire a "pretty looking blonde" as his counsellor, Rodger says that:

> even though it was all fake, I really enjoyed it. [...] But then, I thought about how unfair it was that I could only get a fake little taste of such an experience [...]. It has the same effect as hiring a prostitute, I imagine. It temporarily feels good for the moment, but afterward it makes one feel like a pathetic loser.
>
> *(MTW, 120)*

What Rodger wants then is the genuinely free exercise of distinctively human capacities in selective and directed ways. A hired simulation provides fleeting comfort, but quickly proves profoundly unsatisfying. Second, objectification does not make sense of why incels' complaints against women are so distinctively second-personal. In a video uploaded before his attack, Rodger said "I don't know why you girls aren't attracted to me, but I will punish you all for it. It's an injustice, a crime."[13] Rodger's moralistic tone and his charges of personal wrongdoing presuppose women are human, that they have "agency, autonomy, and the capacity to be *addressed* by him."[14] Objectification misses then key aspects of incel desire and incel hatred.

This brings us to entitlement. On this hypothesis, incels desire women not as objects but as subordinated humans, bound by patriarchal norms to offer them sex and love. Much like a feudal lord sees his servants as personally owing him their loyalty, so incels represent women as owing them a hierarchical allegiance. However, in contemporary reality, women actually see themselves as having no such obligation, and many even positively refuse such a hierarchical picture of gender relations. Incel hatred is then a reaction to this thwarting of hierarchical expectations. Their violence is a form of punishment for this perceived disobedience and a way to put women back in their place.[15] What enrages incels is then not that women assert themselves as humans, but rather as *equal* humans.

While there is something deeply intuitive about this hypothesis, entitlement has two crucial weaknesses. First, entitlement leaves unexplained the exterminatory character of incel violence. Incel attackers do not just want to put women back in their proper place—they want to rid the world of women altogether. Consider the delusional fantasy that Rodger sketches at the end of his manifesto: a "fair and pure world" where women have been rounded up and starved to death in concentration camps, sex is outlawed, and a few women are "kept and bred" in secret labs (*MTW*, 136). But, if the problem is an insolent servant, why fantasize about a world purged of all servants and the great work they do? Second, the claim that incels are punishing the assertion of women's equality is at odds with the facts. Incel attacks are notoriously *not* directed at feminists or women perceived as bucking patriarchal norms. On the contrary. They target 'hot' sororities, yoga studios, and erotic massage parlors—places associated with the very hyperfemininity that incels are obsessed with and that they encapsulate in the 'Stacy' meme. The 'Stacy' is described as "naturally curvy," with "natural," "sexy, majestic long blonde hair," "make up on point," and as letting 'Chad' (her 'alpha-male' counterpart) "dominate her" and abuse her. She is also unintelligent, vain, lazy, manipulative, and sociopathic. For most men, she is out of reach and she's dangerous, exploiting them for money and favors.[16] At the end of the day, the 'Stacy' organizes her life around pleasing the most patriarchal men. And yet she is reviled and targeted for violence. It seems then that the behavior being punished by incels is not feminist-inspired insurrection, but high compliance with the norms of gender hierarchy. The problem of ambivalence remains: why do incels hate what they love and love what they hate?

Beauvoir on Woman as 'Other'

The extreme ambivalence that incels exhibit towards women may seem odd, but it is far from idiosyncratic. In *The Second Sex*, Beauvoir points to it as central to patriarchal social relations and to the culture that sustains them:

> Delilah and Judith, Aspasia and Lucretia, Pandora and Athena, woman is both Eve and the Virgin Mary. She is an idol, a servant, source of life, power of darkness [...] woman embodies no set concept; through her the passage from hope to failure, hatred to love, good to bad, bad to good takes place ceaselessly. However she is considered, it is this ambivalence that is the most striking.[17]

Men have represented women in a myriad of ever-changing, contradictory ways. This oscillation, according to Beauvoir, is the only constant content of patriarchal representations of women.[18] The task she sets for herself is then that of giving an account of these oscillating attitudes.

According to Beauvoir, the key to understanding the way men see women is to first understand the way men see themselves. As human beings, all of us experience our existence as both active agents in the world and fixed beings under the eyes of others—as both *subjects* and *objects*. This gives rise to "a tension between our drive to transcend ourselves and our drive to cement our identities in ways that we and others will find ceaselessly praiseworthy," as Nancy Bauer puts it.[19] We want to do things in the world, but we worry about the uncertain judgment of others. We would like to be successful, but success requires taking up the risk of doing things. Many men try to resolve this tension by embracing a certain cultural myth of masculinity that dissolves this problematic human ambiguity.[20] They become, in their own eyes, what Beauvoir calls "sovereign subjects": pure active agents in the world (*TSS*, 86, 159).[21]

Sovereign subjects refuse to think of themselves as objects. They see themselves as only subjects in the world, unconstrained by facts about who they are, what they have done, or what their bodies are like. At the same time, sovereign subjects attempt to make their capacity to transcend themselves a 'cemented' characteristic of who they are. This means they experience their capacity for action as if it were a static characteristic, like a deep and stable essence. These two things—being just a subject and being a fixed subjectivity—are deeply connected. To think of yourself as *just* an actor, and never as someone who has done certain actions, is to experience your capacity for acting in a distorted way, as if it was a *fixed* feature of who you are. In adopting this attitude, sovereign subjects are trying to be successful without taking any risk. Failure is something we only experience as objects of evaluation. If you are never an object, you can never fail. Moreover, because their only fixed feature is subjectivity itself, sovereign subjects can think themselves permanently successful: all they are is great actors, who can never be disgraced by their actions.

The problem is that this dreamed 'sovereignty' is impossible. To experience oneself as a subject is to experience oneself as an active process of self-fashioning, of *becoming* oneself. The idea of a fixed subjectivity is therefore profoundly incoherent: "to 'be' something, once and for all [e.g. a sovereign subject], is precisely not to be a subject."[22] Put differently, to be a praiseworthy actor one must be open to the risk of evaluation as an object, since there is no heroism without the possibility of failure. But these men see themselves as heroes, regardless of the quality of their actions. They are engaged in a form of "bad faith": an ethically reprehensible denial of their ambiguous freedom, of its risks and its responsibilities.[23] They are thereby *alienating* themselves from their own agency and identifying instead with a flattering fiction.

Men who see themselves as sovereign subjects need to have their paradoxical self-conception shored up constantly. They need an impossible confirmation that they are only activity, once and for all, to drown out their constant experience of human ambiguity. Beauvoir points to two kinds of entities to which they turn. The first is 'Nature': the natural world of impersonal forces, of life and death, of geological and organic processes. Sovereign man can experience himself as being only activity through some ways of relating to Nature: as its master, reaping its fruits, contemplating its landscapes, conquering its mountains. However, according to Beauvoir, this conquest will always be unsatisfying for an aspiring sovereign. Either he is not successful, and Nature remains a foreign obstacle; or, if Nature is successfully conquered, it is destroyed or assimilated: "in both cases, he [i.e. the sovereign subject] remains alone; he is alone when touching a stone, alone when digesting a piece of fruit" (*TSS*, 159). There is no one there to confirm what he has done. He can be only a subject, but he cannot experience his subjectivity as something he *is* in the fixed, object-like sense.

After all, it is only by being captured in the eyes of other humans that we find confirmation of what we are. Other humans are capable of judging us and of making us experience ourselves as fixed beings of some kind or other. It is this experience that the sovereign subject needs to accomplish himself as a fixed subjectivity. But humans pose another problem. A judging peer can never confirm him as *only* an active subject. By the mere act of judging, the other makes the aspiring sovereign a constrained object of their gaze. To be confirmed as a subject by another human, we must also embrace the fact that we are objects in the world in relation to them.[24] Sovereign subjects are incapable of this. They want to be praised but they cannot stand the risk of scrutiny, and so they try to eliminate it by attempting to master others, like they did Nature. However, unlike natural objects, humans fight back. For self-alienated men, interaction with others turns then into an intolerable conflict (*TSS*, 159).[25]

The aspiring sovereign subject is caught in a bind: the natural world is too unlike him, and the peer resembles him too much (*TSS*, 160). He has then a "dream." He wishes he could experience himself as just a subject, in relation to another consciousness who would confirm him as such.

> This embodied dream is, precisely, woman [...]. She pits neither the hostile silence of nature nor the hard demand of a reciprocal recognition against him; by a unique privilege she is a consciousness, and yet it seems possible to possess her in the flesh.
>
> *(TSS, 160)*

'Woman'—or, strictly speaking, this representation of women—is the perfect creature that uniquely allows men to accomplish themselves as sovereign subjects. This is the representation that Beauvoir terms woman as 'Other'. Feminist readings of Beauvoir have often interpreted this term as referring to a representation of women as objects or 'things.'[26] However, the passage above tells a more complex story. In Beauvoir's technical sense, a feminine 'Other' is an entity that is *both* another human consciousness and an embodiment of Nature. She is like other humans in that she can judge and give man the confirmation that mountains and pieces of fruit cannot. But, unlike other men, she can be truly dominated because she embodies Nature.[27] In being Nature and a peer, the Other is neither. She is a *sui generis* invention, an "interesting amalgam," and a paradoxical entity.[28]

The myth of Woman as Other provides sovereign subjects with a "marvelous hope" of escape from the silence of Nature and the struggle with other men (*TSS*, 217, 161). Unlike Nature, she offers him not just the experience of doing things, but of seeing himself as a doer in her eyes. Unlike other men, she is fully conquerable, meaning that he can relate to her as just a subject. Even when he is being judged by her, sovereign man is never a helpless object, and so he can never fail. However, this great power is purchased at a price. Woman is only Other if she is assimilated to Nature, and Nature can only be gloriously conquered because it is a dangerous obstacle.

> Man seeks the Other in woman as Nature and as his peer. But Nature inspires *ambivalent* feelings in man. He exploits it, but it crushes him; he is born from and he dies in it; it is the source of his being and the kingdom he bends to his will.
>
> *(TSS, 163; emphasis mine)*

The promise of the Other ultimately depends on her embodiment of the risk and danger of impersonal and uncontrollable natural forces. Man's ambivalent attitude towards Nature becomes then an ambivalent attitude towards woman as the embodiment of Nature. As Other, she becomes "the stuff of action and its obstacle, man's grasp on the world and its failure" and she acquires a permanent "double face" (*TSS*, 213, 163). This produces an eroticism that is profoundly ambivalent, marked by "hesitation between fear and desire, between the terror of being possessed by uncontrollable forces and the will to overcome them" (*TSS*, 172).

One of Beauvoir's key insights is that, in chasing this impossible fantasy, men doom themselves to a bitter disenchantment (*TSS*, 211, 184). Because "man seeks himself entirely in her and because she is All," Woman as Other "is never exactly *this* that she should be; she is everlasting disappointment" (*TSS*, 213; emphasis original). Just like his aspiration to be only a subject once and for all, man's desire for Woman as Other is impossible to fulfill. He wants the lush beauty of Nature, but not its destructive forces; a docile alterity, but not a full subjectivity facing him. He wants "to subdue her, as an untamed animal."[29] He dreams of a real victory without risk, of a glorious conquest without possible failure, of being a subject without ever being an object. But these aspects cannot be detached from each other. These self-alienated men are then trapped in a disappointing "game" in their relationship with women (*TSS*, 201, 208). In this game, Woman as Other must act aloof. The man must then 'tame' her, not into subjugation but into a willing adoration. However, if he wins the game, she is 'had'—her danger is neutralized and so is her erotic appeal (*TSS*, 204–205). Sovereign man needs to move on to yet another affair, each time destroying the mysterious quality he sought in woman. But if she remains aloof, then this is an actual refusal (*TSS*, 208). Sovereign man's insecure sense of himself crumbles faced with this disapproving judgment. The Other becomes then a natural obstacle, like a crushing rock. Her dangerous allure turns into an uncontrolled threat and she "becomes praying mantis or ogress" (*TSS*, 262). Sooner or later, the Other inevitably turns out to be nothing but a "mirage" (*TSS*, 272).

Woman as Other is then a patriarchal myth tailor-made to fulfill the needs of masculine bad faith. Men want to do things in the world, but they worry about the risk of failure. Woman gives them hope of evading this risk by allowing them to embrace the cultural myth of masculinity as pure, unconstrained activity. Through the Other, men can see themselves as essentially heroes, as fixed transcendent subjectivities. To fulfill this function, Woman as Other must be simultaneously another subject and an embodiment of Nature: someone who can judge and someone whose judgment can be completely conquered. But this representation is paradoxical, and always bound to collapse. Men cannot help but be aware of this, and therefore they see her as "a double and deceptive image" (*TSS*, 213).

This Beauvoirian model of patriarchal representation incorporates what is intuitive about the objectification and entitlement models, but remains distinct from them.[30] As Other, a woman is both an object and a vassal, in a certain sense. But, in being both, she is neither. She is a 'freedom', with a subjective perspective; but, unlike other men, she is not a competing rival. She is an object to be possessed, but not a mere tool to be used for one's purposes. She is a natural object filled with ambiguous powers: like the ocean that is calm and submissive but can engulf and kill you; or the ripe and fragrant fruit that can contain disease and putrefaction. For Beauvoir, "nymphs, dryads, mermaids" and others animistic goddesses are paradigmatic Others (*TSS*, 174–176). They are impossible feminine figures that embody the natural world, with its promise and peril, while retaining a distinct human consciousness.

Elliot Rodger or the Dream of Sovereignty

So far, I have argued that existing feminist proposals to explain incel violence fail to adequately do so. Objectification misses the fact that incels presuppose women's agency in important ways. And entitlement cannot account for why women excelling by patriarchal standards are singled out for extermination. I want to suggest that a Beauvoirian approach can do better. To see this, consider the following Beauvoir-inspired interpretation of Elliot Rodger's *My Twisted World*.

One of the manifesto's central themes is Rodger's search for a sense of accomplishment as a great actor: "as I've always believed, *I am destined for great things*" (*MTW*, 79; emphasis original). Rodger narrates his life as a heroic tale, driven by a clear sense not just of superiority but of extraordinary agentic power. In Beauvoirian terms, Rodger seems to think of himself as a sovereign subject. He constantly talks about himself as "a creator" and a "living god"—a trope Beauvoir associates explicitly with this kind of masculine alienation (*MTW*, 109–110, 113–114, 117–118, 131, 133, 135; *TSS*, 164). Recounting his early childhood, Rodger revels in the security and stability of this sovereign self-image. He climbs the "Big Rock" in his neighborhood, enjoys flying kites and 'conquering' new lands in his travels with his family (*MTW*, 3, 12–14). He wins games with other children and amasses card collections. The admiring regard of others is reliably his. But problems arise when Rodger notices he may not always be seen as the best. At nine years old, he realizes he is short for his age and that tall boys get more "respect." These are his "first feelings of inferiority" (*MTW*, 15). Soon he discovers that school hierarchies are not based on card collections but on wealth, race, height, and "coolness" (*MTW*, 17). Rodger finds himself judged by others in ways that he cannot control and that threaten to make him a 'loser'.

His reaction is then to double down. To maintain his god-like view of himself, he adamantly refuses to be an object of appraisal, and tries to turn all facts about who he is into new games that he is determined to win. This is when he becomes obsessed with social status and competition (*MTW*, 17)—something common to many incels.[31] He takes up skateboarding, dyes his hair blond, buys new clothes, and demands that his parents become rich overnight. He embraces white supremacist and classist ideals, and repositions himself as a 'winner' in these hierarchies by putting others down: "I am descended from British aristocracy. He is descended from slaves"; "I am a beautiful, magnificent gentleman and he is a lowclass, pig-faced thug" (*MTW*, 84, 90). But, try as he might, he cannot fully dictate who he is and what others think of him. He is still an object of their uncertain, and often negative, scrutiny. This unbearable lack of control leads Rodger to turn resolutely inwards: he feels acutely jealous and envious of everyone, leaves rooms crying in frustration, ends friendships, refuses to get a job, drops out of college, and spends more time alone. Because life is a competition that he cannot stand to lose, Rodger flees risk altogether and ends up as a passive thing shut in his room. He becomes living proof that to try to be a sovereign subject is precisely to not be a subject at all.[32]

Where do women fit into the story? In middle school, Rodger starts noticing that 'getting girls' is integral to gaining the respect of other boys (*MTW*, 11). But he also quickly learns that, more than just a trophy, a girl is someone who can *herself* make you feel like a winner. He "was one hundred-times more satisfied from getting a hug from a pretty girl than getting a high five from a popular boy. It was a new experience that enrapture every fiber of my being" (*MTW*, 28). Gaining "female validation" is uniquely satisfying (*MTW*, 13). It is itself a conquest—like climbing a "Big Rock"—and a recognition of that conquest—like a "high five." Navigating the world with a "beautiful girlfriend" becomes then Rodger's ultimate dream of complete and acknowledged mastery over reality (*MTW*, 69). This is a conception of Woman as Other, as both a natural thing to be conquered and a docile freedom that admiringly smiles back. She is an escape from hierarchical struggle, a promise of glorious rest and heroic victory once and for all.

As Rodger gets older and does less and less with his life, his sense of himself as sovereign becomes increasingly unmoored from reality. His need for recognition becomes harder to satisfy as the gap between his and others' views of himself widens. This is precisely why he comes to have "an absolute need" of Woman as Other (*TSS*, 202). Only she can recognize him as a 'god' now. "A man is judged by his fellow men by what he does, objectively and according to general standards." But a woman's regard is different: "it allows itself to be charmed" (*TSS*, 202–203). Woman as Other holds the unique promise of validation, without actual achievement. She is a way of winning *by magic*, of being acclaimed as a hero without heroic deeds. And this is increasingly the only way for Rodger to secure his sense of sovereignty.

However, invested with this power, Woman as Other becomes both the be-all and *the end-all* of existence. If her regard can bestow ultimate triumph, it can also bestow ultimate failure. After all, she cannot be seen as a subject without the risk of negative judgment creeping back in. This leads Rodger to have an increasingly "intense fear of girls" (*MTW*, 42). Consider his description of passing a woman on a beach:

she was like a goddess who came down from heaven. [...] *I was scared*. I was scared she might view me as nothing but an inferior insect who's [sic] presence ruins her atmosphere. Her beauty was intoxicating! And then, just as we passed each other, she actually *looked at me*. She looked at me and *smiled*. [...] I had never felt so euphoric in my life. *One smile*. One smile was all it took to brighten my day. The power that beautiful women have is unbelievable.

(MTW, 76; emphasis original)

The gaze of the Other is so powerful that Rodger's desire becomes ambivalent, involving an almost religious "fear of her judgement" (*MTW*, 99). The smile from a goddess is a great accomplishment because it is freely given to those who are worthy. But if a smile leads to euphoria, a frown can lead to the depths of despair. Feminine reactions become then unbelievably momentous, the doing and undoing of men like Rodger.

And the reaction we see most often from women is indifference, as they go about their lives taking no notice of Rodger. However, because these are Others, their indifference is an intolerable rejection. Invested with all this importance, their lack of response makes Rodger's sense of himself as sovereign crumble. He has not been anointed by them as a living god, secretly destined for greatness. His world is turned upside down and his dreams are destroyed. When confronted with this disappointment, many people would rethink their attitude towards life; but Rodger is so unwilling to take on the risk of being a subject in the world that he just keeps going down a spiral of self-alienation. By the end of his manifesto, it seems too late to step back from this entrenched delusion. He is cut off from the world, with no friends and no accomplishments. There is no alternative source of meaning to start rebuilding a sense of himself as something other than a fallen god, and so the Other, and the magical victory she could bring, is his only way out.

We can now see how Rodger arrives at his declaration of a "War on Women" (*MTW*, 132). First, recall that, within the myth of Woman as Other, fear and desire are always intertwined. In making the Other such a powerful figure by having an absolute need of her, Rodger also amplifies her threatening side. Second, recall that men can only confirm themselves as sovereigns through a feminine Other insofar as they can conquer her and experience themselves as pure subjects in relation to her. But, for Rodger, there is no hope left of taming the Other, of making her his beautiful girlfriend. She is now only an *amplified* and *uncontrollable* threat: no longer a radiant goddess, but only a destructive "praying mantis" (*TSS*, 262). The only way to control this uncontrollable Other is to destroy her (*MTW*, 112). In this way, extreme violence allows Rodger to establish himself as sovereign through Woman: "on the Day of Retribution, I will truly be a powerful god" (*MTW*, 135).

Hot, blonde, young women—the dream girlfriends—are first in Rodger's firing line. If they were the be-all of life, now they are the end-all precisely for the same reasons. In this mode of extermination, they continue to be Others. They are still a choosing subjectivity—one that Rodger can resent in a distinctively second-personal tone. As "the main instigators of sex" "they control which men get it and which men don't" (*MTW*, 136). But, alongside this logic of agency and moralistic blame, there is a logic of immutable and natural evil (*MTW*, 89). Women are "flawed creatures," "wired" wrongly, and "the ultimate evil behind sexuality" because they also embody ambiguous Nature (*MTW*, 136). If before they were its promising, beautiful face, now they are its dark and threatening side.

This is why, in the latter portion of *My Twisted World*, the most desirable women, the 'Stacys', are depicted as embodying dark and distinctively *natural* forces. These blonde goddesses turn out to be "vicious, stupid, cruel animals" capable only of "animal-like thinking," "completely controlled by their primal, depraved emotions and impulses," attracted to "beast-like men" and "beasts themselves" (*MTW*, 117). As such, they should not be given any rights in a society that sets itself above Nature, that is "civilized." They "must be quarantined" in order to attain a "pure" world (*MTW*, 117, 136). This characterization of the Other as an "avid and devouring beast" is precisely one of the tropes Beauvoir associates with masculine disappointment (*TSS*, 208). These attractive and threatening women become then troubling "object[s] of disgust and reverence at the same time."[33] They are unruly, contagious Others: a "plague" that can be resented (*MTW*, 136). Against such a threat, Rodger casts himself as a civilizing force, transcending Nature and heroically reclaiming mastery over the world. He becomes the "wronged, avenging hero" "fighting evil forces against the odds" that incel communities have come to idolize.[34] More than a revenge plot, his killing spree is a desperate attempt to be the great actor he thought himself to be.

Unbecoming Sovereign

On this Beauvoirian reading, incel violence is not a reactionary form of backlash against feminism and the sexual revolution. It is the predictable implosion of a profound form of self-alienation. There could never be a woman that satisfied Rodger because his desires are unsatisfiable. What he wants is not a woman, a relationship, or even a sexual encounter. What he wants *from* women is a way of being acclaimed and adored while also escaping the perils of being judged by others. That is something no real person can provide. In desiring women as this chimerical Other, Rodger also turns them into his most haunting and formidable "enemies" (*MTW*, 125–

126). This is the price he pays for his vanity (*TSS*, 208). In seeing himself as sovereign, he becomes engaged in the doomed pursuit of a mirage.

This Beauvoirian account fills the gaps left by other feminist explanations. Unlike *objectification*, it explains why incels are attracted to women as choosing subjectivities, and why they engage in seemingly punitive retaliation. For Rodger, it is important that women freely choose him to confirm his value; and, when this confirmation is not forthcoming, this freedom licenses ascriptions of blame. But notice that this second-personal register is found alongside proclamations of essential feminine evil. Woman as Other remains then an incoherent amalgam of Nature and subjectivity. In contrast with *entitlement*, this Beauvoirian model can tell us why attacks target women who conform to patriarchal norms, and why they are not just punitive but also exterminatory in tone. 'Stacys' are the perfect instantiation of the myth of Woman as Other. This makes them the alluring erotic object of incel fixation, but also makes their indifference threatening and intolerable. Their connection to Nature as quasi-animistic goddesses gives them the contours of a plague that must then be exterminated. This alternative Beauvoirian model therefore conceptualizes incel violence not as a response to the violation of patriarchal norms, but as the outcome of a form of patriarchal desire that is already profoundly ambivalent.

Notes

1 The term 'incel' was coined in the 1990s by a Canadian woman who created an involuntary celibate online space. In interviews, she has distanced herself from subsequent developments: Peter Baker, "The Woman Who Accidentally Started the Incel Movement," *Elle*, March 1, 2016, https://www.elle.com/culture/news/a 34512/woman-who-started-incel-movement/; Ben Zimmer "How 'Incel' Got Hijacked," *Politico*, May 8, 2018, https://www.politico.com/magazine/story/2018/05/08/intel-involuntary-celibate-movement-218324.
2 Bruce Hoffman, Jacob Ware, and Ezra Shapiro, "Assessing the Threat of Incel Violence," *Studies in Conflict & Terrorism* 43, no. 7 (2020): 569–572, https://doi.org/10.1080/1057610X.2020.1751459; Joseph Brean, "Incel Charges in Toronto Massage Parlour Killing Marks New Milestone in Terrorist Prosecution in Canada," *National Post*, May 19, 2020, https://nationalpost.com/news/canada/terror-charges-laid-in-toronto-massage-parlour-stabbing-that-left-one-dead.
3 Stephane J. Baele, Lewys Brace, and Travis G. Coan, "From 'Incel' to 'Saint': Analyzing the Violent Worldview behind the 2018 Toronto Attack," *Terrorism and Political Violence* 33, no. 8 (2021): 1685. https://doi.org/10.1080/09546553.2019.1638256. See also Amanda Marcotte, "Accused Toronto Killer May Have Roots in Online Misogynist Underworld: Is He a Terrorist?," *Salon*, April 25, 2018, https://www.salon.com/2018/04/25/accused-toronto-killer-may-have-roots-in-online-misogynist-underworld-is-he-a-terrorist/; Laura Bates, *Men Who Hate Women: From Incels to Pickup Artists, the Truth About Extreme Misogyny and How It Affects Us All* (London: Simon & Schuster, 2020), 11; Hoffman, Ware, and Shapiro, "Assessing the Threat," 568.
4 Baele, Brace, and Coan, "From 'Incel' to 'Saint'," 1667.

5 Among those who mentioned Rodger directly are: Chris Harper-Mercer, who killed nine people in Oregon in 2015; Alek Minassian, who drove a van through a crowded street in Toronto, killing ten; and Nikolas Cruz, who killed 17 people in a high school in Florida, on Valentine's Day. See Hoffman, Ware, and Shapiro, "Assessing the Threat," 570–571; Baele, Brace, and Coan, "From 'Incel' to 'Saint'," 1684.
6 Elliot Rodger, "My Twisted World: The Story of Elliot Rodger" (unpublished manuscript, May 23, 2014), 76, https://assets.documentcloud.org/documents/1173619/rodger-manifesto.pdf (hereafter cited in text as *MTW*); Jia Tolentino, "The Rage of Incels," *New Yorker*, May 15, 2018, https://www.newyorker.com/culture/cultural-comment/the-rage-of-the-incels.
7 Tolentino, "Rage of Incels." On 'femcels' see Nick Chester, "Meet the Women of the Incel Movement: The Truth about Femcels," *Huck*, December 5, 2018, https://www.huckmag.com/art-and-culture/tech/meet-the-women-of-the-incel-movement/; Isabelle Kohn, "Inside the World of 'Femcels'," *Mel Magazine*, February 10, 2020, https://melmagazine.com/en-us/story/femcels-vs-incels-meaning-reddit-discord. Another relevant example is Rodger's description of his friend James, who is also a virgin and initially understands his anxieties (*MTW*, 60). As Rodger turns hateful towards women, James distances himself. When confronted about his virginity, James says "he didn't pay attention to it, and focused on his strengths" (*MTW*, 75).
8 Kate Manne, *Down Girl: The Logic of Misogyny* (New York: Oxford University Press, 2018), 37–41; Bates, *Men Who Hate Women*, 3, 50.
9 Tolentino, "Rage of Incels."
10 Baele, Brace, and Coan, "From 'Incel' to 'Saint'," 1675; Bates, *Men Who Hate Women*, 29. For discussion of the capacities denied in this kind of objectification see Linda LeMoncheck, *Dehumanizing Women: Treating Persons as Sex Objects* (Totowa, NJ: Rowman & Allanheld, 1985); Martha C. Nussbaum, "Objectification," *Philosophy and Public Affairs* 24, no. 4 (1995): 249–291, https://www.jstor.org/stable/2961930; Rae Langton, *Sexual Solipsism: Philosophical Essays on Pornography and Objectification* (Oxford: Oxford University Press, 2009).
11 Tolentino, "Rage of Incels."
12 Manne, *Down Girl*, 150; see also Kate Manne, *Entitled: How Male Privilege Hurts Women* (London: Allen Lane, 2020), 25.
13 Elliot Rodger quoted in Manne, *Entitled*, 15.
14 Manne, *Down Girl*, 150; emphasis original; see also Manne, *Entitled*, 26.
15 Amia Srinivasan, "Does Anyone Have a Right to Sex?," *London Review of Books* 40, no. 6 (2018), https://www.lrb.co.uk/the-paper/v40/n06/amia-srinivasan/does-anyone-have-the-right-to-sex; Baele, Brace, and Coan, "From 'Incel' to 'Saint'," 1684; Manne, *Down Girl*, 150–158; Marcotte, "Accused Toronto Killer."
16 Rebecca Jennings, "Incels Categorize Women by Personal Style and Attractiveness," *Vox*, April 28, 2018, https://www.vox.com/2018/4/28/17290256/incel-chad-stacy-becky; "Stacy," Incels Wiki, last modified April 11, 2022, https://incels.wiki/w/Stacy; "Gigastacy," Incels Wiki, last modified February 11, 2022, https://incels.wiki/w/Gigastacy.
17 Simone de Beauvoir, *The Second Sex*, trans. Constance Borde and Sheila Malovany-Chevallier (New York: Vintage, 2011), 162–163 (hereafter cited in the text as *TSS*).
18 Zeynep Direk, "Immanence and Abjection in Simone de Beauvoir," *Southern Journal of Philosophy* 49, no. 1 (March 2011): 68, https://doi.org/10.1111/j.2041-6962.2010.00044.x.
19 Nancy Bauer, *How to Do Things with Pornography* (Cambridge, MA: Harvard University Press, 2015), 47.
20 Women also try to resolve this tension in a problematic way. Feminine self-alienation involves a paradoxically active renunciation of the drive to transcendence.

See Nancy Bauer, *Simone de Beauvoir, Philosophy, and Feminism* (New York: Columbia University Press, 2001), 176; Bauer, *How to Do Things*, 39–51; Charlotte Knowles, "Beauvoir on Women's Complicity in Their Own Unfreedom," *Hypatia* 34, no. 2 (Spring 2019): 242–265, https://doi.org/10.1111/hypa.12469; Manon Garcia, *We Are Not Born Submissive: How Patriarchy Shapes Women's Lives* (Princeton: Princeton University Press, 2021).

21 See also Debra B. Bergoffen, "Simone de Beauvoir and Jean-Paul Sartre: Woman, Man, and the Desire to Be God," *Constellations* 9, no. 3 (September 2002): 412, https://doi.org/10.1111/1467-8675.00290; Sonia Kruks, *Simone de Beauvoir and the Politics of Ambiguity* (New York: Oxford University Press, 2012): 16–17, 69; Bonnie Mann, *Sovereign Masculinity: Gender Lessons from the War on Terror* (New York: Oxford University Press, 2014), 42–45.
22 Bauer, *How to Do Things*, 48.
23 Bauer, *Simone de Beauvoir*, 208, 263, 27; Bauer, *How to Do Things*, 48.
24 Bauer, *Simone de Beauvoir*, 186.
25 Beauvoir is here drawing on Hegel's master–slave dialectic, as a dynamic from which women as Other are excluded (Direk, "Immanence and Abjection," 53, 60). For a congenial and detailed analysis of this aspect of Beauvoir's argument see Bauer, *Simone de Beauvoir*, 172–199.
26 See for example LeMoncheck, *Dehumanizing Women*, 31–32, 115; Langton, *Sexual Solipsism*, 1–2, 316; Ann J. Cahill, *Overcoming Objectification: A Carnal Ethics* (New York: Routledge, 2010), 2–4; Garcia, *Not Born Submissive*, 125.
27 Beauvoir is here connecting the domination of Nature and of women in a way that anticipates later ecofeminist and ecowomanist authors, for whom she was a key influence. See Charlene Spretnak, "Ecofeminism: Our Roots and Flowering," in *Reweaving the World: The Emergence of Ecofeminism*, ed. Irene Diamond and Gloria Orenstein (San Francisco: Sierra Club Books, 1990), 5; Janet Biehl, *Rethinking Ecofeminist Politics* (Boston: South End, 1991), 14; Trish Glazebrook, "Ecofeminism" in *Encyclopedia of Quality of Life and Well-being Research*, ed. Alex C. Michalos (Dordrecht: Springer, 2014), 1765, https://doi.org/10.1007/978-94-007-0753-5. For critical ecofeminist engagements with Beauvoir see Val Plumwood, "Ecofeminism: An Overview and Discussion of Positions and Arguments," *Australasian Journal of Philosophy* 64, issue sup1: Women and Philosophy (1986): 120–138, https://doi.org/10.1080/00048402.1986.9755430; Ynestra King, "The Ecology of Feminism and the Feminism of Ecology," in *Healing the Wounds: The Promise of Ecofeminism*, ed. Judith Plant (Philadelphia: New Society, 1989), 18–28; Marcia Morgan, "An Existential Ecofeminism and a Renewed Critical Theory of Nature: An Imagined Dialogue between Simone de Beauvoir and Jürgen Habermas," *Ideias* 8, no. 1 (2017): 179–202, https://doi.org/10.20396/ideias.v8i1.8649780.
28 Shannon M. Mussett, "Conditions of Servitude: Woman's Peculiar Role in the Master–Slave Dialectic in Beauvoir's *The Second Sex*," in *The Philosophy of Simone de Beauvoir: Critical Essays*, ed. Margaret A. Simons (Bloomington: Indiana University Press, 2006), 280.
29 Karen Vintges, *A New Dawn for the Second Sex: Women's Freedom Practices in World Perspective* (Amsterdam: Amsterdam University Press, 2017), 139, https://doi.org/10.1515/9789048522279.
30 Beauvoir herself explains how the myth of Woman as Other, as a general model, can feed into attitudes resembling objectification in her discussion of Montherlant (*TSS*, 218), and entitlement in her discussion of Claudel (*TSS*, 243).
31 Baele, Brace, and Coan, "From 'Incel' to 'Saint'," 1676.
32 Bauer, "How to Do Things", 48; Mussett, "Conditions of Servitude," 282.
33 Direk, "Immanence and Abjection," 67.
34 Bates, *Men Who Hate Women*, 13.

References

Baele, Stephane J., Lewys Brace, and Travis G. Coan. "From 'Incel' to 'Saint': Analyzing the Violent Worldview behind the 2018 Toronto Attack." *Terrorism and Political Violence* 33, no. 8 (2021): 1667–1691. https://doi.org/10.1080/09546553.2019.1638256.

Baker, Peter. "The Woman Who Accidentally Started the Incel Movement." *Elle*, March 1, 2016. https://www.elle.com/culture/news/a34512/woman-who-started-incel-movement/.

Bates, Laura. *Men Who Hate Women: From Incels to Pickup Artists, the Truth About Extreme Misogyny and How It Affects Us All*. London: Simon & Schuster, 2020.

Bauer, Nancy. *How to Do Things with Pornography*. Cambridge, MA: Harvard University Press, 2015.

Bauer, Nancy. *Simone de Beauvoir, Philosophy, and Feminism*. New York: Columbia University Press, 2001.

Beauvoir, Simone de. *The Second Sex*. Translated by Constance Borde and Sheila Malovany-Chevallier. New York: Vintage, 2011.

Bergoffen, Debra B. "Simone de Beauvoir and Jean-Paul Sartre: Woman, Man, and the Desire to Be God." *Constellations* 9, no. 3 (September 2002): 409–418. https://doi.org/10.1111/1467-8675.00290.

Biehl, Janet. *Rethinking Ecofeminist Politics*. Boston, MA: South End Press, 1991.

Brean, Joseph. "Incel Charges in Toronto Massage Parlour Killing Marks New Milestone in Terrorist Prosecution in Canada." *National Post*, May 20, 2020. https://nationalpost.com/news/canada/terror-charges-laid-in-toronto-massage-parlour-stabbing-that-left-one-dead.

Cahill, Ann J. *Overcoming Objectification: A Carnal Ethics*. New York: Routledge, 2010.

Chester, Nick. 2018. "Meet the Women of the Incel Movement: The Truth about Femcels." *Huck*, December 5, 2018. https://www.huckmag.com/art-and-culture/tech/meet-the-women-of-the-incel-movement/.

Direk, Zeynep. "Immanence and Abjection in Simone de Beauvoir." *Southern Journal of Philosophy* 49, no. 1 (March 2011): 49–72. https://doi.org/10.1111/j.2041-6962.2010.00044.x.

Garcia, Manon. *We Are Not Born Submissive: How Patriarchy Shapes Women's Lives*. Princeton, NJ: Princeton University Press, 2021.

Glazebrook, Trish. "Ecofeminism." In *Encyclopedia of Quality of Life and Well-being Research*, edited by Alex C. Michalos, 1764–1769. Dordrecht: Springer, 2014. https://doi.org/10.1007/978-94-007-0753-5.

Hoffman, Bruce, Jacob Ware, and Ezra Shapiro. "Assessing the Threat of Incel Violence." *Studies in Conflict & Terrorism* 43, no. 7 (2020): 565–587. https://doi.org/10.1080/1057610X.2020.1751459.

Jennings, Rebecca. "Incels Categorize Women by Personal Style and Attractiveness." *Vox*, April 28, 2018. https://www.vox.com/2018/4/28/17290256/incel-chad-stacy-becky.

King, Ynestra. "The Ecology of Feminism and the Feminism of Ecology." In *Healing the Wounds: The Promise of Ecofeminism*, edited by Judith Plant, 18–28. Philadelphia: New Society, 1989.

Knowles, Charlotte. "Beauvoir on Women's Complicity in Their Own Unfreedom." *Hypatia* 34, no. 2 (Spring 2019): 242–265. https://doi.org/10.1111/hypa.12469.

Kohn, Isabelle. "Inside the World of 'Femcels'." *Mel Magazine*, February 10, 2020. https://melmagazine.com/en-us/story/femcels-vs-incels-meaning-reddit-discord.

Kruks, Sonia. *Simone de Beauvoir and the Politics of Ambiguity*. New York: Oxford University Press, 2012.

Langton, Rae. *Sexual Solipsism: Philosophical Essays on Pornography and Objectification*. Oxford: Oxford University Press, 2009.

LeMoncheck, Linda. *Dehumanizing Women: Treating Persons as Sex Objects*. Totowa, NJ: Rowman & Allanheld, 1985.

Mann, Bonnie. 2014. *Sovereign Masculinity: Gender Lessons from the War on Terror*. New York: Oxford University Press, 2014.

Manne, Kate. *Down Girl: The Logic of Misogyny*. New York: Oxford University Press, 2018.

Manne, Kate. *Entitled: How Male Privilege Hurts Women*. London: Allen Lane, 2020.

Marcotte, Amanda. "Accused Toronto Killer May Have Roots in Online Misogynist Underworld: Is He a Terrorist?" *Salon*, April 25, 2018. https://www.salon.com/2018/04/25/accused-toronto-killer-may-have-roots-in-online-misogynist-underworld-is-he-a-terrorist/.

Morgan, Marcia. "An Existential Ecofeminism and a Renewed Critical Theory of Nature: An Imagined Dialogue between Simone de Beauvoir and Jürgen Habermas." *Ideias* 8, no. 1 (2017): 179–202. https://doi.org/10.20396/ideias.v8i1.8649780.

Mussett, Shannon M. "Conditions of Servitude: Woman's Peculiar Role in the Master-Slave Dialectic in Beauvoir's *The Second Sex*." In *The Philosophy of Simone de Beauvoir: Critical Essays*, edited by Margaret A. Simons, 276–293. Bloomington: Indiana University Press, 2006.

Nussbaum, Martha C. "Objectification." *Philosophy and Public Affairs* 24, no. 4 (1995): 249–291. https://www.jstor.org/stable/2961930.

Plumwood, Val. "Ecofeminism: An Overview and Discussion of Positions and Arguments." *Australasian Journal of Philosophy* 64, issue sup1: Women and Philosophy (1986): 120–138. https://doi.org/10.1080/00048402.1986.9755430.

Rodger, Elliot. "*My Twisted World: The Story of Elliot Rodger*." Unpublished manuscript, last modified May 23, 2014. https://assets.documentcloud.org/documents/1173619/rodger-manifesto.pdf.

Spretnak, Charlene. "Ecofeminism: Our Roots and Flowering." In *Reweaving the World: The Emergence of Ecofeminism*, edited by Irene Diamond and Gloria Orenstein, 3–14. San Francisco: Sierra Club Books, 1990.

Srinivasan, Amia. "Does Anyone Have a Right to Sex?" *London Review of Books* 40, no. 6 (2018). https://www.lrb.co.uk/the-paper/v40/n06/amia-srinivasan/does-anyone-have-the-right-to-sex.

Tolentino, Jia. "The Rage of Incels." *New Yorker*, May 15, 2018. https://www.newyorker.com/culture/cultural-comment/the-rage-of-the-incels.

Vintges, Karen. *A New Dawn for the Second Sex: Women's Freedom Practices in World Perspective*. Amsterdam: Amsterdam University Press, 2017. https://doi.org/10.1515/9789048522279.

Zimmer, Ben. "How 'Incel' Got Hijacked." *Politico*, May 8, 2018. https://www.politico.com/magazine/story/2018/05/08/intel-involuntary-celibate-movement-218324.

3

MUST WE ELIMINATE ALL MYTHS?

Simone de Beauvoir and the Myth-Affirmative Feminist Tradition

Adam Kjellgren

The primary aim of this chapter is to examine how Beauvoir's writings on myth can contribute to the development of a toolkit with the help of which it becomes possible to think through contemporary challenges. But to achieve this objective, it is necessary to revisit her relationship with those later feminist theorists, who belong to what I will call *the myth-affirmative feminist tradition*.[1] When compared to the latter, Beauvoir—who devotes a large part of *The Second Sex* (1949) to the role myth plays in the oppression of woman—has been portrayed as representing an antithetical, entirely negative approach to myth. To explain why she takes up this negative approach, some scholars have, furthermore, argued that Beauvoir postulates a genderless, universal human subject, the existence of which myth, according to the view ascribed to her, is thought only to conceal. The present chapter challenges both of these assumptions, which obscure the continued relevance of Beauvoir's writings on myth.

As we will see, Beauvoir never states that all myths must be eliminated. Though her work renders visible why many myths are problematic from a feminist perspective, I will demonstrate that she can still be read as lending support to myth-affirmative strategies. This is important to stress because it enables us to ask what, according to her, distinguishes harmful from non-harmful myths—a question that would make no sense if we were to conclude that she rejects all myths. In answering this question, I will argue that Beauvoir develops an ethically (rather than ontologically) grounded critique of myth, according to which harmful myths are those that have negative consequences in that they circumscribe human freedom. However, because this existentialist argument rests upon and reproduces a myth of its own—namely, the myth of freedom as an absolute value—I conclude by suggesting that the success of Beauvoir's argument follows in part from her capacity as a myth-maker.

DOI: 10.4324/9781003366089-5

"Literary" and "Deep" Myths Today

Current events have once again made visible the far-reaching impacts of arational forces—such as emotionally charged symbols, images, and narratives—within the sphere of contemporary politics. This development has, in turn, generated a renewed interest in questions concerned with the societal impact of myth.[2] But what are we actually talking about when we talk about myth?

In a recent work, political theorist Tae-Yeoun Keum identifies two ways in which this word is often used. Historically, myth has most frequently been employed to denote stories that belong to "a unique form of orally transmitted narrative fiction, featuring fantastical or supernatural elements, which we tend to encounter as the cultural artifacts of ancient or otherwise remote civilizations."[3] This is how the word is used when we speak, for instance, of Greek or Roman myths. Because such stories are thought to belong to a specific literary genre, Keum calls them "literary" myths.[4] But today the word myth is also ascribed another, more wide-ranging meaning. Contemporary theorists of myth thus tend to employ it to denote not stories of a particular type, but "tacit, deeply entrenched imaginative frames" that influence how we experience the world yet escape critical examination, in part because they are not rooted in verifiable facts.[5] Keum refers to such tacit, arational frameworks—held to constitute the "implicit lenses through which we view reality"—as "deep" myths.[6]

Although literary myths are "a distinctly pervasive feature of non-modern cultures," Keum maintains that they "occupy a comparatively marginal place in contemporary culture," the inhabitants of which seldom ascribe to such stories any literal truth.[7] By contrast, she points out that many commentators believe that the influence of *deep myths* has recently increased, at the expense of more rational forces. Having noted that myth has "become a current term in our politics," Keum states:

> The turn to this language comes against the background of a yawning gap between contemporary political developments and the more narrowly rationalist visions that dominated much of twentieth-century liberal thought. In times of mounting disillusionment in the power of facts and reasoned arguments to provide an enduring foundation for politics, worries about the rise of myths in society and culture go beyond a concern about misinformation […]. At stake instead is the existential threat posed by the growing influence of cultural forces that appear immune to correction altogether—forces that are endemic to our imagination and move us at a more elusive level. Just as writers in the early and mid-twentieth century feared that fascism signaled a resurgence of myth, commentators today are alarmed by the extent to which the

worldviews of political actors are governed by grand narratives and symbolic frameworks that resist critical scrutiny.[8]

Though it might thus seem as if literary and deep myth share but a common name, Keum argues that these two meanings of myth have, on the contrary, been "composed together" and "posed as a unified problem in philosophy and politics." This problem, she continues, "rests on the presupposition that deep myths [...] are modern analogues for that which was expressed in the literary myths of ancient or otherwise non-modern cultures."[9] Hence, the continued presence of deep myths in so-called 'modern' societies suggests, to some, that the process of modernization—commonly held to have replaced a typically 'primitive' belief in literary myths with a worldview rooted in facts and scientific knowledge—actually remains incomplete. To see this process through, it is often claimed that:

> contemporary society ought to eliminate the deep myths that it takes for granted—just as it has found a way to shed its strange, magical tales—and replace these residual structures with paradigms and ideas that can be expressed in a corresponding language that makes them available for critical examination.[10]

However, there is also evidence that seems to suggest that we will never be able to eliminate all deep myths.

> Indeed, a growing body of empirical scholarship suggests that our conceptual systems operate figuratively [...] and these studies indicate, in turn, that our propensity for myth may be much more ingrained in our thinking than we might care to acknowledge.[11]

Keum contends that, if this is correct, we might have to accept "a messier political reality," where deep myth constitutes an "enduring fixture" whose power ought to be harnessed rather than denied.[12] Such strategies must not, however, be embraced naively. "It is worth emphasizing," Keum writes, "that engaging our contemporary myths on their own terms brings substantive risks, including the very dangers that have led so many political theorists to be wary of them." "In particular," she continues, "it raises the problem of having to differentiate, in the absence of a clear framework of guiding principles, between myths that are harmful and those that are not."[13]

How do we handle this problem, made visible by Keum? In the following, I argue that Beauvoir offers several important insights of continued relevance. However, as mentioned in the Introduction, this fact will not become fully noticeable unless we first revisit the relation between her and representatives of what I have termed the myth-affirmative feminist tradition.

The Myth-Affirmative Feminist Tradition

In the introduction to *A Feminist Mythology* (2021), philosopher Chiara Bottici writes that "we become women [...] by re-telling the myths we have inherited, as well as those we have ourselves created."[14] Instead of trying to "bring myth to an end," feminists must therefore make use of myth.[15] Though this proposal may appear controversial to some, Bottici is not the first to argue that feminists ought to approach myth as a resource. Since the late 1960s, several influential feminist theorists have discussed myth in positive terms. One may thus speak of a relatively well-established myth-affirmative feminist tradition.

Borrowing from poet and literary scholar Alicia Ostriker, some feminists could be said to have taken up a "revisionist" approach to myths, trying to appropriate supposedly masculine (literary) myths for altered ends.[16] In her celebrated essay "The Laugh of Medusa" (1975)—"perhaps the most sustained exploration of myth's inspirational potential for feminism," according to classists Vanda Zajko and Miriam Leonard[17]—Hélène Cixous, for instance, describes men as the Sirens to which women "only have to stop listening [...] for history to change its meaning" and Medusa as "beautiful" and "laughing" rather than deadly.[18] By contrast, philosopher AnaLouise Keating argues that feminist theorists like Audre Lorde, Paula Gunn Allen and Gloria E. Anzaldúa are not attempting to re-write Greek or Roman literary myths but to *replace* them, by incorporating into their work non-Western variants wherein the feminine is already conceptualized differently.[19] Other feminists, such as Mary Daly, have turned instead toward a supposedly forgotten past, seeking to retrieve a "more ancient, more translucent myth,"[20] which the "patriarchal Greek mythmakers (re-makers)" are described as having distorted.[21] Finally, a fourth group of feminist theorists, to which Donna Haraway and Rosi Braidotti belong, portray themselves as trying to create new "political" myths, centered on figures like the "cyborg" and the "nomadic subject" instead of gods and goddesses.[22]

But what about Beauvoir? Though much has been published on the relationship between her and later feminist theorists, scholars have seldom approached her writings on myth from a comparative perspective. There are a few exceptions however, such as philosopher Pamela Sue Anderson in "Myth and Feminist Philosophy" (2002). In her study, Anderson argues that Beauvoir takes up an "existential-liberal feminist approach" in that she "addresses the danger of false assumptions about women by proposing to expose and eliminate myth."[23] This characterization of Beauvoir as a stark enemy of myth is also common among other scholars. For instance, in an article tellingly titled "Beauvoir the Mythoclast" (2010), philosopher Michèle Le Doeuff states that

> according to *The Second Sex* there are facts and there are myths, with the myths [...] to be stripped away so as to reduce the facts of everyday life to what they are. In essence, this is about a refusal of all "mythologization"—a term that I propose to describe the gaze's flight towards a dream (or nightmare) already dreamt by numerous others.[24]

Likewise, literary scholar Meryl Altman argues that Beauvoir "investigates myth in order to demystify," and that her "ultimate goal is demystification, to stop believing lies, lying to oneself, lying to others."[25] But what makes Anderson's text especially interesting is the fact that she compares Beauvoir to later feminists, such as Luce Irigaray and Haraway, both of whom are held to represent "a progressive-poststructuralist feminist approach" to myth. Unlike the liberal-existentialist one, Anderson emphasizes that this approach is "accompanied by an insistence that myth cannot be simply retrieved, exposed or negated."[26] Irigaray and Haraway consequently seek to refigure rather than to eliminate myth.

According to Anderson, this divergence between existentialist-liberals and progressive-poststructuralists is related to their different philosophies regarding subjectivity. "Both Irigaray and Haraway rely upon the possibility of refiguring myths as a way out of conventional, philosophical accounts of subjectivity."[27] The aim of the progressive-poststructuralist approach, Anderson states elsewhere, "is the disruption of any universal—and univocal—identity. And this disruption is to be accompanied by the production of sexually specific identities."[28] In contrast, Beauvoir is portrayed as wanting to eliminate myth because she postulates a genderless, universal human subject, the existence of which myth only obscures:

> Basically, then, the liberal-existentialist feminist maintains that myth only reinforces the false conceptualizations of woman as the other who lacks autonomy and equality. [...] In the end, Beauvoir's liberal-existentialist feminist approach to myth attempts a critical reading of philosophy which would eliminate not only patriarchal myth, but gender. The assumption is that a gender-neutrality would restore to women their autonomy and so their subjectivity as rational beings. In other words, women would be able to achieve the liberal ideals of individual autonomy, equality and fraternity. And these ideals would give a gender-neutral identity.[29]

In Anderson's view, this approach remains highly flawed. "Beauvoir's proposed gift of 'humanity' to women offers only a contradictory conception of woman as identical to man," she concludes.[30] A similar reading has been put forward by philosopher Drucilla Cornell, who writes that Beauvoir's "call to dethrone mythology is based on an underlying truth that, in spite of the imposition of femininity, we [women] are still subjects like them [men]."[31]

> At the heart of de Beauvoir's analysis of myth is her desire to return Woman to humanity. Men and women are to affirm "their brotherhood" as fellow human creatures, irreducible to their supposed divergent essences as males and females. [...] The goal of feminist politics is to be like them, no longer burdened by the demands of the species and the constraints of a structure of gender identity in which "the male seems infinitely favored."[32]

But is this interpretation correct? There are two problems with Anderson's and Cornell's reading of Beauvoir. First, they suggest that the latter's approach to myth is entirely negative, in the sense that she wishes to eliminate all myths. Second, we will see that there is little evidence to support the assumption that Beauvoir holds that women are, or should strive to become, identical to men. Hence, attempts to explain her writings on this subject with reference to her supposed belief in a universal subject are destined to remain fruitless.

In the following section, I will demonstrate that, although she does make visible that myths have contributed to the oppression of women, Beauvoir does not argue that all myths must be eliminated.

Literary Myths and Patriarchal Oppression

Most feminists mentioned in the preceding section seem to employ the term myth to denote what I, along with Keum, have termed literary myths (the exceptions are Haraway and Braidotti, who, as mentioned, explicitly argue that they seek to invent new *political* myths). As we will see, Beauvoir too devotes considerable attention to such narratives, which she sometimes refers to as "myths" (*mythes*) and sometimes as "legends" (*légendes*). Mimicking the methodology of comparative mythology—defined by the anthropologist C. Scott Littleton as a "systematic comparison of myths and mythic themes drawn from a wide variety of cultures," one aim of which is to "abstract common underlying themes"[33]—Beauvoir refers to many different stories of this sort in order to demonstrate that they all share the same pattern.[34] However, because she approaches these narratives from a distinctively feminist perspective, she is able to identify a pattern overlooked by most previous scholars of myth. To be more precise, Beauvoir argues that all literary myths portray woman as the 'Other' of man.[35]

Yet, it is important to note that this pattern is noticeable not only in literary myths. According to Beauvoir, it also appears in works of modern literature as well as in philosophical and scientific texts.[36] To account for this fact, Beauvoir postulates *another kind of myth*, active on a deeper level. This myth is not a literary myth, but a myth that many such stories (as well as other types of discourse) tend to *reflect*[37]—wherefore I, in accordance with Keum, argue that it can be referred to as a deep myth. This is the phenomenon that Beauvoir, in the introduction to *The Second Sex*, speaks of as "the myth of Woman, of the Other" (*le mythe de la Femme, de l'Autre*).[38] With reference to this myth, she later states:

> There are different kinds of myths. This one, sublimating an immutable aspect of the human condition—that is, the "division" of humanity into two categories of individuals—is a static myth [...] Thus, to the dispersed, contingent, and multiple existence of women, mythic thinking opposes the Eternal Feminine, unique and fixed; if the definition given is contradicted by the behavior of real flesh-and-blood women, it is women who are wrong: it is said not that Femininity is an entity but that women are not feminine.[39]

As we can see, Beauvoir argues here that the myth of Woman rests upon and reinforces the notion of Femininity (with a capital F) as a static essence that all 'real' women supposedly share. Because this essence has been defined in more than one way, she sometimes speaks of a "multiplicity of incompatible myths."[40] Yet all these myths of Woman have one thing in common. "In concrete reality," Beauvoir explains, "women manifest themselves in many different ways; but each of the myths built around woman tries to summarize her as a whole"—which is to say that the many myths that together compose the myth of Woman all ascribe to her a singular, defining quality.[41] In the next section, we will see that Beauvoir believes that this particular myth ought to be phased out rather than refigured. But when it comes to literary myths, I maintain that her position is more ambivalent.

Let us begin by looking at the novel critique that Beauvoir directs toward literary myths. According to her, all preserved literary myths were created by men. "By the time humankind reaches the stage of writing its mythology and laws," she writes, "patriarchy is definitively established: it is males who write the codes."[42] Now this claim has been put forward by mythographers before her. Beauvoir herself cites the anthropologist James Georges Frazer, who concludes that men "make gods" while women "worship" them.[43] But, whereas the latter seems to assume that myth-making, by its very nature, represents a male activity, Beauvoir is among the first to connect the assumed absence of women-produced literary myths with women's *subject position* (or rather, with their lack thereof). Myth-making, she writes, entails "a Subject who projects its hopes and fears toward a (*vers un*) transcendent heaven."[44]

> Not positing themselves as Subject, women have not created the virile myth that would reflect their projects; they have neither religion nor poetry that belongs to them alone: they still dream through men's dreams. They worship the gods made by males. And males have shaped the great virile figures for their own exaltation: Hercules, Prometheus, Parsifal; in the destiny of these heroes, woman has merely a secondary role. Undoubtedly, there are stylized images of man as he is in his relations with woman [...] but men are the ones who have established them, and they have not attained the dignity of myth; they are barely more than clichés.[45]

Why, then, do women not posit themselves as subject? One reason, Beauvoir writes, is that they often "derive satisfaction" from their role as a non-subject.[46] But the act of positing oneself as a subject is also portrayed as one that can be facilitated or obstructed by others. And, as readers familiar with *The Second Sex* will know, Beauvoir argues that man has actively sought to hamper the subject-becoming of woman. "He is pleased to remain the sovereign subject, the absolute superior, the essential being; he refuses to consider his companion concretely as an equal."[47] Hence, it remains impossible to explain the lack of women-produced myths without taking into consideration the *oppression* that women have suffered at the hands of men.

However, the absence of women-produced myths is described not only as a circumstance that *reflects* the existence of patriarchal oppression, but also as one that has helped *reinforce* it. Men who have sought to justify their supremacy are, for example, said to have "found ammunition" in the "legends" of Pandora and Eve.[48] Having noted that man views woman "as the absolute Other," Beauvoir moreover states: "All the creation myths express this conviction that is precious to the male," whereafter she gives the Genesis-story as an example.[49]

Importantly, Beauvoir's argument suggests that such literary myths are not a thing of the past, but continue to influence life in so-called modern societies. When she discusses the little girl's upbringing, she thus notes:

> Her historical and literary culture, the songs and legends she is raised on, are an exaltation of the man. [...] Eve was not created for herself but as Adam's companion and drawn from his side [...] Mythology's goddesses are frivolous or capricious, and they all tremble before Jupiter; while Prometheus magnificently steals the fire from the sky, Pandora opens the box of catastrophes.[50]

In fact, this quote implies that literary myths have done more than *justify* patriarchal oppression; they have also helped produce the very subject (or non-subject) that suffers from it, as well as the (male) subjects that uphold it. "One is not born, but rather becomes, woman," Beauvoir famously states.[51] The above-quoted passage suggests that literary myths, because they condition the upbringing of both young girls and boys, shape what this becoming entails. Beauvoir's argument thus challenges the orthodox Marxist understanding of discourses (such as literary myths) as part only of the ideological superstructure, which *validates* an oppressive system. Instead, literary myths are here portrayed as one of the mechanisms through which the oppressed subject itself is constituted (and constituted as a subject that it is possible to oppress).

This critical part of Beauvoir's analysis serves as an important reminder that literary myths are neither neutral nor inconsequential narratives. Whereas we have seen that Keum claims that literary myths "occupy a comparatively marginal place in contemporary culture," Beauvoir's argument suggests that such stories still constitute an important, political factor. Compared to the political myths utilized by, among others, right-wing populists, literary Greek and Christian myths—taught to children and reproduced both on stage and through mass media—might not constitute a serious threat to the *established* political order. On the contrary, Beauvoir's analysis suggests that such stories often help reproduce it. But as long as we live in a patriarchy, this is precisely what makes many literary myths problematic.

And yet I maintain that Beauvoir does not believe that all literary myths must be eliminated. Here we should note that she holds that myths are subject to change, as pointed out by philosopher Karen Vintges.[52] Toward the end of the myth section in *The Second Sex*, Beauvoir concludes that "a new aesthetic" has been born. Men still expect the feminine body "to be flesh," but now "discreetly so," in the sense that it "must be slim and not burdened with fat."[53] Beauvoir then continues by stating "a new form of eroticism seems to be coming about: perhaps it will produce new myths."[54] Though it seems unclear to me whether these "new myths" will be better than the old, this passage does demonstrate that Beauvoir believes that our shared mythology is not static. Therefore, the fact that all literary myths inherited from the past were created by men does not mean that this narrative genre must be rejected in its entirety.

In one sense, Beauvoir's argument points toward the same conclusion as Bottici's, referenced above. As noted, Bottici states that "we become women [...] by re-telling the myths we have inherited, as well as those we have ourselves created," while Beauvoir demonstrates that literary myths (about, for instance, frivolous or capricious goddesses) condition the upbringing of young girls. Obviously, these two theorists differ in the sense that Beauvoir focuses on the negative effects of literary myths created by men, while Bottici highlights the positive potential of myths created (or re-written) by women themselves. However, as Beauvoir does accentuate the relation between myth and subjectivity, her argument could still be read as anticipating Bottici's. If our inherited literary myths, as Beauvoir argues, influence the becoming of women in a regressive sense, does it not follow that new or revised myths could have a progressive function? After all, her argument implies that literary myths have helped men realize themselves as full subjects by offering them what one might call *models of transcendence*, such as Prometheus—that is, mythographical heroes with which young boys have identified. Would not women, then, have something to gain were they to produce their own myths? Although this conclusion is never made explicit, I hold that Beauvoir can be read as lending it support.

As we have already concluded, Beauvoir writes that women "have not created the virile myth that would reflect their projects; they have neither religion nor poetry that belongs to them alone: they still dream through men's dreams." In the introduction to *The Second Sex*, she depicts this absence as one of the factors that sets the situation of women apart from that of other oppressed groups, who have been able to establish themselves as collective subjects.[55] Unlike proletarians and black people, women do not say 'we' about themselves, writes Beauvoir. "It is that they lack the concrete means to organize themselves into a unit that could posit itself in opposition. They have no past, no history, no religion of their own," she continues.[56] Here, it seems to me as if she identifies one of the main problems to which many later, myth-affirmative feminists will offer myth as a solution. As noted, Beauvoir holds that women lack the means to organize themselves, in part because they have not yet developed any shared cultural expression that could help generate a politically productive, common identity. This situation is in part *caused* by man-made literary myths, which have helped uphold the oppression that has, in turn, kept women from partaking in the conceptualization of the world. But because the situation is due to an absence, it cannot be *solved* simply by abolishing all myths. In other words, Beauvoir's argument suggests that, because women of today suffer from a lack, it is not enough to dismantle the prevailing, patriarchal ideology. Instead, such negative practices need to be paired with positive ones. When she discusses literature written by women, Beauvoir explains:

> When they [women writers] pull away the veils of illusion and lies, they think they have done enough: nonetheless, this negative daring still leaves us with an enigma; for truth itself is ambiguity, depth, mystery: after its presence is acknowledged, it must be thought, re-created. It is all well and good not to be duped: but this is where it all begins; the woman exhausts her courage in dissipating mirages, and she stops in fear at the threshold of reality.[57]

One should note that Beauvoir does not state that re-creation of truth must encompass women-produced myths. Yet she never rejects this notion either. On the contrary, Beauvoir seems to hold that revisionist myth-making constitutes a valid, political tactic. In a talk on existential theater, most likely delivered in 1947, she thus defends Jean-Paul Sartre's decision to base his play *The Flies* (1943) on the Electra myth. This play was produced while France was still being occupied by Germany. It was, Beauvoir explains, "intended to bring a message of hope to oppressed people who were reduced to silence and for whom action was only clandestine and very difficult."[58] This message could not, however, be communicated directly, or it would have been censored:

> For this reason Sartre chose to take shelter behind a historical myth [...] And to all appearances, he tells the story of Orestes who returns to Argos [...]. But from this drama, Sartre makes not only a classic story, but [...] truly the drama of freedom.[59]

This quote illustrates that Beauvoir believes that literary myths (or "historical" myths as she here calls them) can be approached in a revisionist manner, which has the potential of altering their original meaning and thus causing them to acquire new functions.

To conclude, I argue that the relationship between Beauvoir and later, explicitly myth-affirmative feminists must not be conceptualized as one characterized solemnly by discontinuity. Beauvoir, before any other feminist theorist, demonstrates *i*) the gendered nature of literary myths; *ii*) the link between such stories and subjectivity; and *iii*) that it is possible to alter their meaning so that they acquire new functions. I hold that Beauvoir might just as well be understood as having provided the fundament upon which this tradition rests.

The Myth of Woman as a Deep Myth

Thus far, I have focused first and foremost on the different roles that Beauvoir ascribes to literary myths. In the following, I turn to the myth of Woman.

Given how Beauvoir herself defines this phenomenon, I have claimed that the myth of Woman can be characterized as a deep myth. It is not a story that belongs to a specific literary genre, but a deep-rooted imaginative framework. Centered on the patriarchal concept of Femininity as a static essence, this myth governs both what (mythical, literary, philosophical, and scientific) stories we tell and which such stories we recognize as plausible. Hence, the myth of Woman is reflected in all types of discourses. It is ingrained both in tradition and in contemporary culture. This, in turn, means that the myth of Woman cannot be totally eliminated, at least not in one stroke. Perhaps, writes Beauvoir, it "will go out (*s'éteindra-t-il*) one day: the more women assert themselves as human beings, the more the marvelous quality of Other dies in them."[60] However, by making visible that the myth of Woman is everywhere—that it penetrates not only literary myths but also works of modern literature, philosophy, and science—her argument still suggests that this process, the final aim of which must be a complete cultural transformation, will not be realized any time soon.[61]

How, then, should one approach such deep myths? As we have seen, Anderson and Cornell argue that Beauvoir wishes to expose and eliminate the myth of Woman, in part because of her supposed belief in a genderless, universal human subject. According to this reading, Beauvoir seeks to abolish the myth of Woman to make visible that women and men, the feminine and the masculine, are actually identical. But this interpretation is hard to sustain if one looks at what Beauvoir actually writes, for she does not hold that femininity is a deviation that women must overcome. On the contrary, she explicitly states: "Man is a sexed human being; woman is a complete individual, and equal to the male, only if she too is a sexed human being. Renouncing her femininity means renouncing part of her humanity."[62] Furthermore, though Beauvoir maintains that the patriarchal concept of Femininity as a static essence ought to be rejected, she does not argue against all attempts to speak about the specificity of the feminine. With reference to Michel Leiris's autobiographical novel *Manhood* (1935), she writes that when Leiris "describes his vision of female organs, he provides significations and does not develop a myth."[63] She continues by stating:

> Wonder at the feminine body and disgust for menstrual blood are apprehensions of a concrete reality. There is nothing mythical in the experience of discovering the voluptuous qualities of feminine flesh, and expressing these qualities by comparisons to flowers or pebbles does not turn them into myth. But to say that Woman is Flesh, to say that Flesh is Night and Death, or that she is the splendor of the Cosmos (*du Cosmos*), is to leave terrestrial truth behind and spin off into an empty sky.[64]

From the phenomenological perspective that Beauvoir adopts here, an individual could very well be understood to have experienced feminine flesh as flower-like. The feminine body is a concrete reality that generates genuine, lived experiences of various kinds. Hence, if one seeks to express this experience through a simile (stating that feminine flesh *is like* a flower or pebble), one is not necessarily committing any error, according to Beauvoir. But if one instead states that Woman (with a capital W) *is* something (like Flesh, Night, Death, or the splendor of Cosmos)—that is, if one abandons the similes in favor of metaphors that do not uphold but collapse the distinction between the two entities in question—one postulates a static feminine essence. Only at this point does one's discourse become mythical and thereby problematic.

But if Beauvoir does not, *pace* Anderson and Cornell, seek to eliminate the myth of Woman in order to erase all differences between men and women, the feminine and the masculine, then how might one more accurately describe her position with regard to this and other deep myths? In accordance with her existentialist philosophy, Beauvoir denies that there exists such a thing as a static, feminine essence. "An existent *is* nothing other than what he does; the possible does not exceed the real, essence does not precede existence: in his pure subjectivity, the human being *is nothing*."[65] Yet what makes Beauvoir's argument so interesting is that she acknowledges the impossibility of convincing those who already believe in the myth of Woman of this alternative, existentialist ontology. For, whereas claims about, for instance, women's and men's physical bodies can often, as she herself demonstrates, be either vindicated or refuted with reference to verifiable facts, Beauvoir argues that there are no facts capable of proving or disproving the existence of static essences. This is because deep myths such as the myth of Woman constitute the very background against which specific facts are ascribed meaning and this meaning is interpreted. We have thus already seen that, according to Beauvoir, the contradictory behavior of "flesh-and-blood women" will fail to convince most men that there is no such thing as a static, feminine essence[66]—for, in the eyes of those who believe in the myth of Woman, this behavior proves nothing but that some women are not feminine. Beauvoir thus concludes: "Experiential denials cannot do anything against myth."[67] The myth of Woman "escapes all contention because it is situated beyond the given; it is endowed with an absolute truth."[68]

But if we agree that deep myths such as the myth of Woman—because they are too ingrained both in tradition and in contemporary culture—will not disappear anytime soon, while we also follow Beauvoir in assuming that there are no facts with reference to which such myths can be effectively challenged, then were does this leave us? If we cannot once and for all refute oppressive myths, must we then accept them?

I argue that Beauvoir offers a way out of this dead-end by developing an ethically (rather than ontologically) rooted critique of the myth of Woman. In the introduction to *The Second Sex*, Beauvoir explains that the perspective she adopts "is one of existentialist morality."[69] She continues by stating:

> Every subject posits itself as a transcendence concretely, through projects; […] there is no other justification for present existence than its expansion toward an indefinitely open future. Every time transcendence

lapses into immanence, there is degradation of existence into "in-itself," of freedom into facticity; this fall is a moral fault if the subject consents to it; if this fall is inflicted on the subject, it takes the form of frustration and oppression; in both cases it is an absolute evil.[70]

From this ethical standpoint, it is easy to argue that the myth of Woman is highly problematic in that it ascribes to all women a static feminine essence, believed to limit what roles women may play. This myth turns women into objects instead of subjects—'being-in-itself' rather than 'being-for-itself'— both in their own eyes and in the eyes of men. Hence, it contributes to the oppression of women as well as to women's consent in this oppression, both of which Beauvoir, as we just saw, describes as absolute evils. In this way, Beauvoir is able to put forward a critique of the myth of Woman, the effectivity of which does not presuppose the acceptance of any specific ontological claim about human beings.

And yet, one could argue that Beauvoir's way of reasoning here rests upon and reproduces a deep myth of its own, which may be termed *the myth of Freedom*. This is the myth according to which freedom constitutes an absolute value. Now, in calling this belief a myth, I am not saying that freedom is not valuable. However, just like the belief in a static feminine essence, the belief in the absolute value of freedom is not rooted in verifiable facts, but functions instead as the background against which the meaning of specific facts, such as the oppression of women, is interpreted.

Interestingly enough, Beauvoir herself suggests something along these lines. In an essay called "Moral Idealism and Political Realism" (1945), she writes that:

> [Whether man] takes it upon himself to recapture the ideal of his ancestors, of a faction, or of a party, whether he loses himself in the violence of a passion or is fascinated by a myth it is always man who fashions the great idols to which he devotes his life. [...] Whether one fights for his country's independence, his integrity, prestige, or prosperity, whether he fights for the happiness of man, for peace, justice, comfort, or freedom, the goal to be reached is an unreality.[71]

As we can see here, political projects driven by myth end up on the same side as projects motivated by the fight for freedom, in the sense that both are portrayed as being centered on unrealities. Though it might be that Beauvoir, in this particular context, is talking about literary rather than deep myths, her point is that human beings remain the ultimate source of all meaning. Hence, there are no absolute values. According to Beauvoir, the tendency to pretend otherwise is an expression of the 'serious' attitude. In the essay *The Ethics of Ambiguity* [1947], she explains that "the characteristic of the spirit of seriousness is to consider values as ready-made things."[72] The connection between seriousness and myth is, in turn, reinforced in *The Second Sex*, where Beauvoir states: "The myth is one of those traps of false objectivity into which the spirit of seriousness falls headlong."[73]

Against this background, I argue that the myth of Freedom ought to be understood as a similar trap, into which Beauvoir could either be said to fall, herself—or to strategically employ, in the service of feminism. In either case, it seems to me that the success of her argument follows in part from the fact that she (whether intentionally or not) acts as a myth-maker.

Conclusion

In this chapter, I have sought to demonstrate that Beauvoir's writings on myth offer several important insights of continued relevance. To achieve this, I have employed Keum's distinction between literary and deep myths. According to my reading, Beauvoir's writings suggest that: *i*) although many literary myths reproduce patriarchal beliefs and help produce more easily oppressed subjects (or non-subjects)—wherefore *ii*) they cannot be said to occupy a marginal place in contemporary culture—*iii*) the meaning of such stories can still be altered so that they come to perform positive, political functions. Furthermore, I have argued that, according to Beauvoir, *iv*) there are no verifiable facts with reference to which deep myths, such as the myth of Woman, can be challenged—which implies that *v*) such myths must be criticized from an ethical rather than ontological perspective. However, I have also suggested that Beauvoir's ethical critique rests upon and reproduces a deep myth of its own, which further amplifies the impossibility of escaping myth altogether.

Notes

1 The expression 'the myth-affirmative feminist tradition' is used here to refer to feminist theorists who speak of myth in positive terms—i.e., as a phenomenon that can facilitate the emancipatory efforts of feminism—independently of how they define the word 'myth'. Among the more notable representatives of this tradition, one might mention Mary Daly, Luce Irigaray, Merlin Stone, Audre Lorde, Hélène Cixous, Alicia Ostriker, Paula Gunn Allen, Estella Lauter, Julia Kristeva, Gloria E. Anzaldúa, Donna Haraway, Carol P. Christ, Judith Plaskow, Adriana Cavarero, Rosi Braidotti, Drucilla Cornell, Pamela Sue Anderson, and Chiara Bottici. For references to specific works, see the notes to Section 2.
2 Chiara Bottici, *A Philosophy of Political Myth* (Cambridge: Cambridge University Press, 2007), 1–3. Since the publication of Bottici's seminal work, the interest in this topic has only increased.
3 Tae-Yeoun Keum, *Plato and the Mythic Tradition in Political Thought* (Cambridge, MA: Belknap Press of Harvard University Press, 2020), 7.
4 Ibid.

5 Ibid., 9.
6 Ibid., 5, 7.
7 Ibid., 8.
8 Ibid., 232–233.
9 Ibid., 9.
10 Ibid., 11.
11 Ibid., 235.
12 Ibid., 237–238.
13 Ibid., 237–238.
14 Chiara Bottici, *A Feminist Mythology*, trans. Sveva Scaramuzzi and Claudia Corriero (London: Bloomsbury Academic, 2021), 7.
15 Ibid., 1.
16 Alicia Ostriker, "The Thieves of Language: Women Poets and Revisionist Mythmaking," *Signs* 8, no. 1 (1982): 68–90.
17 Vanda Zajko and Miriam Leonard, *Laughing with Medusa: Classical Myth and Feminist Thought* (Oxford: Oxford University Press, 2006), 3.
18 Hélène Cixous, "The Laugh of the Medusa," *Signs* 1, no. 4 (1976): 885.
19 AnaLouise Keating, "Myth Smashers, Myth Makers: (Re)Visionary Techniques in the Works of Paula Gunn Allen, Gloria Anzaldúa, and Audre Lorde," *Journal of Homosexuality* 26, no. 2–3 (1993): 74–75.
20 Mary Daly, *Gyn/Ecology: The Metaethics of Radical Feminism* (Boston, MA: Beacon, 1990), 47.
21 Ibid., 40–41.
22 Donna Haraway, "A Cyborg Manifesto: Science, Technology, and Socialist-Feminism in the Late Twentieth Century," in *Simians, Cyborgs, and Women: The Reinvention of Nature* (London: Free Association Books, 1991), 149; Rosi Braidotti, *Nomadic Subjects: Embodiment and Sexual Difference in Contemporary Feminist Theory* (New York: Columbia University Press, 2011), 29.
23 Pamela Sue Anderson, "Myth and Feminist Philosophy," in *Thinking through Myths: Philosophical Perspectives*, ed. Kevin Schilbrack (London: Routledge, 2002), 118.
24 Michèle Le Doeuff, "Beauvoir the Mythoclast," *Paragraph* 33, no. 1 (2010): 91.
25 Meryl Altman, *Beauvoir in Time* (Leiden: Brill Rodopi, 2020), 368, 341.
26 Anderson, "Myth and Feminist Philosophy," 109.
27 Ibid., 111.
28 Ibid., 110.
29 Ibid., 107–108.
30 Ibid., 108.
31 Drucilla Cornell, *Beyond Accommodation: Ethical Feminism, Deconstruction and the Law* (Lanham, MD: Rowman & Littlefield, 1999), 193.
32 Ibid., 192.
33 C. Scott Littleton, *The New Comparative Mythology: An Anthropological Assessment of the Theories of Georges Dumézil* (Berkeley: University of California Press, 1973), 32.
34 Compare with Altman, *Beauvoir in Time*, 399.
35 Already in 1947, Beauvoir writes: "In mythologies [...] women are always assigned the same roles. They are Ariadne abandoned, Penelope at her needlework, Andromeda in chains. [...] They are the ones who wait, who cannot find their place in the world except through the love of a man." Simone de Beauvoir, "Femininity: The Trap," in *Simone de Beauvoir: Feminist Writings*, ed. Margaret A. Simons and Marybeth Timmermann (Urbana: University of Illinois Press, 2015), 44.
36 Compare with Sara Heinämaa, *Toward a Phenomenology of Sexual Difference: Husserl, Merleau-Ponty, Beauvoir* (Lanham, MD: Rowman & Littlefield, 2003),

127: "Beauvoir shows that women have been represented as half-persons by men not just in religious texts and poetry but also in empirical and philosophical sciences, which claim to describe reality or its metaphysical structures."
37 "Children's literature, mythology, tales, and stories *reflect* the myths created by men's pride and desires." Simone de Beauvoir, *The Second Sex*, trans. Constance Borde and Sheila Malovany-Chevallier (New York: Vintage, 2011), 350, emphasis added.
38 Ibid., 34 (trans. modified). Simone de Beauvoir, *Le Deuxième Sexe 1. Les Faits et les Mythes* (Paris: Gallimard, 1949), 26; *Le Deuxième Sexe 2. L'Expérience Vécue* (Paris: Gallimard, 1949). In volume one (*DSI*) and two (*DSII*) of *Le Deuxième Sexe*, Beauvoir employs the expression *le myth de la femme* (spelled with a lowercase f) five times (*DSI*, 235, 296, 298 383, 391) and *le myth de la Femme* (with a capital F) twice (ibid., 26, 392). In the latest English translation, *The Second Sex* (*TSS*), Borde and Malovany-Chevallier sometimes leave the article out and translate *le myth de la femme* and *le myth de la Femme* as "the myth of woman" (*TSS*, 196, 240, 315) and "the myth of Woman" (ibid., 322). Other times, they keep the article and translate these expressions as "the myth of the woman" (ibid., 242, 321) and "the myth of the Woman" (ibid., 34). However, as the translators themselves argue, when "used alone without an article," the word "woman" in English refers to "woman as an institution, a concept" (ibid., 17). Hence, I hold that the article should always be left out when one refers to mythical notions of woman.

In addition to "the myth of woman/Woman," Beauvoir speaks of "the feminine myth" (*du mythe féminin*) (*TSS*, 256/*DSI*, 311), "the myth of the eternal feminine" (*le mythe de l'éternel féminin*) (*TSS*, 258, trans. modified/*DSI*, 314–315), and "the myth of femininity" (*le mythe de la féminité*) (*TSS*, 328/*DSII*, 9). Yet there is nothing to suggest that these expressions refer to different entities. Hence, after having spoken only of "the myth of woman" and "the myth of Woman" in the first chapter of *Mythes*, Beauvoir begins the second chapter by stating that she will now seek to "confirm this analysis of the feminine myth" (*TSS*, 256) by studying the works of five authors—only to then begin chapter three by writing that her study of these authors has demonstrated that "[t]he myth of woman plays a significant role in literature" (ibid., 315).
39 Beauvoir, *The Second Sex*, 315.
40 Ibid.
41 Ibid.
42 Ibid., 114.
43 Ibid., 111, 727.
44 Ibid., 196 (trans. modified). *Le Deuxième Sexe 1*, 235.
45 Beauvoir, *The Second Sex*, 196.
46 Ibid., 30.
47 Ibid., 849.
48 Ibid., 31.
49 Ibid., 194.
50 Ibid., 350.
51 Ibid., 330.
52 Karen Vintges, *A New Dawn for the Second Sex: Women's Freedom Practices in World Perspective* (Amsterdam: Amsterdam University Press, 2017), 87.
53 Beauvoir, *The Second Sex*, 323.
54 Ibid., 324.
55 Ibid., 28.
56 Ibid.
57 Ibid., 841. Interestingly, this line of argument is later picked up by Daly, according to whom Beauvoir "sadly notes" that "women who have perceived the

reality of sexual oppression usually have exhausted themselves in breaking through the discovery of their own humanity, with little energy left for constructing their own interpretation of the universe." This suggests that Daly in Beauvoir identifies an ally whose writings could be invoked in support of her own myth-affirmative feminism. Mary Daly, *Beyond God the Father: Towards a Philosophy of Women's Liberation* (London: Women's Press, 1986), 7.
58 Simone de Beauvoir, "Existentialist Theater," in *"The Useless Mouths" and Other Literary Writings*, ed. Margaret A. Simons and Marybeth Timmermann (Urbana: University of Illinois Press, 2011), 138.
59 Ibid., 138–139.
60 Beauvoir, *The Second Sex*, 196 (trans. modified). *Le Deuxième Sexe 1*, 235. In the introduction to the second volume of *The Second Sex* (328), Beauvoir also states that contemporary women are in the process of "overthrowing the myth of femininity; they are beginning to affirm their independence concretely."
61 Elsewhere, I have argued that Beauvoir's approach is deeply committed to historical materialism in the sense that the myth of Woman, according to her, cannot be fully dethroned as long as the dominant power structure of patriarchal society remains intact. Adam Kjellgren, "The Myth of Woman: Simone de Beauvoir and the Anthropological Discourse on Myth," *History of European Ideas* (10 May 2023), https://doi.org/10.1080/01916599.2023.2198542.
62 Beauvoir, *The Second Sex*, 815–816.
63 Ibid., 317.
64 Ibid. (trans. modified). *Le Deuxième Sexe 1*, 386.
65 Beauvoir, *The Second Sex*, 319.
66 Ibid., 315.
67 Ibid.
68 Ibid.
69 Ibid., 37.
70 Ibid.
71 Simone de Beauvoir, "Moral Idealism and Political Realism," in *Philosophical Writings*, ed. Margaret A. Simons, Marybeth Timmermann, and Mary Beth Mader (Urbana: University of Illinois Press, 2004), 179.
72 Simone de Beauvoir, *The Ethics of Ambiguity*, trans. Bernard Frechtman (New York: Open Road Integrated Media, 2018), 35.
73 Beauvoir, *The Second Sex*, 322.

References

Altman, Meryl. *Beauvoir in Time*. Leiden: Brill Rodopi, 2020.
Anderson, Pamela Sue. "Myth and Feminist Philosophy." In *Thinking through Myths: Philosophical Perspectives*, edited by Kevin Schilbrack, 101–122. London: Routledge, 2002.
Beauvoir, Simone de. *Le Deuxième Sexe 1. Les Faits et les Mythes*. Paris: Gallimard, 1949.
Beauvoir, Simone de. *Le Deuxième Sexe 2. L'Expérience Vécue*. Paris: Gallimard, 1949.
Beauvoir, Simone de. "Moral Idealism and Political Realism." In *Philosophical Writings*, edited by Margaret A. Simons, Marybeth Timmermann and Mary Beth Mader, 175–193. Urbana: University of Illinois Press, 2004.
Beauvoir, Simone de. "Existentialist Theater." In *"The Useless Mouths" and Other Literary Writings*, edited by Margaret A. Simons and Marybeth Timmermann, 137–150. Urbana: University of Illinois Press, 2011.

Beauvoir, Simone de. *The Second Sex.* Translated by Constance Borde and Sheila Malovany-Chevallier. New York: Vintage, 2011.
Beauvoir, Simone de. "Femininity: The Trap." In *Feminist Writings*, edited by Margaret A. Simons and Marybeth Timmermann, 42–48. Urbana: University of Illinois Press, 2015.
Beauvoir, Simone de. *The Ethics of Ambiguity.* Translated by Bernard Frechtman. New York: Open Road Integrated Media, 2018.
Bottici, Chiara. *A Philosophy of Political Myth.* Cambridge: Cambridge University Press, 2007.
Bottici, Chiara. *A Feminist Mythology.* Translated by Sveva Scaramuzzi and Claudia Corriero. London: Bloomsbury Academic, 2021.
Braidotti, Rosi. *Nomadic Subjects: Embodiment and Sexual Difference in Contemporary Feminist Theory.* New York: Columbia University Press, 2011.
Cixous, Hélène. "The Laugh of the Medusa." *Signs* 1, no. 4 (1976): 875–893.
Cornell, Drucilla. *Beyond Accommodation: Ethical Feminism, Deconstruction and the Law.* Lanham, MD: Rowman & Littlefield, 1999.
Daly, Mary. *Beyond God the Father: Towards a Philosophy of Women's Liberation.* London: Women's Press, 1986.
Daly, Mary. *Gyn/Ecology: The Metaethics of Radical Feminism.* Boston, MA: Beacon, 1990.
Haraway, Donna. "A Cyborg Manifesto: Science, Technology, and Socialist-Feminism in the Late Twentieth Century." In *Simians, Cyborgs, and Women: The Reinvention of Nature*, 149–182. London: Free Association Books, 1991.
Heinämaa, Sara. *Toward a Phenomenology of Sexual Difference: Husserl, Merleau-Ponty, Beauvoir.* Lanham, MD: Rowman & Littlefield, 2003.
Keating, AnaLouise. "Myth Smashers, Myth Makers: (Re)Visionary Techniques in the Works of Paula Gunn Allen, Gloria Anzaldúa, and Audre Lorde." *Journal of Homosexuality* 26, no. 2–3 (1993): 73–96.
Keum, Tae-Yeoun. *Plato and the Mythic Tradition in Political Thought.* Cambridge, MA: Belknap Press of Harvard University Press, 2020.
Kjellgren, Adam. "The Myth of Woman: Simone de Beauvoir and the Anthropological Discourse on Myth," *History of European Ideas* (10 May2023): 1–16. https://doi.org/10.1080/01916599.2023.2198542.
Le Doeuff, Michèle. "Beauvoir the Mythoclast." *Paragraph* 33, no. 1 (2010): 90–104.
Littleton, C. Scott. *The New Comparative Mythology: An Anthropological Assessment of the Theories of Georges Dumézil.* Berkeley: University of California Press, 1973.
Ostriker, Alicia. "The Thieves of Language: Women Poets and Revisionist Mythmaking." *Signs* 8, no. 1 (1982): 68–90.
Vintges, Karen. *A New Dawn for the Second Sex: Women's Freedom Practices in World Perspective.* Amsterdam: Amsterdam University Press, 2017.
Zajko, Vanda, and Miriam Leonard. *Laughing with Medusa: Classical Myth and Feminist Thought.* Oxford: Oxford University Press, 2006.

4

BEAUVOIR, BARDOT, AND *BURQINIS*

Making Sense of Modern France

Catherine Raissiguier

In August 1959 Simone de Beauvoir published a short piece in English for *Esquire* magazine titled "Brigitte Bardot and the Lolita Syndrome." The essay was reprinted and published in England in 1960 under the same title as a short book illustrated by a copious selection of photographs of the young actress.[1] *Brigitte Bardot and the Lolita Syndrome* opens with Beauvoir's brief reflection on Bardot's performance and reception by French viewers on the 1958 New Year Eve's French television special *Parade de fin d'année* (End of the Year Parade).

> On New Year's Eve, Brigitte Bardot appeared on French Television. She was got up as usual—blue jeans, sweater and shock of tousled hair. Lounging on a sofa, she plucked at a guitar. "That's not hard," said the women. "I could do just as well. She's not even pretty. She has the face of a housemaid." The men could not keep from devouring her with their eyes, but they too snickered. Only two or three of us, among thirty or so spectators, thought her charming. Then she did an excellent classical dance number. "She can dance," the others admitted grudgingly. Once again I could observe that Brigitte Bardot was disliked in her own country.[2]

In the opening paragraph Beauvoir lays out the premise of her musings about the iconic French actress.[3] The essay offers Beauvoir's analysis of Bardot's less than warm reception within France despite her great success and renown at the time. In a nutshell, Beauvoir sees Bardot, at the beginning of her career, as challenging normative expectations of French (white) women's femininity and petty bourgeois morality and, in the process, eliciting the ire of many of her compatriots. It must be noted, however, as Beauvoir documents later in the essay, that Bardot's reception in France was in fact much more nuanced and often contradictory. Indeed, at the beginning of her career Bardot drew both sharp criticism and adulation from the French public—a pattern that has continued throughout her life. What is certain is that Beauvoir "was struck by how differently Brigitte Bardot was treated in America and in France."[4]

Brigitte Bardot and the Lolita Syndrome[5] sets out to examine this differential treatment. Through the lens of gender equality, Beauvoir wrote the essay specifically for an American audience, in part as a response to Bardot's phenomenal success *outre Atlantique* but also because Beauvoir believed that there was greater formal gender equality in the United States than in France, and that this difference framed Bardot's reception in the two countries.[6] It must be noted, however, that when Beauvoir traveled to the United States in 1947, she did not find the kind of gender equality and freedom she had expected to encounter: "Personally, on the strength of all these reports, I'd imagined women here would surprise me with their independence. 'American woman,' 'free woman'—the words seemed synonymous." Instead, she surmised that:

> Their demanding, defiant attitude is proof that American women are not really on [an] equal footing with men. They feel contemptuous, often with good reason, of the servility of French women, who are always ready to smile at their men and humor them. But the tension with which they twist around on their pedestal conceals a similar weakness. In both cases, through docility or arbitrary demand, man remains king; he is essential, and woman is inessential.[7]

It is interesting to note here that Beauvoir slips into the kind of orientalist language commonly used at the time to oppose and draw parallels between the two groups of women. In the next sentence the French woman becomes the "submissive harem girl" (*la servante soumise du harem*) who is placed in opposition to the praying mantis (the American woman). "The praying mantis is the antithesis of the harem girl, but both depend on the male," concludes Beauvoir.[8]

The Lolita Syndrome sets out to unpack the Bardot phenomenon, to analyze the character that Roger Vadim (and other film directors) helped create,[9] and to examine the new model of women's sexuality that it embodies.[10] Indeed, by the mid-1950s, Bardot had become "an icon of rebellious youth, 'natural' sexuality, and beyond that of French womanhood both in and out of France."[11] Beauvoir's short essay argues that Bardot ushered in new forms of sexual behavior and subjectivity that connote freedom, autonomy, and agentic power. The essay's main argument is that this new model poses a threat to dominant understandings of womanhood in post-war France.

Unlike the few critical commentaries that debate whether Beauvoir is right in championing Bardot's subversive representation of women's sexual agency in the essay, this chapter aims to mine *The Lolita Syndrome* for what it might tell us about Brigitte Bardot as an ambiguous yet representative piece of the collective construction of modern France. The chapter is organized around two parts that build on one another. In the opening section, I look at the ways in which Beauvoir writes about Bardot's power to trouble common understandings of what constitutes France and French womanhood. Bardot's persona, Beauvoir argues, both helps to anchor and rewrites the eternal feminine myth upon which patriarchal power is erected. In the second part, I build on Beauvoir's analysis to examine the 'Bardot phenomenon' both at its point of emergence in post-war France and in its lingering impact in relation to recent controversies surrounding the Muslim body and face coverings. Here I analyze Bardot as a component of a modern French identity—or, in other words, as a core component of a modern national myth.[12]

In the summer of 2016, some 30 French beach towns issued local bans on the wearing of *burqinis* (full body swimwear donned by a handful of Muslim women in France). The mayors of these towns framed *burqinis* and the women who wore them as symbols of Islamic extremism, and thus a direct threat to French values in general and France's deep attachment to *laïcité* (the French form of secularism). In the midst of extensive media coverage, internal debates, and criticism from around the world, France's highest administrative court ruled that the bans violated basic civil rights. Many middle-of-the-road French republicans as well as far-right extremists like Marine Le Pen (leader of the French National Rally) embraced the executive orders as logical extensions of previous bans on body and head covering, and welcomed them as an appropriate tool to fend off the 'threat' that these 'fully clothed' women posed to the country and its national identity. Others rejected the orders as ludicrous and discriminatory. Marine Le Pen's blog, in the summer of 2016, reminded French people that the nation's beaches were not spaces where women went to cover up. Instead, she wrote: "The French beaches are those of Bardot and Vadim."[13]

This chapter drills down on Beauvoir's insights on the ambiguous qualities of Bardot as a persona to suggest that the ongoing French love/hate relationship with their most famous actress might also be read as a sign of the discomfort with which they see themselves (and their nation) reflected in that persona. It is precisely such complexity and contradictions that animate the analysis I deploy in this chapter. Indeed, "functioning as the image of permissiveness and a slap in the face of bourgeois morality, as well as 'classic' object of male desire,"[14] Bardot can be seen as a "transitional figure"[15] whose complicated persona has attracted and continues to attract the attention of feminist scholars since Beauvoir's insightful analysis.[16] Throughout, I aim to inflect my own feminist analysis of Bardot with an intersectional sensibility that invites us to think about the ways in which race, gender, and sexuality frame our understanding of Bardot and her impact on the construction of a modern French identity. Here, I suggest that *The Lolita Syndrome* might help us reflect on and better understand current disputes about public dress and displays of femininity in contemporary France. Beauvoir's analysis of Bardot as a myth and a commodity prefigures and helps frame the analysis of Bardot as a piece of a collective French imaginary deployed in this chapter.

Bardot: A Rewriting of the Eternal Feminine

> *Brigitte Bardot n'est pas Simone de Beauvoir, mais avec son personnage libre et libre de son corps, elle a parlé aux femmes de cette époque. BB a été l'un des signes forts dans une période d'ascétisme, avec la volonté de faire bouger les choses.*[17]
>
> Brigitte Bardot is not Simone de Beauvoir, but with her free spirit and the freedom of her body, she spoke to her female contemporaries. BB was one of the strong signs in a time marked by asceticism, with the will to shake things up.
>
> *(Francoise Picq, historian of French feminism)*

The Lolita Syndrome is often read as an extension of Beauvoir's work on the 'Eternal Feminine' myth in *Le Deuxième Sexe*.[18] In the essay, Beauvoir examines the Bardot *persona*—the carefully crafted, widely reproduced, and astutely marketed image of the actress and the ideological work it performs within France. The *Lolita Syndrome* is loosely organized into three sections. In the first, Beauvoir points out the many ways in which the Bardot persona ('BB') re-articulates familiar constructs of 'woman' as an object fabricated by and for men. This is followed by a section in which Beauvoir examines aspects of BB that subvert patriarchal constructions of womanhood. The essay then concludes with some reflections on the limits and the future of the BB phenomenon. At the time of the essay's writing Beauvoir saw the subversive potential of BB as being eroded, and her character as "in the process of evolving" in the direction of greater conformity and heteronormative bourgeois morality.[19]

In *The Lolita Syndrome*, Beauvoir carefully documents how the characters Bardot played in the films in which she starred between 1952 and 1959 re-articulate core woman/nature/object v. man/culture/subject dualities that construct 'woman' as the ultimate Other.[20] These characters, however, also present subversive elements that reframe the Eternal Feminine myth.

Beauvoir claims that Bardot departs from the Eternal Feminine in two fundamental ways: firstly, Bardot ignores moral norms; and, secondly, Bardot's authenticity and her active (sexual) subjectivity place her outside the frame of the object. Both, according to Beauvoir, present a direct challenge to dominant constructions of sex and gender in 1950s France.

The concept of a Lolita syndrome is based on Beauvoir's belief, at the time, that women in France (and elsewhere) were making significant gains in terms of gender equality. As a result, new forms of female character representation emerged not only in movies but also in theater and literary productions, most notably with Nabokov's novel that inspired the title of the essay. One of Beauvoir's claims in *The Lolita Syndrome* is that erotic tension needs and builds on difference: "Love can resist familiarity; eroticism cannot."[21] In an age when women are moving into the province of men (they drive cars, speculate on the stock exchange, and, perhaps singularly in the case of France, display their bodies on public beaches), Beauvoir argues, film and literature have been hard at work creating female characters who embody new forms of eroticism that re-establish and yet transform the social distance between men and women:

> The adult woman now inhabits the same world as the man, but the child-woman moves in a universe which he cannot enter. The age difference re-establishes between them the distance that seems necessary to desire. At least that is what those who have created a new Eve by merging the "green fruit" and "femme fatale" types have pinned their hopes on.[22]

Brigitte Bardot emerged as a perfect example of this new type: a *"garçon manqué* or tomboy, child-woman, whose ambiguous androgyny manages to suggest childhood innocence and sexual availability simultaneously."[23]

> Seen from behind, her slender, muscular, dancer's body is almost androgynous. Femininity triumphs in her delightful bosom. The long voluptuous tresses of Mélisande flow down to her shoulders, but her hair-do is that of a negligent waif. The line of her lips forms a childish pout, and at the same time her lips are very kissable. She goes about barefooted, she turns up her nose at elegant clothes, jewels, girdles, perfumes, make-up, at all artifice.[24]

It is important to note here that what Beauvoir sees as Bardot's androgyny must be placed in relation to more traditional forms of feminine embodiment. The gender-neutral (or, rather, gender-bending) quality of her slim, narrow-hipped body is emphasized by the type of clothing that Bardot wears on and off screen. Likening Bardot to Madonna, Ginette Vincendeau, for instance, notes that BB "experimented with wearing clothes usually seen in different contexts [...] with 'diverting' their original meaning, or with unusual juxtapositions" such as sailor jerseys, cut-off shorts, men's shirts, etc.[25]

Indeed, from her clearly 'modern' get-up—blue jeans, sweater, and tousled hair—to her 'common' face akin to that of a 'housemaid,' BB was departing from pre-war norms of femininity and ushering in new forms of feminine behaviors that would become much more common in the decades to follow. What is interesting here is the clear class inflection when Bardot's face is likened to that of a housemaid. This is a direct reference to the ways in which Bardot's aesthetic—despite or perhaps because of her bourgeois upbringing—embraces a working-class female sensibility. Such a sensibility departs from that of the great French actresses who preceded her (e.g. Michèle Morgan[26]), whose infallible fashion sense and demeanor gave them 'class' and indeed aligned them with the tastes of the French bourgeoisie.

As a harbinger of deep transformations in the dominant sex–gender system, Bardot emerged as a contradictory figure of post-war France. So, while Beauvoir notes and emphasizes the ire BB provokes, the text also suggests that she is greatly appreciated by many women and men alike. Indeed, Beauvoir notes: "Brigitte receives three hundred fan letters a day, from boys and girls alike, and every day indignant mothers write to newspaper editors and religious and civil authorities to protest against her existence."[27] Beauvoir then admits to the dual and contradictory effects that BB has on her fellow citizens—adored by the young (boys and girls alike) and despised by mothers, who sense in her very existence the danger posed to existing patriarchal norms and conventions. It is precisely the adoration and effects that BB produces among young people—imagined as a spell or an incitement to do bad—that these mothers want to stamp out. According to Beauvoir, in the wake of a murder committed by three young men near Angers, their school's parent–teacher association denounced BB's influence on the youth: "It was *she*, they said, who was responsible for the crime. *And God Created Woman* had been shown in Angers; the young people had been immediately perverted."[28]

At the end of the essay Beauvoir, however, moves away from this generational reading of the BB phenomenon towards a more political one. Indeed, Beauvoir writes that BB elicits in young and old alike (and I would add women and men alike) the animus of those who "want mores to be fixed once and for all."[29] In other words, with Beauvoir, we can see Bardot's troubling force as a foreboding of the political/cultural wars that would be ushered in a decade later by students in 1968.

It is important to note that the persona that BB represents is complicated by the rise of a new form of celebrity culture that emerged at the same time as Bardot was acquiring her iconic status. The BB persona then comes into being at the intersection of media representations of Bardot's private life, the imaginary characters Bardot inhabits in films, and media representations of Bardot the star/celebrity—all three representing BB as a "monument of immorality."[30] Beauvoir insists that this persona is a modern rewriting of the old myth of the Eternal Feminine that re-inscribes woman as other but does so by draping her within a "new type of eroticism." It is, according to Beauvoir, precisely "this novelty"—this reframing—"that entices some people and shocks others."[31]

> Her clothes are not fetishes and, when she strips, she is not unveiling a mystery. She is showing her body, neither more nor less, and that body rarely settles into a state of immobility. She walks, she dances, she moves about. Her eroticism is not magical, but aggressive. In the game of love, she is as much a hunter as she is prey. The male is an object to her, just as she is to him. And that is precisely what wounds masculine pride. In the Latin countries, where men cling to the myth of the "woman as an object," BB's naturalness seems to them more perverse than any possible sophistication. To spurn jewels and cosmetics and high heels and girdles is to refuse to transform oneself into a remote idol. It is to assert that one is man's fellow and equal, to recognize that between the woman and him there is mutual desire and pleasure.[32]

For Beauvoir, Bardot exudes "aggressive" eroticism—she is on an equal footing with men in "desire and pleasure," and she is as much a "hunter as she is a prey."[33] And this is precisely "why Bardot is so unpopular in France."[34] Throughout, Beauvoir explains much of the negative critical reception of the BB persona in France by the feminist challenges she presents. Indeed, Beauvoir portrays Bardot as "one of the first post-war, liberated Frenchwomen":[35] a French woman whose unfiltered speech and actions—her raw and "natural" demeanor in general, and in sex more specifically, challenges essentialist notions of what constitutes womanhood and the "repressive sexual standards for women operating in the 1950s" in France.[36]

> BB does not try to scandalize. She has no demands to make; she is no more conscious of her rights than she is of her duties. She follows her inclinations. She eats when she is hungry and makes love with the same unceremonious simplicity. Desire and pleasure seem to her more convincing than precepts and conventions. She doesn't criticize anyone. She does as she pleases, and that is what is disturbing. She does not ask questions, but she brings answers whose frankness may be contagious.[37]

Film critic Ginette Vincendeau analyzes the ways in which Bardot is perceived by readers of the popular film fan magazine *Cinémonde* by examining their letters to the publication between 1957 and 1959. Vincendeau's study corroborates the idea that the reception among her public—both men and women—was indeed mixed. It also points out that the BB phenomenon (sometimes referred to as *Bardomania*) in France must be understood against the backdrop of an emergent celebrity culture and new forms of stardom that centers primarily on women and is fueled by the "relentless exposure of their bodies and of their private lives."[38] Beauvoir understood the impact of this emerging global stardom culture and the negative impact it was bound to have on women in the industry:

> She is the new idol of American youth. She ranks as a great international star [...]. Not a week goes by without articles in the press telling all about her recent moods and love affairs or offering a new interpretation of her personality, but half of these articles and gossip items seethe with spite.[39]

Vincendeau's analysis of the letters also suggests that Bardot's controversial impact lies not so much in her overt sexuality, but rather in the fear that her power—including economic—produces in post-war France: "In this respect the outrage at Bardot's earnings among [readers] revealingly mirrors journalists who at the time criticized her for her efficient management of her wealth."[40]

The kind of provocative freedom that Beauvoir and others underscored in their reading of BB continued unabated throughout Bardot's life. She married early and many times (four times to date), she refused to play the expected roles of good wife and mother that her bourgeois upbringing had laid out for her, and she rejected wholesale post-war French patriarchal morality: "Bardot is neither rebellious nor immoral; this is why morality hasn't got a chance with her. Good and evil are part of conventions to which she would not even think of bowing."[41]

Despite the very mixed reception in her own country that ignites Beauvoir's reflection in *The Lolita Syndrome*, it is fascinating to see that Brigitte Bardot becomes, at the height of her success, not only a fixture of French cultural life but also a core component of an emerging idea about what constitutes a modern French identity. This idea is deployed within France and exported abroad through popular culture. Indeed, it might not be an overstatement to suggest that Brigitte Bardot, by the mid-1950s, had become part and parcel of the brand 'France.' It is to the construction of this myth and the deployment of this brand and its lingering impact that I now turn.

Bardot: The Making of a National Myth

> *[Brigitte Bardot] est une proprieté nationale, comme la régie Renault.*[42]
> Like Renault, Brigitte Bardot is a national brand.
>
> *(Raoul Levy, film producer/director)*

Impoverished, weakened, and humiliated by the tremendous losses it had incurred during World War II, France entered the post-war era with a fierce desire to rebuild the country's infrastructure and to regain, in a rapidly changing geo-political context, its standing as a first-class nation. How to get there and how to draw from France's past were questions raised by the nation's political, intellectual, and technological elite of the time.[43] Questions that pertained to France's role and place in the world and its policy choices were discussed differently in a variety of settings, but invariably embraced and promoted *une certaine idée de la France* (a certain idea of France). The phrase, penned by General Charles de Gaulle in his war memoirs[44] and reiterated in a televised interview with Michel Droit during the 1965 presidential election campaign, claimed the long-standing and much-envied exceptional quality of the nation:

> *Il est tout à fait vrai, je dirais que c'est ma raison d'être, il est tout à fait vrai que depuis toujours et aujourd'hui, je me fais, en effet, de la France une certaine idée. Je veux dire par là qu'à mon sens, elle est quelque chose de très grand, de très particulier. C'est, du reste, je le pense, ressenti par le monde entier [...] C'est vrai, la France est une chose, à mes yeux, très considérable, très valable.*[45]

> It is completely true, I will say that it is my *raison d'être*, it is completely true that forever and to this day I have had a certain idea of France. What I mean by this is that, in my mind, it is something great and very particular. Something which, I believe, is felt by people the world over [...] It's true, France is a thing that, in my eyes, is very great, is very considerable, very valuable.

This "certain idea of France" can be seen as a very successful, long-standing, and fluid narrative—a national myth of sorts—that articulates and deploys through multiple means notions about France's crucial role in the establishment of civil liberties and human rights, its universalist egalitarian political project, and its valuing of all things beautiful. In post-war France, this narrative was also vulgarized and exported through popular culture such as movies, the mainstream print media, and the growing medium of television.[46] And Brigitte Bardot, whom French film critic André Bazin once described as *notre BB nationale* (our national BB), saturated every aspect of France's post-war culture.[47]

It must be noted here that Brigitte Bardot's career as an actress coincided almost exactly with the period known as *Les Trentes Glorieuses* (The Thirty Glorious Years). Indeed, Bardot burst on to the French cultural/media scene in 1949, when, at the age of 15, she made the front cover of the popular women's magazine *Elle*. Her acting career began in 1952, when she appeared in *Le Trou Normand* (Crazy for Love), and ended when she quit acting in

1973, at the age of 39. Simultaneously, between 1945 and 1975 France experienced tremendous economic growth (it was the fastest growing economy in Europe during the period) and its attendant dramatic social and cultural changes. With increased economic power came new forms of consumerism, including leisure and tourism activities. *Les Trentes Glorieuses* came to a brutal halt with the economic downturn of the 1970s. The first decade of this exceptional period (1949–1959)—the one that frames Beauvoir's analysis—was particularly busy for the young actress. Bardot started with a few modeling stints when she was still a teenager; at 18 she married film director Roger Vadim and started acting in France and abroad; and by the decade's end she had divorced and remarried, had featured in no fewer than 24 films, and had become a household name not only in France but also internationally. Brigitte Bardot's sensational presence on the world stage offered France an opportunity to regain and expand its cultural reach and radiance, and to make noteworthy economic gains.[48]

In the mid-1980s, before Brigitte Bardot's fame and influence had been mired by her growing rapprochement with the extreme right and her repeated racist and homophobic statements, French author Catherine Rihoit wrote an insightful biography of Bardot and her central role in France, titled *Brigitte Bardot: Un Mythe Français*. The book deploys the concept of national myth as a central lens through which one can read Bardot's acting persona (BB) as well as her private self (Brigitte): "*Brigitte Bardot deviendra un mythe, une légende, et un mythe, une légende, c'est précisément cela: un personage, une histoire qui dépasse l'individu et l'instant, pour exprimer toute une époque.*" (Brigitte Bardot will become a myth, a legend, and a myth, a legend, is precisely that; a persona, a story that transcends the individual and the moment to express an epoch in its entirety.)[49] Throughout, Rihoit discusses the various ways in which Bardot emerged both as an enduring symbol of a modernizing post-war France and as a core component of French culture both inside and outside the hexagon: "*Brigitte est considérée désormais comme une institution française. Le public lui demande donc de se conduire en institution.*" (Brigitte is now considered as a French institution, and as such her audience asks of her to behave like an institution.)[50]

In the above quote Rihoit evokes the unique role that Bardot, at the time, was being asked to assume: to be and to act like a national institution—a daunting task for anyone, but especially for a young woman not 'destined' to take on such a responsibility. Indeed, in a 1970 radio interview, journalist Jacques Chancel asks the 35-year-old actress if sometimes she imagines herself as another woman, in another world, to which Bardot replies:

> *Bien sûr, j'étais destinée à tout à fait autre chose [...] mais pour moi c'est miraculeux. Je n'arrive pas à imaginer que je suis Brigitte Bardot par exemple. J'y pense pas. Alors, de temps en temps, je me rends*

> *compte, j'ai une prise de conscience et là, je me dis bon il faut quand même vraiment que je sois sérieuse, que je fasse mon métier sérieusement parce que je représente quelque chose d'important. Mais quand je n'y pense pas, pour moi je suis Brigitte, une femme comme les autres.*[51]
>
> Of course, I was destined to something completely different [...] but for me it is miraculous. I cannot imagine, for instance, that I am Brigitte Bardot. I do not think about it. So occasionally, I realize, I have a flash of self-consciousness, and then I tell myself: alright I must really be serious, I must do my job seriously because I represent something important. But when I don't think about it, for me, I am simply Brigitte, a woman like all the others.

In this section of the chapter, I draw on Rihoit's analysis to suggest that Brigitte Bardot must be seen not only as a myth that has currency inside the nation, but also as a key component of a national 'brand' that France deployed inside and outside its borders during the years that immediately followed World War II.[52] By the mid-1950s, after the release of Roger Vadim's *Et Dieu créa la femme*, Bardot's fame was such that spelling out her name was no longer necessary. Brigitte Bardot had simply become BB. These two initials conveniently shorten the actress's full name, connote in French *bébé*/baby (the "green fruit" evoked by Beauvoir in *The Lolita Syndrome*),[53] and capture the market and cultural value that the actress had fully acquired by then.

> When *And God Created Woman* was shown in first-run houses on the Champs Elysées, the film, which had cost a hundred and forty million francs, brought in less than sixty. Receipts in the USA have come to $4,000,000, the equivalent of the sale of 2,500 Dauphines [cars]. BB now deserves to be considered an export product as important as Renault automobiles.[54]

Indeed, Brigitte Bardot, only ten years after the end of the war, embodied an idea of modern France that would inflect not only the nation's sense of itself at the time but also its global impact for years to come. As part of the branding apparatus that modernizing France deploys during these three 'glorious' decades in terms of fashion, culture, and national identity, Brigitte Bardot, I argue, can be read not only as a product of France's *Trentes Glorieuses* (with its euphoric optimism, openness to change, and democratizing ideals) but also as a representation of the period's more sinister elements, including racism and post-colonial resentment.

Bardot's ability to reinforce at the same time as she troubles common sense ideas about French womanhood frames her contradictory reception in France. One might add that Bardot's own complex and ambiguous personality echoes a central tension at the heart of modern Frenchness—an anchoring in tradition combined with an irreverent rejection of some of its precepts: "*Bardot [...] se rebellera contre la tradition, pour mieux s'en proclamer l'héritière.*" (Bardot [...] will rebel against tradition to better claim its heritage.)[55] Bardot's rebelliousness and sexual autonomy, however, did not have the same appeal to all segments of the French population. As noted by Beauvoir, Bardot's rewriting of the French sex/gender system through her characters as well as in her personal life has encountered much disapproval in her home country. Perhaps because the changes such rewriting introduces are too dramatic and costly outside the "well-tempered"[56] bohemian sensibilities of a growing new French bourgeoisie, Bardot is seen as scandalous by those who want mores "to be fixed once and for all."[57]

> *Il y aura toujours chez Brigitte ces deux courants apparemment contradictoires, mais dont la coexistence sera une des raisons du succès et du charme d'une personnalité complexe. Ce mélange de bohème et de convention annonce la nouvelle bourgeoisie qui ne sera plus celle de l'austérité et du bas de laine, mais de la jouissance bien tempérée.*[58]
>
> There will always be within Brigitte those two apparently contradictory currents whose co-existence nevertheless will be one of the reasons for the success and the charm of such a complex personality. This mélange of bohemian sensibility and convention announces the new bourgeoisie, which will no longer be that of austerity and penny-pinching, but rather that of a well-tempered, pleasure-affirming attitude.

Indeed, Brigitte Bardot was not simply a product to be bought and sold; but her image also helped sell and export other commodities, certain trends, and abstract ideas about modern France. For instance, BB popularized the bikini in France and in Europe generally. Bardot's style (her hair, her clothes, her bare body) ushered in French and European-wide fashion trends. According to Ginette Vincendeau, "Bardot's championing of new fashion coincided with important changes in the clothing industry."[59] The French fashion industry in the 1950s experienced not only the decline of *haute couture* but also the related emergence of the democratizing and lasting trend of *prêt-à-porter* (ready-to-wear), and the importance of young people as a consumer group. Such championing was also part and parcel "of the export effort of the French fashion business [...] This was particularly necessary at a time when French fashion was fast losing its world hegemony. Bardot was thus bankable in France and eminently exportable."[60]

The exportability of Bardot and what she represented at the time is to be found among other things in the troubling erotic sensibility she exudes and the unabashed nudity she displays. Like her fashion tastes, such eroticism "proved a bankable commodity."[61] BB also participated in and helped create the image of the beach as a privileged space for pleasure and leisure activities in post-war France. By setting up residence in St-Tropez, and by filming in its setting, she also helped popularize it as a unique beach-vacation destination. By baring her body and offering her nudity to the desirous gaze of men and women the world over—including that of Beauvoir—Bardot helped shape a particular idea of modern France where women are not covered and where the relation between the sexes is not seen as a source of danger that needs regulating. Instead, it is perceived as a form of playful and healthy banter, and a clear sign of modernity and democracy where

> [the] visibility of the bodies of women and men, their easy accessibility to one another, the free play of seduction, [are] taken to be hallmarks of liberty and equality, the expression on the personal level of what it means to live in a politically free society.[62]

By promoting Bardot as a national good that can be featured and consumed on French TV during holidays such as New Year's Eve, and by exporting her all over the world (but especially to 'America') through French cinema, the French TV and film industry has indeed contributed to the making of a French brand. In the process, it has also helped frame the dominant narrative about France's identity in which certain ideas about gender and sexuality have center stage, and ideas about race, religion, and immigration provide a powerful and lasting subtext.

> *Brigitte ne représente pas la sexualité des bars et des boites de nuits; avec elle, l'érotisme français sort de l'obscôvre de l'alcôve pour célébrer joies du plein air et du soleil. Le sexe, désormais, ce n'est plus la maladie, l'épuisement, la dégénérescence mais au contraire la santé.*[63]
>
> Brigitte does not represent the sexuality found in bars and nightclubs; with her, French eroticism comes out of the obscurity of the bedroom to celebrate the joys of the sun and the outdoors. From now on, sex is no longer disease, exhaustion, and degeneracy, but rather health.

Like the rest of her persona, Bardot's sexuality is ambiguous: it is at one and the same time perceived as visibly festive and healthy and as unbridled and audaciously provocative:

> She is showing her body, neither more nor less, and that body rarely settles into a state of immobility. She walks, she dances, she moves about. Her eroticism is not magical, but aggressive. In the game of love, she is as much a hunter as she is a prey. The male is an object to her, just as she is to him.[64]

Bardot embodies forms of feminine agentic desires and pleasures that unsettle sexual and gender mores in post-war France.

Both perceptions, however, in different but parallel ways connote race and class. Imagined fears of 'unbridled,' thus dangerous, sexualities have long been used to mark the bodies of stratified others. In a similar way, the kind of newly celebrated 'healthy' sexuality that Bardot embodies, according to Rihoit, has historically been opposed to that of the colonized others in France and elsewhere.[65] Through the deployment of new forms of racialized sexual imaginaries, BB troubles the contours of French identity and emerges, in the process, as a "monument of immorality."[66] The infamous mambo scene in *Et Dieu créa la femme* renders crystal clear the kind of racialization to which I am referring here. At the end of the film, "Bardot goes into a frenzy of dancing to the black band's music (which at this point includes a lot of drum beat); Bardot is a whirl of bare feet, wild hair, syncopated movements as if 'possessed' by the music."[67] This *mise-en-scène*, Vincendeau comments, constructs Bardot's body (and her sexuality) not only as close to nature but also as "primitive."[68] Such connection with the primitive is crassly present when Curd Jürgens, the actor who plays the role of the older man pining after Juliette in *Et Dieu créa la femme*, describes Bardot, at the time of the filming, as a n——— *blonde* (a blond n———). According to Vincendeau, Jürgens' description, "despite, but also because of, its racism" reveals the constructed nature of her persona, and—I would add—the racial underpinnings of the Bardot phenomenon.[69] Marguerite Duras' depiction of Bardot for *France-Observateur* in 1958 also points to the racial subtext of Bardot's persona in general and of her sexuality more specifically: "*La Reine Bardot se tient juste là où finirait la moralité et, à partir de quoi la jungle serait ouverte de la liberté amoureuse. Un pays d'où l'ennui chrétien est banni.*" (Queen Bardot stands precisely where morality ends and whence the *jungle* of free love opens. A country where Christian boredom is banned.)[70]

Such racialized understandings of Bardot's ambiguous morality and sexuality are not to be found in *The Lolita Syndrome*—in part because Beauvoir did not have the privilege of a *longue durée* look at Bardot's life span, and because the actress's problematic relationship with questions of race and immigration had not yet fully taken shape. It is also due to Beauvoir's own blind spots and the locational limits of her analysis, which some have described as Beauvoir's 'white problem.'[71] While it is well beyond the scope of this chapter to engage the debate surrounding Beauvoir's own complex relationship with whiteness and white supremacy, it is clear that a growing body of intersectional critiques of Beauvoir's oeuvre in general, but of *The Second Sex* more specifically, help us interrogate such blind spots.[72] Since the mid-nineties, Brigitte Bardot has been condemned by French courts, and fined six times for inciting racial hatred. While Bardot's racist rants and her anti-Muslim position are regularly (and justifiably) criticized in France, very few commentators have analyzed the racial underpinnings of her key role in the construction of a modern French identity. This may be attributed to the staying power of 'a certain idea of France,' and its attendant belief that the French republic is indeed exceptional in all things, including matters of 'race' and racial equality.

Conclusion

> Perhaps the hatred she has aroused will calm down, but she will no longer represent anything for anyone. I hope that she will not resign herself to insignificance in order to gain popularity. I hope she will mature, but not change.[73]

This is how Beauvoir ends *The Lolita Syndrome*. This final note follows Beauvoir's reflections on the ways in which the Bardot image, in her films and in the media, was going through a form of rehabilitation. Indeed, Beauvoir documents what she sees as a new focus, in 1959, on Bardot's connection to the earth (her love of animals) and the nation, and her capacity to be a wife and mother.

This is an interesting—albeit half mistaken—prevision for the future impact of Brigitte Bardot on France. Brigitte Bardot the person never became 'insignificant.' Quite the contrary: Bardot's continued significance in France is due to her short but spectacular career as an actress; her continued presence on the French cultural scene as a singer well into the 1970s and beyond;[74] her multiple and often avant-garde contributions to the animal rights cause; her rapprochement with the French radical right; and her repeated condemnations for incitement to racial hatred. We are, in fact, seeing a renewed interest in her as a 'phenomenon' as well as an individual. Each year new books and articles are penned around some aspect of Brigitte Bardot's life, activism, and political inclination; and in 2020 the radio channel France Culture aired a five-part series titled *Brigitte Bardot, à nu* (Brigitte Bardot bared). In fact, Brigitte Bardot is part and parcel of the complex and contradictory story that we must reckon with and tell about modern France.

This chapter has built on Beauvoir's analysis of Bardot to reflect on common understandings of modern France and the women who live there. Bardot's own ambiguity and ambiguous impact continue to intrigue and fascinate. In her book, Catherine Rihoit ponders whether Brigitte, the woman, was fully aware of how outstanding she was and what that meant for France and for herself.

> *A-t-elle dès le début de sa carrière saisi combien elle était exceptionnelle—comme lorsqu'elle répondra à Jacques Chancel qui lui dit:*

*"Finalement vous êtes un bonne petite Française." "Non, je suis une grande Française."*⁷⁵

Did she realize from the beginning of her career how exceptional she was—like when she responded to Jacques Chancel when he told her [in a radio interview]: "At the end of the day, you are a good little French woman." "No, I am a great French woman."

By defining herself as a *grande Française*, Brigitte Bardot, with her well-known sense of repartee, not only rejects Chancel's diminutive "good little French woman" formula, but also claims her own central role in French national identity post-war affairs and discourse. Her *grande Française* status—whether we like it or not—is also evidenced by the fact that, in 1969, Charles de Gaulle chose Brigitte Bardot to be the model for Marianne—the first time an actress would receive this honor. Bardot's sculpted bust, at the height of the actress's success, appeared as a representational emblem of the French republic in town halls all over the country. In 1985 Bardot was granted the high distinction of becoming a knight of the Legion of Honor. While it would be unthinkable today for Bardot to officially represent the nation, it is interesting to note that she emerges again and again as a central character in nationalist and populist narratives that invite us to imagine and embrace a time and space when Frenchness was as simple and beautiful as Bardot on a St-Tropez beach.

When Eric Zemmour produced his much-criticized video-montage bid for the French presidential election in 2022, he, like Marine Le Pen in 2016, called on Brigitte Bardot to evoke a nation that, according to him, is fast disappearing and that, with his party (*La Reconquête*), he aims to save.⁷⁶ The montage, which included clips of brown and black people in France and random scenes of social unrest, provided the visual backdrop for Zemmour's delusional yet dangerous depiction of the French nation he claims has been lost. In the speech and the visual text that accompanies it, Bardot and other French icons are called upon to remind us of the country they need to reconquer:

> Do you recall the country you knew when you were a child, do you remember the country that your parents described to you, do you remember the country that you rediscover in films and books; the country of Joan of Arc and Louis the XVI, the country of Bonaparte and General de Gaulle; [...] the country of Gabin and Delon, of Brigitte Bardot and Belmondo.⁷⁷

By occupying such a central role in France's post-war national reach for grandeur and radiance, Brigitte Bardot was then (and still is to this day) called on to function as a bridge between France's past and its future. In *The*

Radiance of France: Nuclear Power and National Identity after World War II, Gabrielle Hecht sheds light on the complex dynamics that inflect the construction of national identities, and the need for a temporal bridge between past and present in the making of national identities:

> Discussions of national identity typically refer back to the past. But ultimately national identity discourse is not about the past per se, or even about the present. Instead, it is about the future. National identity discourse constructs a bridge between a mythologized past and a coveted future. Nations and their supposedly essential characteristics are imagined though a telos in which the future appears as the inevitable fulfillment of a historically legitimated destiny.[78]

As in 1959, when Beauvoir pondered Bardot's mixed reception in France, Bardot continues to mesmerize and appall. It is her complex role at the juncture of the two myths of the eternal feminine and of the French republic that such strong and contradictory reactions must be analyzed and understood.

Acknowledgements

I would like to extend my thanks to the members of the Hunter College Faculty Writing Seminar (2020–2021) whose feedback on an early draft of this chapter helped steer it in the right direction.

Notes

1 "Brigitte Bardot and the Lolita Syndrome" was not published in France until 1979. It is assumed that the original French version of the text must have been lost since it was translated into French from the English version when the essay was included in Claude Francis, Fernande Gontier, and Simone de Beauvoir, *Les écrits de Simone de Beauvoir: la vie, l'écriture* (Paris: Gallimard, 1979). The text was published again in English in 2015 without the photographs, with an introduction by Elizabeth Fallaize, and with minor adjustments to the English original in Margaret A. Simons and Marybeth Timmerman, eds., *Simone de Beauvoir: Feminist Writings* (Urbana: University of Illinois Press, 2011), 114–125.
2 Simone de Beauvoir, *Brigitte Bardot and the Lolita Syndrome*, trans. Bernard Frechtman (London: André Deutsch and Weidenfeld & Nicolson, 1960), 5.
3 Even though some critics claim that *Brigitte Bardot and the Lolita Syndrome* was one of Beauvoir's favorite essays, it has garnered relatively little critical interest. See Denise Warren, "Beauvoir on Bardot: The Ambiguity Syndrome," *Dalhousie French Studies* 13 (Fall/Winter 1987): 39–50, and Pilar Godayol, "*Brigitte Bardot and the Lolita Syndrome*, by Simone de Beauvoir: Censored under Francoism," *Translation & Interpreting* 12, no. 2 (2020): 36–47.
4 Kate Kirkpatrick, *Becoming Beauvoir: A Life* (London: Bloomsbury Academic, 2019), 305–306.
5 Hereafter referred to as *The Lolita Syndrome*.

6 See Warren, "Beauvoir on Bardot."
7 Simone de Beauvoir, *America Day by Day*, trans. Carol Cosman (Berkeley: University of California Press, 1999), 330.
8 Ibid. Beauvoir scholars and feminists have engaged the philosopher's use of the term 'harem,' and debated whether or not it authorizes the kind of essentialist dualist framing that her work aims to dismantle. Engaging this debate is beyond the scope of this chapter.
9 Brigitte Bardot married Roger Vadim in 1952, when she was 18. In 1954, Vadim directed *Et Dieu créa la femme* (*And God Created Woman*), which launched Bardot's international career and fame. They divorced in 1957.
10 Perhaps I need to remind readers who might not be familiar with the French actress that Brigitte Bardot appeared in over 40 films during her acting career, that she was also a successful and prolific singer, and that her image saturated the French cultural landscape in the 1950s and 60s. During that time, she was featured relentlessly on TV (through specials, documentaries, and news segments). She appeared on the front cover and inside numerous magazines, newspapers, and books. She was also widely pictured in cartoons, advertisements, postcards, and posters. Her style was copied by other actresses and ordinary French women alike. She modelled for the bust of Marianne—the symbolic representation of the French republic—and was famous enough to be recognized by her initials alone: BB. See Ginette Vincendeau, "The Old and the New: Brigitte Bardot in 1950s France," *Paragraph* 15, no.1 (March 1992): 73–96; and Dana W. Sherwood, "Integration by Popular Culture: Brigitte Bardot as a Transnational Icon and European Integration in the 1950s and 1960s" (MA Thesis, University of Ottawa, 2011).
11 Vincendeau, "The Old and the New," 73.
12 Feminist scholars have long analyzed and rendered visible the gendered and racial underpinnings of nation and national identity. Among others, see George L. Mosse, *Nationalism and Sexuality: Respectability and Abnormal Sexuality in Modern Europe* (New York: Howard Fertig, 1985); Cynthia Enloe, *Bananas, Beaches, and Bases: Making Feminist Sense of International Politics* (Berkeley and Los Angeles: University of California Press, 1989); Nira Yuval-Davis, *Gender and Nation* (London: SAGE, 1997); and Ida Blom, Karen Hageman, and Catherine Hall, eds., *Gendered Nations: Nationalisms and Gender Order in the Long Nineteenth Century* (Oxford and New York: Berg, 2000).
13 Quoted in Sophie Fuggle, "Brigitte Bardot vs. the Burkini," *Foreign Policy: The Global Magazine of News and Ideas*, 23 August 2016.
14 Vincendeau, "The Old and the New," 83.
15 Ibid.
16 See Catherine Rihoit, *Brigitte Bardot: Un Mythe Français* (Paris: Club France Loisirs, 1986); Warren, "Beauvoir on Bardot"; and Catherine Rodgers, "Beauvoir Piégée par Bardot?" in "Beauvoir in the New Millennium," special issue of *Simone de Beauvoir Studies* 17 (2000–2001): 127–148.
17 Quoted in Agence France Presse, "'Et Dieu … créa la femme': quand Bardot bousculait les tabous," *Le Point Culture*, 23 December 2016. Unless stated otherwise, all translations are mine.
18 Warren, "Beauvoir on Bardot."
19 Beauvoir, *The Lolita Syndrome*, 32.
20 Warren, "Beauvoir on Bardot."
21 Beauvoir, *The Lolita Syndrome*, 8.
22 Ibid., 10.
23 Elizabeth Fallaize, "Introduction," to "Brigitte Bardot and the Lolita Syndrome" by Simone de Beauvoir, in Simons and Timmermann, *Simone de Beauvoir:*

Feminist Writings, 109–110. Beauvoir is not the only one to see BB as androgynous. Serge Gainsbourg, one of her many lovers, noted for instance that Bardot had "the hips of a young man." Rihoit, *Un Mythe Français*, 33, quoted in Rodgers, "Beauvoir Piégée par Bardot?," 140.
24 Beauvoir, *The Lolita Syndrome*, 11.
25 Vincendeau, "The Old and the New," 80.
26 Michèle Morgan was a French actress whose leading roles marked French cinema from the 1930s to the end of the1950s. She continued to act in the 1960s and beyond, but in much lesser roles, and died in 2016 at the age of 96.
27 Beauvoir, *The Lolita Syndrome*, 6.
28 Ibid., 7.
29 Ibid., 36.
30 Ibid., 7.
31 Ibid., 8.
32 Ibid., 20–21.
33 Ibid., 20.
34 Fallaize, "Introduction," 110.
35 Goyadol, "Censored under Francoism," 42.
36 Fallaize, "Introduction," 110.
37 Beauvoir, *The Lolita Syndrome*, 17.
38 Ginette Vincendeau, "A Star is Torn (To Pieces): Brigitte Bardot Seen through Readers' Letters in *Cinémonde*," *Contemporary French and Francophone Studies* 19, no.1 (2015): 98. *Cinémonde* is a popular magazine devoted to cinema, featuring abundant images of movie stars (especially women). It is also in the pages of magazines like *Cinémonde* that new forms of popular cinephilia, including emerging feminine ones, developed in the 1950s.
39 Beauvoir, *The Lolita Syndrome*, 6.
40 Ginette Vincendeau, *Brigitte Bardot* (London: BFI/Palgrave Macmillan, 2013), 84–91.
41 Beauvoir, *The Lolita Syndrome*, 16.
42 Quoted in Rihoit, *Un Mythe Français*, 189.
43 See Gabrielle Hecht, *The Radiance of France: Nuclear Power and National Identity after World War II* (Cambridge, MA: MIT Press, 2009).
44 Charles de Gaulle, *Mémoires de guerre, vol. I: L'Appel, 1940–1942* (Paris: Plon, 1954).
45 Charles de Gaulle, "Interview du général de Gaulle, candidat à la Présidence de la République, entre les deux tours de l'élection présidentielle," by Michel Droit, 13 December 1965, video (Paris: INA). https://www.ina.fr/ina-eclaire-actu/video/caf89046845/charles-de-gaulle.
46 In 1956 only 10 percent of French households owned a TV set. See Rihoit, *Un Mythe Français*, 170.
47 Quoted ibid., 161.
48 See Sarah Leahy, "The Matter of Myth: Brigitte Bardot, Stardom and Sex," *Studies in French Cinema* 3, no. 2 (2003): 71–81.
49 Rihoit, *Un Mythe Français*, 38.
50 Ibid., 182.
51 Brigitte Bardot, interview by Jacques Chancel. Radioscopie. Office national de radiodiffusion télévision française. 5 February 1970, audio. https://www.youtube.com/watch?v=2bVXoxAarIA.
52 Adapted from the work of Wally Olins and others, I am using the terms 'brand' and 'branding' rather loosely in this chapter to signal the multifaceted aspects of this phenomenon, which not only refers to the political, social, and cultural mechanisms that construct national identities and project national imaginaries,

but also the economic ones that profit from them. Wally Olins, "Branding the Nation: Historical Context," *Journal of Brand Management* 9, no. 4/5 (2002): 249–261.
53 Beauvoir, *The Lolita Syndrome*, 10.
54 Ibid, 6.
55 Rihoit, *Un Mythe Français*, 7.
56 Ibid., 9.
57 Beauvoir, *The Lolita Syndrome*, 36.
58 Rihoit, *Un Mythe Français*, 9.
59 Vincendeau, "The Old and the New", 81.
60 Ibid.
61 Ibid., 83
62 Joan Wallach Scott, *The Politics of the Veil* (Princeton, NJ: Princeton University Press, 2007), 168.
63 Rihoit, *Un Mythe Français*, 100.
64 Beauvoir, *The Lolita Syndrome*, 20.
65 See Ann Laura Stoler, *Race and the Education of Desire: Foucault's History of Sexuality and the Colonial Order of Things* (Durham, NC: Duke University Press, 1995); and Anne McClintock, *Imperial Leather: Race, Gender and Sexuality in the Colonial Conquest* (New York and London: Routledge, 1995), 46–56.
66 Beauvoir, *The Lolita Syndrome*, 7.
67 Vincendeaau, "The Old and the New," 90.
68 Ibid.
69 Ibid.
70 Quoted in Dominique Chalant, *Bardot pour toujours* (Paris: Lanore, 2019), 80. Emphasis mine.
71 For a direct engagement with Beauvoir's 'white problem' see T. Storm Heter, "Beauvoir's White Problem," *Chère Simone de Beauvoir*, January 2021. https://lirecrire.hypotheses.org/3404. See also Linda Martín Alcoff, *The Future of Whiteness* (Cambridge: Polity, 2015); Sonia Kruks, "Simone de Beauvoir and the Politics of Privilege," *Hypatia* 20, no. 1 (2005): 178–205; and Nathalie Nya, *Simone de Beauvoir and the Colonial Experience* (Lanham, MA: Lexington, 2019).
72 See Patricia Hill Collins, "Simone de Beauvoir, Women's Oppression and Existential Freedom," in *A Companion to Simone de Beauvoir*, eds. Laura Hengehold and Nancy Bauer (Hoboken, NJ: Wiley Blackwell, 2017), 325–338; Kathryn T. Gines, "Comparative and Competing Frameworks of Oppression in Simone de Beauvoir's The Second Sex," *Graduate Faculty Philosophy Journal* 35, no. 1–2 (2014): 251–273; bell hooks, *Black Looks: Race and Representation* (New York: Routledge, 2015); Audre Lorde, "The Master's Tools Will Never Dismantle the Master's House," in *This Bridge Called My Back: Writings of Radical Women of Color*, eds. Cherrie Moraga and Gloria Anzaldúa (Albany: State University of New York Press: 2015), 94–102; and Margaret Simons, *Beauvoir and The Second Sex: Feminism, Race, and the Origins of Existentialism* (Lanham, MD: Rowman & Littlefield, 1999), 141–151.
73 Beauvoir, *The Lolita Syndrome*, 37.
74 Bardot recorded her last single, *La Chasse* (The Hunt), in 1982.
75 Rihoit, *Un Mythe Français*, 66.
76 Zemmour's video, which was initially available on YouTube, is no longer accessible in France since his conviction for copyright infringement by a French court in March 2022.
77 Eric Zemmour, "Pourquoi je suis candidat," 30 November 2021. Accessed 23 March 2022. https://www.ericzemmour.fr/candidature.
78 Hecht, *The Radiance of France*, 12.

References

Agence France Presse. "'Et Dieu … créa la femme': quand Bardot bousculait les tabous." *Le Point Culture*, 23 December 2016. https://www.lepoint.fr/culture/et-dieu-crea-la-femme-quand-bardot-bousculaient-les-tabous-23-12-2016-2092568_3.php.
Alcoff, Linda Martín. *The Future of Whiteness*. Cambridge: Polity, 2015.
Bardot, Brigitte. Interview with Jacques Chancel. *Radioscopie*. Office national de radiodiffusion télévision française. 5 February 1970. Audio. https://www.youtube.com/watch?v=2bVXoxAarIA.
Beauvoir, Simone de. *Brigitte Bardot and the Lolita Syndrome*. Translated by Bernard Frechtman. London: André Deutsch and Weidenfeld & Nicolson, 1960. First published in *Esquire*, August 1959.
Beauvoir, Simone de. *America Day by Day*. Translated by Carol Cosman. Berkeley: University of California Press, 1999. First published as *L'Amérique au jour le jour 1947*. Paris: Gallimard, 1948.
Blom, Ida, Karen Hageman, and Catherine Hall, eds. *Gendered Nations: Nationalisms and Gender Order in the Long Nineteenth Century*. Oxford and New York: Berg, 2000.
Choulant, Dominique. *Bardot Pour Toujours*. Paris: Lanore, 2019.
Collins, Patricia Hill. "Simone de Beauvoir, Women's Oppression and Existential Freedom," in *A Companion to Simone de Beauvoir*, edited by Laura Hengehold and Nancy Bauer. Hoboken, NJ: Wiley Blackwell, 2017: 325–338.
Enloe, Cynthia. *Bananas, Beaches, and Bases: Making Feminist Sense of International Politics*. Berkeley and Los Angeles: University of California Press, 1989.
Fallaize, Elizabeth. "Introduction" to "Brigitte Bardot and the Lolita Syndrome" by Simone de Beauvoir. In *Simone de Beauvoir: Feminist Writings*, edited by Margaret A. Simons and Marybeth Timmerman. Urbana: University of Illinois Press, 2015: 109–113.
Francis, Claude, Fernande Gontier, and Simone de Beauvoir. *Les écrits de Simone de Beauvoir: la vie, l'écriture*. Paris: Gallimard, 1979.
Fuggle, Sophie. "Brigitte Bardot vs. the Burkini." *Foreign Policy: The Global Magazine of News and Ideas*, 23 August 2016. https://foreignpolicy.com/2016/08/23/brigitte-bardot-vs-the-burkini-france-burqini-ban/.
Gaulle, Charles de. *Mémoires de guerre*, vol. I, *L'Appel, 1940–1942*. Paris: Plon, 1954.
Gaulle, Charles de. "Interview du général de Gaulle, candidat à la Présidence de la République, entre les deux tours de l'élection présidentielle," by Michel Droit, 13 December 1965, video. Paris: INA. https://www.ina.fr/ina-eclaire-actu/video/caf89046845/charles-de-gaulle.
Gines, Kathryn T. "Comparative and Competing Frameworks of Oppression in Simone de Beauvoir's *The Second Sex*," *Graduate Faculty Philosophy Journal* 35, no. 1–2 (2014): 251–273.
Godayol, Pilar. "*Brigitte Bardot and the Lolita Syndrome*, by Simone de Beauvoir: Censored under Francoism." *Translation & Interpreting* 12 no. 2 (2020): 36–47.
Hecht, Gabrielle. *The Radiance of France: Nuclear Power and National Identity after World War II*. Cambridge, MA: MIT Press, 2009.
Heter, T. Storm. "Beauvoir's White Problem," *Chère Simone de Beauvoir*, January 2021. https://lirecrire.hypotheses.org/3404.

hooks, bell. *Black Looks: Race and Representation*. New York: Routledge, 2015.
Kirkpatrick, Kate. *Becoming Beauvoir: A Life*. London and New York: Bloomsbury Academic, 2019.
Kruks, Sonia. "Simone de Beauvoir and the Politics of Privilege." *Hypatia* 20, no. 1 (2005): 178–205. http://www.jstor.org/stable/3810848.
Leahy, Sarah. "The Matter of Myth: Brigitte Bardot, Stardom and Sex," *Studies in French Cinema* 3 no. 2 (2003): 71–81.
Lorde, Audre. "The Master's Tools Will Never Dismantle the Master's House." In *This Bridge Called My Back: Writings of Radical Women of Color*, edited by Cherrie Moraga and Gloria Anzaldúa. Albany: State University of New York Press, 2015: 94–102.
McClintock, Anne. *Imperial Leather: Race, Gender and Sexuality in the Colonial Conquest*. New York and London: Routledge, 1995.
Mosse, George L. *Nationalism and Sexuality: Respectability & Abnormal Sexuality in Modern Europe*. New York: Howard Fertig, 1985.
Nya, Nathalie. *Simone de Beauvoir and the Colonial Experience*. Lanham, MD: Lexington, 2019.
Olins, Wally. "Branding the Nation: Historical Context." *Journal of Brand Management* 9, no. 4/5 (2002): 249–261.
Rihoit, Catherine. *Brigitte Bardot: Un Mythe Français*. Paris: Club France Loisirs, 1986.
Rodgers, Catherine. "Beauvoir Piégée Par Bardot?" In "Beauvoir in the New Millennium (2000–2001)." Special issue of *Simone de Beauvoir Studies* 17 (2000–2001): 127–148.
Scott, Joan Wallach. *The Politics of the Veil*. Princeton, NJ: Princeton University Press, 2007.
Sherwood, Dana W. "Integration by Popular Culture: Brigitte Bardot as a Transnational Icon and European Integration in the 1950s and 1960s." MA Thesis. University of Ottawa, 2011.
Simons, Margaret A. *Beauvoir and The Second Sex: Feminism, Race, and the Origins of Existentialism*. Lanham, MD: Rowman & Littlefield, 1999: 141–151.
Simons, Margaret A. and Marybeth Timmerman, eds. *Simone de Beauvoir: Feminist Writings*. Urbana: University of Illinois Press, 2015.
Stoler, Ann Laura. *Race and the Education of Desire: Foucault's History of Sexuality and the Colonial Order of Things*. Durham, NC: Duke University Press, 1995.
Vincendeau, Ginette, "A Star is Torn (To Pieces): Brigitte Bardot Seen through Readers' Letters in *Cinémonde*." *Contemporary French and Francophone Studies* 19 no. 1 (2015): 90–105.
Vincendeau, Ginette, *Brigitte Bardot*. London: BFI/Palgrave Macmillan, 2013.
Vincendeau, Ginette, "The Old and the New: Brigitte Bardot in 1950s France." *Paragraph* 15, no. 1 (1992): 73–96.
Warren, Denise. "Beauvoir on Bardot: The Ambiguity Syndrome." *Dalhousie French Studies* 13 (Fall/Winter 1987): 39–50.
Yuval-Davis, Nira. *Gender and Nation*. London: SAGE, 1997.

PART II
Lived Ambiguities

5
USES OF AMBIGUITY AS TOOL

A Black Feminist Phenomenologist Reflects on the Year 2020 (and Ambiguous Futures)

Qrescent Mali Mason

> on the anniversary of the deaths of
>
> Breonna Taylor, murdered by the Louisville, Kentucky, police on March 13, 2020
>
> and
>
> George Floyd, murdered by the Minneapolis, Minnesota, police on May 25, 2020,
>
> we remember
>
> the Black and brown victims of state violence
>
> and
>
> the global uprisings of the summer of 2020 ...

Preface

This essay is based on a talk I originally gave at the *Simone de Beauvoir: New Perspectives for the 21st Century* online conference at KU Leuven, Belgium, in May of 2020. I want to thank the conference participants at *New Perspectives* for helping me write and conceive of this piece through their self-reflective contributions.

At the time of this editing, 2022 is nearing its close. In attempting to prepare this piece for this volume, I struggled with how to edit something from the past, about the past, for a future audience. Thanks go to Hanae Victoria Mason, who urged me to think of this as an opportunity to really test the value of offering ambiguity as a tool, not just for the year 2020 but for the many years we have to come. It has been enriching to see how relevant these reflections remain to me, and how ambiguity as a framework continues to lead me into new insights and ways of relating to the world. It was important to me during the original talk to have conference attendees join me in my exploration of the uses of ambiguity by participating in the talk itself through populating an online word cloud. I find that crucial aspects of my thinking have been shaped by being in dialogue/conversation with others, and that this often remains invisible in the contemporary model of single-authorship. Co-exploration, co-constitution, and co-reflection are philosophical praxes that reflect a Black feminist commitment to understanding the self as always already in relation to a community of others. Black feminist philosopher bell hooks writes about the importance of "ongoing conversation" to her theorizing: "my sense [of the work] actually emerged as I talked through it with other people, and not as an internal, silent dialogue with myself."[1] This concern with the interplay of the self and the 'other' points toward an initial connection between ambiguity and Black feminism.

In this chapter, I experiment with recreating the experience of the talk by inviting you, the reader, to interact directly and physically with the text through reflection prompts you will find throughout the text. In this way, I hope that you may not only follow me in the development of my arguments here, but also reflect upon your own contributions to its development and use. I also see this as a mode of ambiguity in praxis.

Introduction

I want to focus on the concept of ambiguity in order to consider contemporary engagements with Simone de Beauvoir's work and the legacies of feminist thinkers who, like Beauvoir, are complex, complicated, brilliant, and also ambiguous. I want to take a moment to think about the ambiguities that emerged for me in the year 2020, inspired by Beauvoir's own phenomenological engagement with the concept. Adding the lens of Black feminist phenomenology, I want to think about ambiguity not only as a philosophical concept that I have inherited from a French existentialist white woman who I will never meet, but also as a concept that helped me heal, have discernment, and live through 2020, a year full of ambiguities.

I want to talk about how I journeyed through having done so myself, and how having done so changed my relationship to Beauvoir; how, in my life and my thinking, I had turned away from her, feeling worn down in certain senses by all the critique of her, of the messiness of her life, of how much there seemed to be to apologize for. The year 2020, however, helped me realize that it was Beauvoir herself who offered me the tools that allowed me to position myself ambiguously toward her as a figure. I want to think about ways that 2020 forced us to confront how we are all, as another feminist philosopher of ambiguity, María Lugones, suggests, imbued with this ambiguity.[2]

I want to think about what being a Black feminist philosopher brings to bear on my relationship to the concept of ambiguity. I want to describe how being so allowed me to access dimensions of ambiguity that I didn't before consider or know. I want to spend time with this Black feminist lens and think through how it inspires me to dig into ambiguity, to expand it. In mapping my own lived experiences as a Black feminist philosopher in the year 2020, I hope to pay homage to Beauvoir and to the ways her thinking continues to impact and inspire contemporary feminist thinkers from around the world.

The title of this essay aims to call to mind the lineages that it hopes to honor: both Beauvoir's and Black feminist Audre Lorde's, whose commitment to the concept of use is evidenced in the titles of her works—"Uses of the Erotic: The Erotic as Power" and "The Uses of Anger."[3] Following queer feminist phenomenologist Sara Ahmed, I want to begin with the idea that:

> the word *use* is a busy word. To start with use is to start small and to start simply [...] Use is a relation as well as an activity that often points beyond something even when use is about something: to use something points to what something is for.[4]

Here, I will be thinking about the uses of ambiguity, how we can understand it as a critical phenomenological concept, and how a (Black) feminist commitment to praxis makes me concerned not only with ambiguity's meaning but also with its usefulness.

What does it mean to me to say that I situate myself as a Black feminist phenomenologist? Like others of us who consider how the structures of consciousness are affected by situations of difference, I situate my work within the context of critical phenomenology. I take critical phenomenology to be a vein of phenomenology that recognizes and attempts to resolve some of the lacunae and oversight of historical phenomenological traditions, particularly with regard to the relationship that phenomenological method and inquiry have—and always already have had—to the power relations embedded within the social.

Gail Weiss, Ann V. Murphy, and Gayle Salamon write in the "Introduction" to *50 Concepts Toward a Critical Phenomenology* that a critical phenomenology is one:

> that mobilizes phenomenological description in the service of a reflexive inquiry into how power relations structure experience as well as our ability to analyze that experience. A critical phenomenology draws attention to the multiple ways in which power moves through our bodies and our lives. It is also an ameliorative phenomenology that seeks not only to describe but also to repair the world, encouraging generativity, respect and compassion for the diversity of our lived experiences. Such a project can never be an individual endeavor, moreover, but requires coalitional labor and solidarity across difference.[5]

In this way, I take critical phenomenology to be calling for us to consider how difference affects not only the phenomenological process but also our possible ontological accounts. As such (and in the tradition of other Black feminist thinkers who are at the heart of my teaching, research, and writing) I begin and end with offering my own situational specificities—those differences that make the difference—in recognition of the aforementioned. I am Qrescent Mali Mason, a 38-year-old, bisexual, Black feminist assistant philosophy professor at what is known as a 'selective private liberal arts college.' I live in West Philadelphia, Pennsylvania, in the United States, and my people are from Montgomery, Alabama, and Montego Bay, Jamaica/Brooklyn, New York. I am a third-generation college graduate whose mother is also a professor. I was initially trained in philosophy at Spelman College, a private Black women's liberal arts college in Atlanta, Georgia.

I name these positions, what I take to be salient dimensions of my situation, in order to make these positions explicit in an attempt to resist any claim to universality. Instead, I want to make a rather extreme claim to specificity and difference at the outset. Hence, my positionality is not masked in my writing or in my philosophizing. I am interested in the kinds of phenomenological writing and thinking that do the same, as I hope they might provide more possibilities for theorizing difference. Like Lugones,

> If I am right, it is not just those who theorize about difference who need to worry about it when theorizing. Difference makes the kind of difference that makes inappropriate the theoretical division of labor between those of us who work on difference and those of us who don't.[6]

In other words, although I am foregrounding those differences of mine as a Black feminist commitment, I believe there are theoretical treasures we all might discover in doing so, Black feminist or not.

Already, I am wading into ambiguous waters; but at the very least I want to make it clear that being a Black feminist phenomenologist orients me to having an almost doubled interest in the liberatory and ameliorative dimensions of phenomenology. In my view, a phenomenology that is not invested in liberation meets neither the criteria of Black feminist nor the criteria of critical. While Black feminist political commitments differ, at the very least being a Black feminist commits me to philosophizing with an investment in the liberation of all oppressed peoples, along axes of race, gender, sexuality, class, ability, age, and other structural social identities. Being a Black feminist places my locus of concern with liberation projects of Black people across the diaspora who have been historically enslaved, colonized, and exploited, and made the targets of violence and death for centuries. I have a particular concern with the lived experiences of Black women and what they come to know and teach us as a result of those experiences.

My Early Relationship with Beauvoir

My initial interest in ambiguity began with my first reading of *The Ethics of Ambiguity* in graduate school at Temple University in Philadelphia, in 2007. At the time, I was half-heartedly working toward a doctorate in philosophy, a discipline I chose to study because it felt like a place where I might fruitfully explore my philosophical interests in Black people and love under the guidance of Lewis R. Gordon. Having initially studied philosophy at Spelman with Al-Yasha Williams, I had fallen in love with the discipline as a means of coming to understand the breadth and depth of a diversity of experiences. In graduate school, I learned that philosophy was for white men, and I was shocked. The home I had chosen for myself had become, for all intents and purposes, quite cold and unwelcoming.

I ended up being a teaching assistant for Lewis' undergraduate class on existentialism and the students were assigned *Ethics*, so I read it too. As I read, I had the feeling of being intellectually seen, borne witness to. In the text, I found Beauvoir to be a totally different woman than the one I had been taught to be impressed by as the author of *The Second Sex*, which, at the time, felt to me outdated and irrelevant. What was delightfully exciting about ambiguity was that I was attracted not only to the concept but also to the figure/persona attached to it.

Hence began a Beauvoir deep dive. I read everything that I could, joined the tribe of existentialism, and was most fascinated by the way Beauvoir lived. I was especially scandalized by her love life and the way it appeared that her experiences with her many loves/lovers (Zaza and Jacques and Sartre and Olga and Bianca and Nelson and Claude, etc.) transformed her each time.[7] I recognized her cycles of translation and conversion, and began to think of places in the Black feminist literature where such cycles and conversions also felt present. I thought first of Lorde's autobiomythographical narrative in *Zami: A New Spelling of My Name*.[8] And then bell hooks, with her naked writing about love in her trilogy—*All About Love: New Visions, Communion: The Female Search for Love*, and *Salvation: Black People and Love*.[9] It seemed to me that there was something profound about the way the erotic (re)orients one again and again to oneself, especially to oneself in relation to the ubiquity of patriarchy. These (re)orientations I termed 'erotic conversions' and began to think that they must have some kind of feminist ethical valence. Getting juicy with Beauvoir's life and wanting to trace how it related to her ethics gave me the motivation to stay in graduate school, study French for a summer at the Sorbonne, and finally finish my dissertation.

In 2014, I completed my dissertation about the connections among ethics, autobiography, feminism, and the erotic. I argued that Black feminist thinkers like Lorde, hooks, and Patricia Hill Collins were, like Beauvoir, also using autobiography as a form of philosophizing; and that that focus on the ethical dimensions of the category of the erotic in their lives revealed their doing so. In the end, I felt that my project lacked cohesion, as if it were invisibly split in two. Though I had pulled together parts that I intuited were related, in the end I didn't feel like I quite articulated the connection. I felt embarrassed by the project, as most of us do about our thesis projects. I didn't then have the presence of mind to realize that my unique positionalities and histories may have afforded me the potential to see linkages where others may not. Nevertheless, I became convinced that the method of autotheoretical writing, following those writers, is a useful and unique form of feminist theorizing. This commitment is additionally supported through my Black feminist and critical phenomenological orientations.

How did you first come into relationship with Simone de Beauvoir's work?

Growing with Beauvoir

I attended my first International Simone de Beauvoir Society Conference in 2016 and found the community of thinkers there to be not only smart but delightful to be around. Through the Society I met Beauvoir scholars I idolized, like Margaret 'Peg' Simons and Sonia Kruks, and had the opportunity to build relationships with others who had been moved by Beauvoir's work. While teaching in the Women's and Gender Studies Program (at what is now known as the bell hooks Center) at Berea College in rural Kentucky—where I had the great honor to become colleagues with bell hooks, who lived and worked there during the last years of her life—I was asked to contribute to an edited volume on feminist phenomenology. While I was teaching about intersectionality in the classroom and having enriching Black feminist conversations with bell, I felt disconnected from the lived experiences of Black women outside of rural Appalachia whose lives seemed to me at the time somehow more representative of Black women's experiences than mine.

Although I was learning much from my students at Berea, my partner and I felt the stress of being racialized minorities in a dry, conservative town far away from our families. I stayed sane during the time by connecting to other Black women around the globe through the social media platform

Instagram. The confluence of situations somehow led me to consider that there might be a connection between intersectionality and ambiguity. I realized that Beauvoir's existential phenomenological lens brought to light under-examined dimensions of the intersectionality literature and provided a ready-made dialogue with which to nestle the concept itself.[10] Intersectional ambiguity continues to be at the core of my philosophical thinking.

In 2019, I was voted President of the International Simone de Beauvoir Society, which I found confusing and intimidating. Though many of my feelings of under-qualification might be chalked up to imposter syndrome, I struggled to inhabit the role. I had moved back to the city of Philadelphia, and back into teaching in a philosophy department. Once again, in my 'home' discipline, it became clear to me that there was a great need for me and others like me to do for my Black feminist heroes like Lorde, hooks, and Collins what was in the process of being done for Beauvoir. I felt that they, too, deserved attention and renewed lenses through which to be met as philosophers. And, simultaneously, thinkers like Kathryn Sophia Belle (formerly Kathryn T. Gines) were leading me to take seriously the ways that Beauvoir erased and neglected the experiences of Black women.[11] On the internet, I read comments sections that provided me with a queer and #MeToo lens through which to view Beauvoir's love life that I had so cherished and in some ways hoped to emulate. In the era of cancellation, Beauvoir and Sartre's self-interested choices during Nazi occupation took on a new cast. In my personal life, I started to feel confused about what it meant to helm a society dedicated to the legacy of this woman whose life—once the inspiration that brought me back into philosophy—now felt so distant from my own. The ambiguities that initially drew me to Beauvoir were those I had come to find conflicting.

2020

Enter 2020.

In January of 2020, I was in the midst of the dissolution of a nine-year partnership that ended, among many reasons, because I wanted children and remained unsure whether my partner did as well. Though broken up, we lived together until March; and, during that time, I began putting feelers out for potential sperm donors, one of whom seemed possibly interested. In March of 2020, during Spring Break, the threat of the COVID-19 virus had spread across the globe, and my college officially announced that we would be conducting all classes online for the rest of the semester. The students—many of whom had left their lives on campus while they vacationed off campus—were told they would not be allowed to return to campus. Philadelphia went into quarantine measures soon thereafter.[12] All of a sudden, everyone was wearing masks, and I was rushing to the grocery store to buy tins and tins of tuna that are still in my cupboard. My ex-partner moved out and, as the world became stranger by the day, I found myself falling in love with the potential sperm donor, a childhood friend, who decided to spend the summer with me and see if we might be compatible both as co-parents and as partners.

On May 25, 2020, word of George Floyd's murder began to spread from the activist circles in Minneapolis to activist groups across the country, including the Philadelphia chapter of Black Lives Matter, with which my sister, Hanae Victoria Mason, had been a central organizer since 2016.[13] As May turned to June, global uprisings began in response to the complex nexus of conditions that include continued state violence against Black people, economic conditions brought on by the coronavirus, and the psychological trauma of uncertainty of the future. In Philadelphia, my sister was pepper-sprayed while protesting. Blocks from my home, on 52nd Street, the Philadelphia police unleashed tear gas on my community, including residences and businesses.[14] Homes and stores were looted and burned. The sounds of rubber bullets, helicopters, fireworks, and sirens droned on without end for more than 36 hours. The National Guard, called upon to 'protect' the community, blocked off streets such that folks in my West Philadelphia neighborhood had to travel miles to go to corner and grocery stores because all of ours were destroyed and boarded up. Meanwhile, nearby suburban white enclaves like the one in which the college I teach at is located remained untouched and unoccupied.

Having decided that he no longer wanted to live in what he felt had become a hostile environment for Black men in the United States, and in fear of the potential response to the 2020 Presidential election, my lover— with whom I had spent the whole summer preparing to build a family and debating the merits of leaving the country—moved to Tanzania in September. I stayed behind to continue teaching online, prepare my dossier for promotion in my academic job in philosophy, and apply for fellowships to support my upcoming sabbatical. During this time, I lived alone for the first time in more than a decade, and attempted to fulfill my social needs via the internet, all the while longing for a child and for the fraying connection between me and my now ex-lover.

In late October 2020, Walter Wallace, Jr., a Black man suffering from a mental health crisis, was murdered by the Philadelphia police a few blocks away from my home.[15] Again, protests erupted and, as a result, the Black and Indigenous students at the college where I teach, led by women, held a strike against the college. The strike, which lasted for two weeks, called the administration and faculty out for the mistreatment and silencing of students of color and of first-generation and low-income students, who are a vast minority on campus. Students provided a set of demands that would have to be met in order for them to return to classes and continue their work-study jobs. The strike divided the campus along racial and political lines as students and faculty were positioned to show solidarity with the strikers by not holding classes.[16] We were extended, instead, the opportunity to 'teach-in.' The strike brought my campus to its knees as the deep divisions that had been percolating became more explicit; and I sat in hours and hours of meetings, positioned to mediate between the students, who trusted me as a Black feminist ally on campus, and the administration, who struggled to meet the demands of students and to understand their deep frustrations.

On November 2, the majority of voting citizens in the United States got rid of a celebrity-cum-fascist President, stoking flames for his supporters' future attempts to disrupt democratic order. Eventually, the college strike ended and we struggled to pull the pieces back together in our classes; and I struggled to pull my pieces together in my home, feeling increasingly isolated and depressed, barely gathering the strength to make the drive south to Alabama to spend the close of the year with my mother and sister in my childhood home.

The World Health Organization (WHO) now estimates that between January and December 2020, excess deaths considered, the coronavirus killed nearly 3 million people worldwide.[17]

What lived experiences of the year 2020 (or, for the future, choose a year to reflect upon) did you find most salient?

_____

_____

_____

On Beauvoirian Ambiguity

Let's return, for a moment, to ambiguity. Generally, in the discipline of philosophy, the basic definition of ambiguity is something in which several (more than one) interpretations are possible.[18] This something cannot be resolved according to some rule or process. As ambiguity is a kind of vagueness, the opposite of ambiguity seeks specific and distinct interpretations. Ambiguity is threatening to disciplines such as philosophy that traditionally seek clarity because their purpose and/or method is to 'disambiguate.'[19]

Beauvoir begins her discussion of the phenomenological dimensions of ambiguity in *Ethics* with the concept of paradox. She offers various descriptors that account for human lived experience and ontology:

Life ←→ death
Reasoning/thinking being ←→ (irrational) animal/plant
Internally powerful ←→ crushed by the weight (of other things)
Past ←→ future
Sovereign and unique ←→ universally the same
Object for others ←→ (subject to self)
Individual ←→ collective

Those familiar with the text know these descriptors, which form the first couple of pages of *Ethics*.[20] Notably, for Beauvoir, ambiguity is neither a synthesis nor exactly a dialectic; rather, as Kruks has described, for Beauvoir, ambiguous "tensions are the very stuff of life itself."[21] They cannot be eliminated.

Beauvoir quickly turns her critical attention to philosophers. She writes:

> As long as there have been men and they have lived, they have all felt this tragic ambiguity of their condition, but as long as there have been philosophers and they have thought, most of them have tried to mask it.[22]

Beauvoir goes on to explain that a reason they must do this is because the task of philosophy appears to be to make things *more* clear, and hence more comprehendible. The philosophers' fault, then, is reduction. The philosopher tries to mask ambiguity by either denying life or denying death. Beauvoir contends that many of the ethics and ethical systems and orientations that people follow—due to their sense that philosophy has authority—seek to eliminate ambiguity. This is their fault and we bear the consequences of these faults.[23]

I want to make note here that Beauvoir infamously goes on to deny the title 'philosopher' as applied to herself.[24] When I read her indictment here in light of my own ambivalent experiences in the discipline, I think, "Ah, yes. Who in their right mind would want to identify as a philosopher under these conditions?" Perhaps that is part of what continues to be wrong with philosophy, and why many diverse practitioners continue to feel ill-suited within it. Either way, rather than do this, Beauvoir wants to begin by assuming ambiguity. In order to do so, she suggests that we begin by assuming failure because it is by virtue of our capacity to fail that we have an ethics at all.

What, then, do non-philosophers think about ambiguity? How has its shadow of uncertainty landed in the minds of others? In an interview, senior New York state actuary Brian Fullilove offered an additional take on ambiguity in the actuary field, stating:

> [In insurance,] ambiguity is defined as something that we haven't yet figured out. We don't know enough about it or something about it is

hard or difficult to measure. Even though this is the case, we still think the thing is "black and white-able."[25]

He goes on to explain that, in a field that is results-driven, a 'no-result result' is "worthless." This intimates ambiguity's general negative valence. This 'intolerance for ambiguity' has even been connected to providing conditions for the possibility of fascism.[26]

As I gather these thoughts on ambiguity, I return to existential phenomenology, seeking further engagements. In his discussion of Black existential philosophy, Lewis Gordon gestures towards additional instantiations of ambiguity, writing:

> No human being is a subject alone, nor an object alone. It is even incorrect to say that a human being is "both." A human being is neither a subject nor an object, but instead, in the language of Simone de Beauvoir and Merleau-Ponty, "ambiguous." This ambiguity is an expression of the human being as a meaningful, multifaceted way of being that may involve contradictory interpretations, or at least equivocal ones.[27]

In other words, ambiguity may also be understood as encompassing multiplicity and paradox. Gordon continues, "Such ambiguity stands out not as a dilemma to be resolved, as in the case of an equivocal sentence, but as a way of living to be described." Hence, "The phenomenological task at hand is thus to draw out a hermeneutic of this ambiguity. [...] In the Africana experience this calls for a description of the ways in which human ambiguity is manifested or evaded."[28] The complexity of ambiguity leads us to how we might best engage it: not in the mode of resolution—but rather as a motivation to more deeply describe our ways of living out and through our fundamental ambiguities, in the movements between and among descriptive categories.

Usefulness as Criteria

We return to the consideration of use. Beauvoir follows me in this as well, writing in the early part of *Ethics* that man makes the "useless" choice to inflict his coming-to-be upon himself.[29] This is because, for Beauvoir, there is no metaphysical/absolute value that founds this choice. Beauvoir continues, the word useful "can only be defined [...] in the human world established by man's projects and the ends he sets up."[30] In other words, what is useful is that which has value with regard to human projects.

What, then, does it mean to take a Black feminist approach to ambiguity, to its meaning and dimensions? A Black feminist orientation toward use also recalls a commitment to use. Following Ahmed:

> I think again of Audre Lorde, who especially in her later work often spoke of her desire to be useful to others. She spoke even of her desire for her own death to be a useful death [...]. She writes of how she thought about death, about how to die (as well as how to live): "rather than just fall into death, any old way, by default, according to somebody else's rules" [...]. Not falling into death, not going the same way others are going, as things have gone before, requires asking questions. Usefulness here is about asking questions about how to do something, how to be something. She notes that you have no choice; mortality is the condition of having to die. But mortality acquires a different meaning for those whose existence is not supported: "We all have to die at least once. Making that death useful would be winning for me. I wasn't supposed to exist anyway, not in any meaningful way in this fucked-up white boys' world" [...]. Usefulness might matter more for those who were not "supposed to exist." Usefulness then becomes a political address, a way of facing outward, toward others. Audre Lorde teaches us that we need to keep the question of use alive not because it does not matter but because it does.[31]

In other words, Lorde leads us into a consideration of the norms used to evaluate the meaning and value of our contributions. She also points us to the connection between praxis and ontology; and, further, recalling the infamous feminist 'the personal is political,' how these are always already couched in the political. Lorde leads us to ask: might usefulness be a valid criterion for the phenomenological task—especially for those whose ambiguous positionalities, like those of Black women, for example, consistently place them in close proximity to death and dying?

In her groundbreaking "How Is This Paper Philosophy?" Black feminist epistemologist Kristie Dotson writes about how a culture of praxis might be more hospitable to diverse practitioners of philosophy. She sets up two criteria for a 'culture of praxis' that the discipline of philosophy might adopt, one based in Black feminist politics:

> 1) Value placed on seeking issues and circumstances pertinent to our living, where one maintains a healthy appreciation for the differing issues that will emerge as pertinent among different populations and 2) Recognition and encouragement of multiple canons and multiple ways of understanding disciplinary validation.[32]

Drawing on the work of Lorde, Dotson concludes that "a culture of praxis within professional philosophy would present a great deal more livable options than it does currently."[33] The embrace of use, then, becomes another *useful* means of mitigating death. Critical phenomenology might add to its understanding of amelioration the necessity for use as a dimension of that which heals or fixes.

As I have adopted an orientation of usefulness for thinking about ambiguity, in trying to further explore the concept, I am thinking about ambiguity as tied to my own projects and the projects to which I connect myself. In this way, ambiguity is *useful* as an orientation that helps us navigate tensions and rest in the idea that we will have to make decisions that are not clear, that are not given foundation by virtue of what Beauvoir refers to as pre-furnished ethical recipes.[34]

What does it mean to make ambiguity useful?

_____

_____

_____

Mapping Ambiguities

Here, I pause in order to bring to light the ambiguities I have shared in this essay. I want to make the point that ambiguities are ubiquitous, and that paying attention to these phenomena in lived experience reveals the extent to which this is so. I want to suggest that navigating these antinomies characterized not only my lived experience in 2020, but perhaps also yours.

Pursuing a goal/dream ←→ pushing/'forcing' it
Love ←→ work
Independence ←→ dependence
Loneliness ←→ solitude
Embodied ←→ disembodied
Erotically alive ←→ wanting to die
Spirituality ←→ analytic brain
Thinker ←→ artist
Self-focused ←→ other-focused
Love like a cooling cenote ←→ rage like a green flame
Students ←→ faculty admin
Rest ←→ active resistance
Institutional change ←→ dismantle the whole shit
Abolish ←→ reform
Self-love/self-care ←→ communal love and care
Systems ←→ chaos
Flexibility ←→ rigidity

Healing ←→ stagnancy
Stay and resist ←→ leave and rebuild
Hope ←→ despair

I note the " ←→ " as the space between the terms on these lists, the tension between the two, among the many. Because I am coming to better understand how these terms need not stand in binary opposition, I am appreciative of the emphasis on the *movement*, the *relationality* between the terms. I borrow this notation from Lugones, who uses it in *Pilgrimages* to describe subjects who are "oppressed ←→ resisting" and, hence, who inhabit constant spaces of ambiguity.[35] In considering 2020, we are reminded of the very circumstances in which Beauvoir turned her thinking to ambiguity: circumstances that were much like our own—personal, global, and uncertain.

In what ways has your lived experience reflected any of the ambiguities described?

_____

_____

_____

As you reflect on your own ambiguities, consider these shared by participants at the conference *Simone de Beauvoir: New Perspectives for the 21st Century*, (see figure 5.1) collected across time zones and subjectivities. Consider, even, how this is itself an exercise in ambiguity, how your interactions (and those of others) with these pages remind us that the ways we take up use are inextricably tied to others'.

Which ambiguities do you share with others? Which appear to be uniquely yours?

_____

_____

_____

On Ambiguity as a Useful Tool

Mapping ambiguities, developing an appreciation for them, finding them in unexpected places helped me get through 2020. In many ways, the ambiguities

FIGURE 5.1 Screenshot of ambiguities suggested by participants at the conference "Simone de Beauvoir: New Perspectives for the 21st Century" (June 2020)

Beauvoir initially helped me identify have deepened and become more entrenched. As a Black feminist, learning how not to grasp for definitive political meaning was especially useful to the task of surviving conditions of uncertainty.

I continue to consider and to question: what does it mean to entrench ambiguities? How can we embrace/imbue ambiguity, like Lugones suggests? I am encouraged by other Black women thinking about ambiguity and its relationship to our lived experience. Examples include Ralina Joseph's analysis of how Black women use strategic ambiguity as a "way of pushing back against that discrimination [in mainstream spaces] anyway through a coded resistance to postracial ideologies";[36] and Zakiyyah Jackson, who analyzes ambiguity in *Becoming Human*.[37]

Even though *Ethics* remains my favorite of all Beauvoir's texts, Beauvoir would go on to decry the juvenility of some of her stances in it. As she moved more squarely into theorizing decolonization, Lugones would also lose some of her connection to the concept. In light of this, I assume, following Beauvoir, the possible future failure of this concept to accurately capture what I have even described here. I can imagine reflecting on even this piece of writing and eventually becoming embarrassed by my own short-sightedness. Despite and perhaps even because of this, I am encouraged that ambiguity always already orients us toward failure and toward embracing our failure.[38] Much like Beauvoir, I no longer feel as if I am writing toward or for a world as usual. I believe in the possibilities of ambiguity to help others make sense of their experiences and for us to connect and form bonds of solidarity across our vast differences. I believe that ambiguity can be useful both for me and for others. When we don't deny ambiguity, we are less likely to fight against it. Not fighting against life makes it livable, perhaps contributes to more ease.

And the list of Black feminist thinkers I want to engage expands: Angela Davis, bell hooks, Audre Lorde, Adrian Piper, Lorraine O'Grady, Kimberlé Crenshaw ...

I had become embarrassed by Beauvoir, where she might have faltered and all the rightful criticism aimed at her. But becoming more mature is becoming again attendant to (and more tolerant of) the ambiguities of others. I have also come into deeper empathy with Beauvoir's dis-identification as a philosopher, as 2021 found me shifting into artistic practice through performance and visual art. I became formally exhausted with the philosopher's need for clarity, that for which I had been trained. Navigating outsider-within status and the shifting histories and exclusions within philosophy has become more tiring than I am willing to give effort. I find myself feeling ambiguous towards this as well. I ask myself: Am I a philosopher? Has this identification kept me from accessing something important within myself?

To live in the United States and many other countries like it is to live in the midst of innumerable ambiguities. I have come to know that the most useful way to do so is ambiguously.

Which ambiguities still have use for you?

_____

_____

_____

Acknowledgement

An infinite well of thanks goes to Liesbeth Schoonheim, whose intellectual generosity and commitment to fostering important conversations are sincere inspirations.

Notes

1 bell hooks and Stuart Hall, *Uncut Funk: A Contemplative Dialogue* (New York: Routledge, 2018), 7.
2 María Lugones, *Pilgrimages/Peregrinajes: Theorizing Coalition against Multiple Oppressions* (Lanham, MD: Rowman & Littlefield, 2003).

3 See "Uses of the Erotic: The Erotic as Power," 53–60 and "The Uses of Anger: Women Responding to Racism," 124–133, in Audre Lorde, *Sister Outsider* (Berkeley, CA: Crossing Press, 1994, Kindle Edition).
4 Sara Ahmed, *What's the Use? On the Uses of Use* (Durham, NC: Duke University Press, 2019), 23.
5 Gail Weiss, Ann V. Murphy, and Gayle Salamon, "Introduction," in *50 Concepts for a Critical Phenomenology*, ed. Gail Weiss, Ann V. Murphy, and Gayle Salamon (Evanston, IL: Northwestern University Press, 2020), xiv.
6 Lugones, *Pilgrimages/Peregrinajes*, 68.
7 Ursula Tidd, *Simone de Beauvoir* (London: Reaktion, 2009); Simone de Beauvoir, *Diary of a Philosophy Student Vol. 1*, ed. Marybeth Timmermann and Margaret A. Simons, trans. Barbara Klaw (Urbana: University of Illinois Press, 2006); Simone de Beauvoir, *Wartime Diary*, ed. Margaret A. Simons and Sylvie le Bon de Beauvoir, trans. Anne Deing Cordero (Urbana: University of Illinois Press, 2009); Simone de Beauvoir, *The Prime of Life*, trans. Peter Green (New York: Lancer, 1973); Simone de Beauvoir, *Memoirs of a Dutiful Daughter*, trans. Hazel Rowley (New York: Harper Perennial, 2005); Simone de Beauvoir, *A Transatlantic Love Affair: Letters to Nelson Algren*, ed. Sylvie Le Bon de Beauvoir (New York: New Press, 1998).
8 Audre Lorde, *Zami: A New Spelling of My Name—A Biomythography* (Trumansburg, NY: Crossing Press, 1982).
9 bell hooks, *All about Love: New Visions* (New York: Perennial, 2001); bell hooks, *Salvation: Black People and Love* (New York: William Morrow, 2001); bell hooks, *Communion: The Female Search for Love* (New York: William Morrow, 2002).
10 Qrescent Mali Mason, "Intersectional Ambiguity and the Phenomenology of #BlackGirlJoy," in *Re-Thinking Feminist Phenomenology*, ed. Sara Cohen Shabot and Christinia Landry (New York: Rowman & Littlefield, 2018), 51–68.
11 Kathryn T. Gines, "Comparative and Competing Frameworks of Oppression in Simone de Beauvoir's *The Second Sex*," *Graduate Faculty Philosophy Journal* 35, no. 1–2 (2014): 251–73; Kathryn T. Gines, "Sartre, Beauvoir, and the Race/Gender Analogy: A Case for Black Feminist Philosophy," in *Convergences: Black Feminism and Continental Philosophy*, ed. Maria del Guadalupe Davidson, Kathryn T. Gines, and Donna-Dale L. Marcano (Albany: State University of New York Press, 2010), 35–51; Kathryn Sophia Belle, "Interlocking, Intersecting, and Intermeshing: Critical Engagements with Black and Latina Feminist Paradigms of Identity and Oppression," *Critical Philosophy of Race* 8, no. 1–2 (2020): 165–98.
12 City of Philadelphia, "Timeline and Updates," Covid-19 Recovery Office, Managing Director's Office. Accessed 1 August 2022. https://www.phila.gov/departments/covid-19-recovery-office/timeline-and-updates/.
13 For more about this, read her essay, "On Being/As I Am," at https://howwestayfree.com/On-Being-As-I-Am. Hanae Victoria Mason, *How We Stay Free: Notes on a Black Uprising*, ed. Christopher R. Rogers, Fajr Muhammad, and Paul Robeson House and Museum (New York: Common Notions, 2022).
14 Associated Press, "Report on Philadelphia Police Response to George Floyd Protests Finds Flaws," *PBS NewsHour*, December 24, 2020. https://www.pbs.org/newshour/nation/report-on-philadelphia-police-response-to-george-floyd-protests-finds-flaws; Ron Todt, "Teargas Used on Philadelphia Crowds as Destruction Continues," *Times Leader*, May 31, 2020. https://www.timesleader.com/wire/state-wire/785919/teargas-used-on-philadelphia-crowds-as-destruction-continues.
15 Jenny Gross, "What We Know about the Death of Walter Wallace Jr. in Philadelphia," *New York Times*, October 29, 2021. https://www.nytimes.com/article/walter-wallace-jr-philadelphia.html.

16 Susan Snyder, "Haverford College Students Launched a Strike Last Fall after a Racial Reckoning: The Impact Still Lingers," *Philadelphia Inquirer*, April 25, 2021. https://www.inquirer.com/news/haverford-college-strike-division-racism-wallace-20210425.html.
17 World Health Organization, "The True Death Toll of COVID-19: Estimating Global Excess Mortality." Accessed August 9, 2022. https://www.who.int/data/stories/the-true-death-toll-of-covid-19-estimating-global-excess-mortality.
18 Kent Bach, "Ambiguity," in *Routledge Encyclopedia of Philosophy* (London: Routledge, 2016).
19 Adam Sennet, "Ambiguity," in *The Stanford Encyclopedia of Philosophy*, ed. Edward N. Zalta (Stanford, CA: Stanford University, Fall 2021). https://plato.stanford.edu/archives/fall2021/entries/ambiguity/.
20 Simone de Beauvoir, *The Ethics of Ambiguity*, trans. Bernard Frechtman, Kindle Edition (Princeton, NJ: Carol Publishing, 1991), 7.
21 Sonia Kruks, *Simone de Beauvoir and the Politics of Ambiguity* (New York: Oxford University Press, 2012), 8.
22 Beauvoir, *The Ethics of Ambiguity*, 7.
23 Ibid., 8.
24 bell hooks, "Beauvoir and Bell: True Philosophers," in *Beauvoir and Western Thought from Plato to Butler*, ed. William S. Wilkerson and Shannon M. Mussett (Albany: State University of New York Press, 2012).
25 Brian Fullilove, telephone conversation with author, May 20, 2021.
26 Else Frenkel-Brunswik, "Intolerance of Ambiguity as an Emotional and Perceptual Personality Variable," *Journal of Personality* 18, no. 1 (1949): 108–43.
27 Lewis R. Gordon, "Existential Dynamics of Theorizing Black Invisibility," in *Existence in Black: An Anthology of Black Existential Philosophy*, ed. Lewis R. Gordon (New York: Routledge, 1997), 72.
28 Ibid.
29 Beauvoir, *The Ethics of Ambiguity*, 11.
30 Ibid.
31 Ahmed, *What's the Use?*, 223 (internal citations omitted).
32 Kristie Dotson, "How Is This Paper Philosophy?," *Comparative Philosophy* 3, no. 1 (2012): 26.
33 Ibid.
34 Beauvoir, *The Ethics of Ambiguity*, 134.
35 Lugones, *Pilgrimages/Peregrinajes*.
36 Ralina L. Joseph, *Postracial Resistance: Black Women, Media, and the Uses of Strategic Ambiguity* (New York: New York University Press, 2018), 3.
37 Zakiyyah Iman Jackson, *Becoming Human: Matter and Meaning in an Antiblack World* (New York: New York University Press, 2020).
38 Kruks, *Simone de Beauvoir and the Politics of Ambiguity*.

References

Ahmed, Sara. *What's the Use? On the Uses of Use.* Durham, NC: Duke University Press, 2019.
Associated Press. "Report on Philadelphia Police Response to George Floyd Protests Finds Flaws." *PBS NewsHour*, December 24, 2020. https://www.pbs.org/newshour/nation/report-on-philadelphia-police-response-to-george-floyd-protests-finds-flaws.
Bach, Kent. "Ambiguity." In *Routledge Encyclopedia of Philosophy*. London: Routledge, 2016. https://doi.org/10.4324/9780415249126-U001-1.

Beauvoir, Simone de. *The Prime of Life*. Translated by Peter Green. New York: Lancer Books, 1973.
Beauvoir, Simone de. *The Ethics of Ambiguity*. Translated by Bernard Frechtman. Kindle Edition. Princeton, NJ: Carol Publishing, 1991.
Beauvoir, Simone de. *A Transatlantic Love Affair: Letters to Nelson Algren*. Edited by Sylvie Le Bon de Beauvoir. New York: New Press, 1998.
Beauvoir, Simone de. *Memoirs of a Dutiful Daughter*. Translated by Hazel Rowley. New York: Harper Perennial, 2005.
Beauvoir, Simone de. *Diary of a Philosophy Student Vol.* 1. Edited by Marybeth Timmermann and Margaret A. Simons. Translated by Barbara Klaw. Urbana: University of Illinois Press, 2006.
Beauvoir, Simone de. *Wartime Diary*. Urbana: University of Illinois Press, 2009.
Belle, Kathryn S. "Interlocking, Intersecting, and Intermeshing: Critical Engagements with Black and Latina Feminist Paradigms of Identity and Oppression." *Critical Philosophy of Race* 8, no. 1–2 (2020): 165–198.
Dotson, Kristie. "How Is This Paper Philosophy?" *Comparative Philosophy* 3, no. 1 (2012): 3–29.
Frenkel-Brunswik, Else. "Intolerance of Ambiguity as an Emotional and Perceptual Personality Variable." *Journal of Personality* 18, no. 1 (1949): 108–143. https://doi.org/10.1111/j.1467-6494.1949.tb01236.x.
Gines, Kathryn T. "Comparative and Competing Frameworks of Oppression in Simone de Beauvoir's *The Second Sex*." *Graduate Faculty Philosophy Journal* 35, no. 1–2 (2014): 251–273. https://doi.org/10.5840/gfpj2014351/212.
Gines, Kathryn T. "Sartre, Beauvoir, and the Race/Gender Analogy: A Case for Black Feminist Philosophy." In *Convergences: Black Feminism and Continental Philosophy*, edited by Maria del Guadalupe Davidson, Kathryn T. Gines, and Donna-Dale L. Marcano, 35–51. Albany: State University of New York Press, 2010.
Gordon, Lewis R. "Existential Dynamics of Theorizing Black Invisibility." In *Existence in Black: An Anthology of Black Existential Philosophy*, edited by Lewis R. Gordon, 69–79. New York: Routledge, 1997.
Gross, Jenny. "What We Know about the Death of Walter Wallace Jr. in Philadelphia." *New York Times*, October 29, 2021. https://www.nytimes.com/article/walter-wallace-jr-philadelphia.html.
hooks, bell. *All about Love: New Visions*. New York: Perennial, 2001.
hooks, bell. *Salvation: Black People and Love*. New York: William Morrow, 2001.
hooks, bell. *Communion: The Female Search for Love*. New York: William Morrow, 2002.
hooks, bell. "Beauvoir and Bell: True Philosophers." In *Beauvoir and Western Thought from Plato to Butler*, edited by William S. Wilkerson and Shannon M. Mussett. Albany: State University of New York Press, 2012.
hooks, bell and Stuart Hall. *Uncut Funk: A Contemplative Dialogue*. New York: Routledge, 2018.
Jackson, Zakiyyah Iman. *Becoming Human: Matter and Meaning in an Antiblack World*. New York: New York University Press, 2020.
Joseph, Ralina L. *Postracial Resistance: Black Women, Media, and the Uses of Strategic Ambiguity*. New York: New York University Press, 2018.
Kruks, Sonia. *Simone de Beauvoir and the Politics of Ambiguity*. New York: Oxford University Press, 2012.

Lorde, Audre. *Sister Outsider*. Berkeley, CA: Crossing Press, 1994.
Lorde, Audre. *Zami: A New Spelling of My Name—A Biomythography*. Trumansburg, NY: Crossing Press, 1982.
Lugones, María. *Pilgrimages/Peregrinajes: Theorizing Coalition against Multiple Oppressions*. Lanham, MD: Rowman & Littlefield, 2003.
Mason, Hanae Victoria. *How We Stay Free: Notes on a Black Uprising*. Edited by Christopher R . Rogers, Fajr Muhammad, and Paul Robeson House and Museum. New York: Common Notions, 2022.
Mason, Hanae Victoria. "On Being/As I Am." Accessed August 1, 2022. https://howwestayfree.com/On-Being-As-I-Am.
Mason, Qrescent Mali. "Intersectional Ambiguity and the Phenomenology of #BlackGirlJoy." In *Re-Thinking Feminist Phenomenology*, edited by Sara Cohen Shabot and Christinia Landry, 51–68. New York: Rowman & Littlefield, 2018.
Sennet, Adam. "Ambiguity." In *The Stanford Encyclopedia of Philosophy*, edited by Edward N. Zalta, Fall Edition. Stanford, CA: Stanford University, 2021. https://plato.stanford.edu/archives/fall2021/entries/ambiguity/.
Snyder, Susan. "Haverford College Students Launched a Strike Last Fall after a Racial Reckoning: The Impact Still Lingers." *Philadelphia Inquirer*, April 25, 2021. Accessed August 2, 2022. https://www.inquirer.com/news/haverford-college-strike-division-racism-wallace-20210425.html.
Tidd, Ursula. *Simone de Beauvoir*. London: Reaktion, 2009.
Todt, Ron. "Teargas Used on Philadelphia Crowds as Destruction Continues." *Times Leader*, May 31, 2020. https://www.timesleader.com/wire/state-wire/785919/teargas-used-on-philadelphia-crowds-as-destruction-continues.
Weiss, Gail, Ann V. Murphy, and Gayle Salamon. "Introduction." In *50 Concepts for a Critical Phenomenology*, edited by Gail Weiss, Ann V. Murphy, and Gayle Salamon, i–xiv. Evanston, IL: Northwestern University Press, 2020.
World Health Organization. "The True Death Toll of COVID-19: Estimating Global Excess Mortality." Accessed August 9, 2022. https://www.who.int/data/stories/the-true-death-toll-of-covid-19-estimating-global-excess-mortality.

6
BEAUVOIR, THE PHILOSOPHY OF FREEDOM, AND THE RIGHTS OF BLACK WOMEN DURING FRENCH COLONIAL TIMES

Nathalie Nya

A great challenge to Simone de Beauvoir's philosophy of freedom, within the field of feminist philosophy and post-colonial philosophy, is how her thoughts on freedom apply to the situation of colonized women or non-white women. I will particularly go into the condition of French colonized women as thematized in the work of French-Martinican writer Paulette Nardal, and compare her view with Beauvoir's stances. Nardal attended the Sorbonne in the 1920s, like Beauvoir, but there is no indication that the two scholars met. Both authors, however, discuss the issue of women's suffrage rights and freedom in a way that allows for a comparison of their work. My assumption is that the philosophy of freedom described by Beauvoir can be representative of women colonizers' perspective. However, through the comparison with Nardal's first-person perspective, we can begin to imagine that Beauvoir's philosophy of freedom is not exclusive to women colonizers, but also includes the position of colonized women. Beauvoir's views on female oppression ought to be currently understood as an attempt to speak alongside and rather than speaking for since, even in the case of white French women, Beauvoir lived a privileged life unattainable to uneducated and financially non-independent women.

In what follows, I first examine Beauvoir's philosophy of freedom as elaborated in her existential philosophy. I then go into the work of Nardal to show her struggle for Martinican women's enfranchisement testified by her trust in the capability of her countrywomen to vote. Finally, I discuss the application of Beauvoir's philosophy of freedom to the situation of colonized or oppressed women.

Existential Ethics or a Philosophy of Freedom

Originally published in France in 1947, Simone de Beauvoir's *The Ethics of Ambiguity* lays out a genealogy of modern ethics that places existential ethics within the field of philosophy. Discussing the previous work of Kant, Hegel, Marx, and Sartre, Beauvoir argues that existential ethics is a philosophy that negates absolute values and moral rules. She states that every action is neither good nor bad, thus putting forward the ambiguity of action. Human action creates situations that are unclear, and in itself can be viewed in more than one way. This contradicts the moral principle that human action should be interpreted from the perspective of either its goodness or its wrongfulness.

According to Beauvoir, the lived experience of human beings shows us the ambiguity of action.[1] She argues that, "as long as there have been men and they have lived, they have all felt this tragic ambiguity of their condition."[2] However, in *The Ethics of Ambiguity*, Beauvoir claims that,

> the notion of ambiguity must not be confused with that of absurdity. [...] To declare that existence is absurd is to deny that it can ever be given a meaning. [...] Absurdity challenges every ethics; but also, the finished rationalization of the real would leave no room for ethics.[3]

Existential ethics is a form of radical humanism, and Beauvoir traces its theoretical underpinning to the tradition of modern philosophy, specifically to the philosophies of Kant, Hegel, and Marx. She borrows the principle of freedom of will from Kant. From Hegel, she gets the historicity of the concept of freedom of action. Finally, from Marx, she takes the subjectivism of the concept of freedom of action. Beauvoir states:

> By affirming that the source of all values resides in the freedom of man, existentialism merely carries on the tradition of Kant, Fichte, and Hegel, who, in the words of Hegel himself, "have taken for their point of departure the principle according to which the essence of right and duty and the essence of the thinking and willing subject are absolutely identical."[4]

However, Beauvoir posits that what gives rise to values and meaning is the understanding of the intentionality of freedom in terms of one's situation, and not in terms of disembodied or uncontextualized moral principles.

The situationality of personal or individual freedom cannot be analyzed without examining its relation to the personal freedom of others. Freedom is the basis of the moral obligation we have toward other people in Beauvoirian ethics. In *The Bonds of Freedom*, Kristana Arp states that Beauvoir "shows how an individual can only develop moral freedom by interacting with other morally free subjects."[5] In freedom, the *me–others* relationship is as crucial as the subject–object relationship.[6] Beauvoir wants to emphasize that the dual nature of the human condition is based not only in ourselves but also in those we perceive as others. This relational dimension of ambiguity is also brought out in the situationality of freedom, insofar as it encompasses both the subjective and the objective dimensions of exerting one's will, and requires the existence of others who are also free. To will oneself free is also to will others free.[7] In her examination of Beauvoir's ethics, Lori J. Marso posits that:

> when confronting others, we should not seek to control them; nor should we see our own freedom as a zero-sum game in competition with the freedom of others. Instead, the meaningful exercise of our own freedom depends on acting to make possible the kind of political conditions that lessen or eliminate violence, including the structural violence of oppression.[8]

Beauvoir focuses on the myriad instances in which the subjective practice of freedom draws one toward bad faith. Bad faith points to the many ways in which people deny their freedom, thus tumbling into the trap of denying the freedom of others.

Beauvoir then examines the many ways human beings are not acting morally and do not care about the freedom of other people. In her analysis of the relationship between personal freedom and the freedom of others, Beauvoir notes that human beings' lack of individual care about the freedom of others leads to oppression. The relationships between oppressor and oppressed, between women and men, colonizers and colonized, blacks and whites, and Arabs and whites are fraught with bad faith and human error—or ethical mistakes. Beauvoir attempts to resolve these issues in her ethics. The relationship between the self and the other is troubled, and may lead to huge ethical mistakes or human error—awful instances of oppression and violence—and the development of political conflicts, war, and intercontinental terror. Beauvoir's ethics points towards concrete, ambiguous, moral choices in processes of liberation, as opposed to the development of moral principles. While the latter are supposedly deduced from transhistorical truths, the former emerge within real struggles for liberation. This struggle starts from the interdependency of my own freedom and that of others: my freedom requires others to be free too. Her existentialist ethics thus is a philosophy of liberating the oppressed—women, black people, Arabs, and all unnamed others.

Nardal on the Rights of Black Colonialized Women

As the purpose of my inquiry is partly to cover the presence of French female colonized subjects from the perspective of the philosophy of freedom and post-colonial philosophy, I now explore the lives of colonized women. Specifically, since my intention is to conduct a comparative analysis of the views on freedom of Beauvoir and French-Martinican writer Paulette Nardal, I focus on the lives of colonized women in Martinique, which was an overseas colony of France.

In 1944, French women were granted the right to vote. Two years later, in 1946, Martinique became an overseas department of France, and thus Martinican women were granted the right to vote and to participate in French general elections.[9] Since 1848, a small number of free black men in the West Indies had had the right to vote. However it was not until 1870 that the black men in that area would begin to vote in French colonial administrative elections. Thus, there were approximately 76 years between Martinican men's suffrage and that of Martinican women.

A few places in the West Indies, such as Guadeloupe, had a culture that encouraged stronger political activism among women than Martinique, which also resulted in relatively early active participation by women from the former in government politics.[10] The leading women in Martinique who became political were, in general, authors by profession. Therefore, women in Martinique who had the opportunity to be political expressed their views on the political prospects and freedom of women and of all Martinicans typically through literary and sociocultural venues.

In 1945, author and journalist Paulette Nardal founded the *Rassemblement Féminin Martiniquais* (Martinican Women's Assembly), the Martinican branch of *L'Union Féminine Civique et Sociale* (the Women's Civic and Social Union, based in France). She had been involved with the latter organization, which examined the situation of the female sex and pushed for the emancipation of women in French territories, as well other French feminist associations.[11] The purpose of establishing its equivalent in Martinique was to get French-Martinican women to the polling booths for the first time, urged on by the fact that French women in France had already voted for the first time on April 29, 1945.[12] Some 33 percent of women in Martinique voted for the first time in 1946 as a result of Nardal's activism.[13] As feminist scholar T. Denean Sharpley-Whiting notes in her Introduction to Nardal's *Beyond Negritude* ("On Race, Rights, and Women"), the *Rassemblement Féminin Martiniquais* enabled Nardal to

> further the interests of women on the island, particularly as they related to, among other matters, race, social justice and its intersection with women's rights and duties as mothers, workers, citizens and newly

enfranchised voters and the colonial hangovers Martinique continued to face even at the dawn of the island's becoming an overseas department of France.[14]

Using her professional status as an author and journalist, Nardal, through her organization, was able to buoy the political rights of women in Martinique and add to their political education.

What we find in the analysis of Nardal is what authors like Beauvoir, Fanon, and Sartre ignore—namely an engagement with the political disenfranchisement of black women. Nardal's contribution was to propel the liberal critique of political disenfranchisement and lack of freedom among colonized women into the discussion of French colonialism. Nardal's ideas give us an opportunity to look into what women in Martinique contributed throughout the cultural venues that formed as Martinique transitioned from being a colony of France to an overseas department. Martinican women certainly were a part of the development of black and Creole national identity in Martinique, which illustrates more generally the importance of black and Creole women for improving the racial condition of people of color.

The immediacy "of her calls to voting as part of women's duty is in no small part a function of the newness of enfranchisement."[15] Nardal viewed the enfranchisement in Martinique as definitely a positive move within women's liberal political achievement. Beauvoir emphasized throughout her work that women's right to vote was necessary but never enough to liberate women. She stated among others that "abstract rights [...] have never been sufficient to guarantee woman a concrete hold on the world: there is not yet real equality today between the sexes." Likewise, she asserts that "the kept woman—wife or mistress—is not freed from the male just because she has a ballot paper in her hands. [...]; work alone can guarantee her concrete freedom." Nardal, on the other hand, seemed more positive, assessing that the enfranchisement of women in Martinique would be crucial for giving a political voice to women. But to her as well, the right to vote was a tool, not a goal.[16] Rather than treating enfranchisement as if it were the *end* of all sexist oppression, Nardal sees the enfranchisement of women as a tool for making *further* progress towards the full emancipation of women.

In "From an Electoral Point of View" [1945], Nardal explains what women bring to political actions. Women's connections to the concrete reality of life, such as the work they do in the home, influence their liberal political perspectives. The different situations that women have experienced let them contribute effectively to society by voting, from their own stances and social perspectives. Although Nardal supports Beauvoir's idea that the situation of women has kept their political status low, she surpasses

Beauvoir by stating that their situation also gives women an upper hand in politics. Nardal wrote and created social and literary organizations that pushed for political action among women and that started from Martinican women's history. Women of color had seen very little political, economic, and social improvement to their lives as they were subject to French imperial control. Nardal felt that action, especially political action, was just as important as her writing, which tried to propel action by challenging the gender and racial discrimination levied on female citizens of Martinique.[17]

To Nardal, the active participation of women in Western institutions had the potential to liberate them from oppression. In her essay "Woman in the City" [1945], in which she contemplates the ascension of Martinican women to the status of citizen, Nardal elaborates on her concept of freedom:

> The social is the aspect of life that interests woman first and foremost. Regarding social duty, she is man's equal. As an individual, she is also intelligent and free. But as a social being, her services are bound to humankind. Like man, she must contribute to the progress of humanity. But this service, owing to the physical and psychological differences that exist between man and woman, will be of a different kind, though not necessarily of lesser value because of its difference. In fulfilling this social obligation, she remains true to her feminine vocation. What does this social duty entail? First, we must free ourselves from old prejudices, from lazy routines, in order to become familiar with social environments different from our own. The women of Martinique will therefore have to study problems concerning the family, the professions, the city [...]. It is to social education work that they are summoned.[18]

The Philosophy of Freedom and the Rights of Black Colonialized Women

Reflecting on Nardal's conception of black women's rights, Nardal's view comes close to Sartre's conception of freedom, insofar as Sartre posits that we must have a strong sense of responsibility for others when we act, and our own freedom depends on it—the sense of responsibility is simply the result or expression of our freedom.[19] Nardal would not have been in favor of a situated concept of freedom as developed by Beauvoir in *The Second Sex* [1949] and *The Ethics of Ambiguity* [1947]. Beauvoir argued that women's freedom is constrained by their situations and physical embodiment.[20] Sartre's model of freedom, similar to Nardal's, gives credence to the interconnectedness of freedom, choice, and responsibility, and provides more freedom to people marginalized by liberalism. Both Sartre and Nardal acknowledge the presence of oppression, while also stressing that the oppressed can act. This view on freedom enabled Nardal to rally for women's right to vote in Martinique. As Robert Bernasconi shows, to Sartre:

> Existentialism's first move is to make every man aware of what he is and to make the full responsibility of his existence rest on him. And when we say that a man is responsible for himself, we do not only mean that he is responsible for his own individuality, but that he is responsible for all men.[21]

According to Sartre, man's choice bears a sense of responsibility of bridging the gap between himself and the rest of mankind. In terms of the responsibility that man has for all men, he will be able to act freely within the concrete circumstances of mankind.[22] For Sartre, our freedom carries responsibility for the wellbeing of all others. In this respect, Nardal's choice to support women's suffrage in Martinique is not just relevant to Martinican women but pertains to all, insofar as freedom is determined by the living circumstances of all people. To Nardal, caring about the needs of all women involves caring about the needs of all.

While Nardal may have supported the sense of universal responsibility built into Sartre's conception of freedom, to her we come to *recognize* our responsibility through certain others and not through everyone in general. Sartre's philosophy posits that individual freedom is influenced by the tangible circumstances of everyone. Through his universal conception of freedom, or conception of everyone's freedom, the specific situation of each person blends with the individual sense of responsibility for everyone.

To Beauvoir, instead, a person's situation—not the person's sense of responsibility for all and the person's choices—determines the freedom of that person. As Sonia Kruks recounts, Beauvoir's objection to Sartre's concept of freedom was based on the problems she saw in the relation of situation to freedom.[23] Beauvoir argued that Sartre's rules, in which he defined individual freedom in all concrete circumstances, could not be consistently applied as a blanket statement to all individuals. She believed that a concrete examination of the circumstances of individuals—and the circumstances of women in particular—reveals that the living situations of some people give them no freedom whatsoever.[24]

Arp notes that, in terms of existentialist philosophy, Beauvoir posited a theory of freedom based more on moral freedom than on ontological freedom—the type of freedom that Sartre emphasizes in *Being and Nothingness*, the freedom that all human beings have.[25] Human freedom, according to *Being and Nothingness*, is the ability of consciousness to rise above its concrete situation. It is 'ontological' in the sense that every human being is free by definition, and can always escape the here and now. Beauvoir's moral freedom is different from Sartre's ontological freedom.[26] According to Arp, Beauvoir's concept of freedom "is the conscious affirmation of one's ontological freedom. And it can only be developed in the absence of certain constraints."[27] Arp tries to show that Beauvoir's concept of freedom serves to criticize material and social constraints, whereby to develop moral freedom requires having relationships with other people.[28]

In *The Ethics of Ambiguity*, Beauvoir elaborates on how specific social circumstances and a reduction to an inferior type of Otherness shape our subjectivity as well as restrict the possible self-interested choices—moral choices—individual people may make. She draws in part on the condition of women to build her analysis. Beauvoir characterizes the condition of women as an apparently childlike state that puts limitations on the choices a woman is able to make within the walls of her social situation.[29] This submissive state of women, however, is debatable: at stake is the question of whether women are even capable of making a moral choice that signals the self-interestedness of self-liberation. Across civilizations women have traditionally been marginalized by sex, generally did not hold positions of power, and were seen as the fairer and weaker sex, unable to contribute to the societies in which they grow up.

Beauvoir reins in the scope of her analysis to specifically explicate how women's actions affect the ways they are treated as grown-up children in Western countries. Even in contemporary Western countries, she argues:

> Among women who have not had in their work an apprenticeship of freedom, there are still many who take shelter in the shadow of men; they adopt without discussion the opinions and values recognized by their husband or their lover, and that allows them to develop childish qualities which are forbidden to adults because they are based on a feeling of irresponsibility.[30]

In Western countries—similar to the situation of women from non-Western origins, such as Asian, African, Arab, and Jewish women—many women have not been informed about the scope of their freedom or the myriad choices that are available to them. Through their relationships with husbands and lovers, they become infantilized and, therefore, irresponsible. This made the majority of women, regardless of their origins or political circumstances, more likely to live with a state of mind that lacked freedom than a mind accustomed to freedom, and this includes colonial and colonized women.

According to Arp, Beauvoir distinguishes between the case of the modern Western woman and the African woman or harem slave of the past (women from other civilizations). There exists a possibility of liberation for the Western woman, but there is no such possibility for these other women. The difference lies in the knowledge about their circumstances available to each woman.[31] The more aware she is of her living constraints and conditions, the more she is in a position to rise above the oppression of being a woman. According to Beauvoir, what is lacking in the lives of many women is education, which can bring the hope and knowledge of their capacity of freedom. Many European women lacked the means to educate themselves, or anyone they could ask, yet many African women innately understood that there were other possibilities for their lives other than slavery. In the case of the African or harem slave, Beauvoir stated that these women lacked the instrument that could ensure their freedom.[32] African or harem slaves, as Arp notes in relation to Beauvoir's ethics, "are not able to realize their moral freedom because they are cut off from creating their own future by their oppressors."[33] They have no access to the knowledge and tools that would make them moral free agents, which prevents them from participating in the creation of their future. In other words, women could not be morally free because they did not *know* that moral freedom was a possibility for them. They simply could not become morally free because there were men and legal structures, among other factors, that were stopping them from being morally free. Women knew nothing about moral freedom, and, as the adage says: 'Knowing is half the battle.'

However, from Nardal's perspective, all women, including the harem slave and Western women, have ontological freedom. They are able to act and make moral choices within the scope of their situation. Beauvoir unfortunately does not appear to believe that women always have the capacity that may set them free.[34] In showing doubt about women's ability to make these moral decisions, Beauvoir doubts women's sense of moral freedom—questioning whether they have the ability to comprehend freedom, choice, and responsibility. In comparing the situation of women to children, her analysis suggests that the state of childhood is missing any sense of self and social responsibility. Because Beauvoir believes that women, in general, are lacking social responsibility, she casts doubt on whether women are intelligent enough to act and free themselves from oppression. Beauvoir asserts that Western women of today are in the "apprenticeship of freedom," or educated to become self-assertive, and the condition of women that she describes encompasses Western women as well as women of other civilizations. However, Beauvoir's approach suggests a debilitating point of view from which women are not able to do very much about their individual situations: being denied the ability to develop moral freedom, women cannot be assigned the status of a moral actor.[35]

The problem, Arp argues, is that "Beauvoir's ethics hinges on the connection she makes between morality and freedom […]. If the oppressed lack moral freedom, the implication is that they somehow are not fully moral."[36] In this respect, Nardal's work is important. To her, in spite of their gender and racial oppression, colonized women are able to conceive of the political and social good.

Nardal clearly saw the racial and gender limitations of her situation as a woman. Yet, she would disagree with Beauvoir's claim in *The Ethics of Ambiguity* and in *The Second Sex* that women's social and physical constraints encumbered their freedom. As Sharpley-Whiting notes:

> If for Beauvoir, woman has always been cast as man's "Other" and *The Second Sex* endeavors to uncover just what that "Otherness" means for woman, Nardal takes this "Otherness" as an affirmation of feminine difference. Nardal's is a question of ontology, of being. Woman simply *is* or *does*. Where such "otherness" does not correspond to Nardal's ideas about women's equality, in effect, where she deems feminine characteristics as male-manufactured, she is quick to dispense with them.[37]

According to Sharpley-Whiting, from an ontological perspective rather than a materialist feminist and existentialist perspective, Nardal associates the condition of women with women's own self and their own actions. In ontologically associating being with action, Nardal visualizes freedom within the situation of women, allowing women to examine and decide for themselves what they feel is right and wrong. From this perspective, "women, like men, are wholly tied to social duty, the obligation to foster and nurture human progress."[38]

As Sharpley-Whiting shows, because of her dedication to Christianity as well as her endorsement of humanist principles, Nardal conceives the social duty of women from a perspective that integrated Western values into her own beliefs.[39] She sees the duties of women as different but not divorced from those of men or from those of humanity in general. Nardal, who frames her discourse on the rights of women in Martinique within dominant Western discourses, asserts that, as women assumed the responsibilities of their station in society, they turned into responsible agents, which benefited the entire country of Martinique.

Despite differences between Nardal's and Beauvoir's conceptions of freedom, Nardal's own biography reinforces one of Beauvoir's necessary conditions for the possibility of freedom of women. Nardal's education and work is a mirror of her apprenticeship of freedom, which illustrates her learned experience of acting responsibly, affirming Beauvoir's belief that education helped the freedom of women.[40] Already having acquired this distinct personality trait during her developmental years, Nardal got her self-assertion—or "apprenticeship of freedom"—through her schooling, initially at the Colonial College for Girls in Martinique and later at the Sorbonne in France.[41] Nardal's sense of self-assertion and freedom was honed in Western educational institutions, and took up ideas from the women she met in French women's organizations. It was also developed through her studies of the solid limitations put on people of color as a result of their race and engendered by her interactions with people of color, such as when she witnessed Anna Julia Cooper's dissertation defense at the Sorbonne in 1925.[42]

Nardal's self-assertive actions in regard to the advancement of women (both European and non-European) during her stay in France, England, and Martinique put her in a unique place to engage in discourse and act upon it.[43] Nardal's education is reflected in her philosophy, which resists the oppression of women by urging participation in Western institutions and the use of Western discourses. Nardal's actions were unexpected for the average Martinican or French woman. Beauvoir's analysis would have explained this by arguing that Nardal's education permitted her to act resourcefully and bypass the racial and gender limitations of her status as a woman of color. Nardal claimed to be a moral subject, and Beauvoir would agree with this claim.

In the early 1960s, when Beauvoir chose to come to the assistance of Algerian war rape victim Djamila Boupacha and aid her counsel, Gisèle Halimi, with the trial, she believed that Boupacha was oppressed and had less freedom than Halimi and herself.[44] While it can be argued that, to Beauvoir, Boupacha was oppressed, one may also posit that Beauvoir regarded Halimi as she may have regarded Nardal—as an exceptionally free minority woman. In Boupacha's trial, Halimi's actions as a highly capable lawyer illustrated that she possessed a sense of agency that allowed her to know what decisions to make—from altering the location of the trial and influencing public opinion to authoring a book on Djamila Boupacha's case.

Conclusion

Comparing Beauvoir's concept of freedom to Nardal's—despite the racial and situational differences between their analyses—I believe that both women would agree that pushing for women's political liberation is a pressing issue for both colonized and colonizer women. Beauvoir believes that the state of independence, without the right kind of education and work advancing toward freedom, was not likely to happen for French women—a situation she likens to the lack of freedom of the African or harem slave of the eighteenth century.[45]

Beauvoir's analysis does not examine the role of white privilege in French women's political liberation. Her analysis in *The Second Sex* of the political limitations of the voting rights of French women in the 1940s does not state why white French women were the first group of women in the empire to receive the right to vote. However, her analysis of the obstacles white women face in overcoming their oppression (i.e., political, economic, and moral) refers to troubles obvious in the oppressive state of affairs of non-white women; her argument for moral freedom coming about through education includes colonial as well as colonized women.

Nardal, on the other hand—through her analysis of the way French-Martinican women adhere to their social duties to become financially and politically free as citizens of Martinique—allows us to conceive of all women as ontologically free, and responsible. Both authors in their own way opened up the conversation on freedom of the oppressed. Both analyses of Beauvoir and Nardal on freedom can give rise to the development of a more elaborative philosophy of freedom within the field of feminist philosophy and post-colonial philosophy, and provide a starting point from which the situation of white women and non-white women can be further defined.

Notes

1 Anne Morgan, "Simone de Beauvoir's Ethics of Freedom and Absolute Evil," *Hypatia: A Journal of Feminist Philosophy* 23, no. 4 (December 10, 2008): 75.
2 Simone de Beauvoir, *The Ethics of Ambiguity*, trans. Bernard Frechtman (New York: Philosophical Library/Open Road, 2015), 6.
3 Ibid., 129.
4 Ibid., 16.
5 Kristana Arp, *The Bonds of Freedom: Simone de Beauvoir's Existentialist Ethics* (Chicago/La Salle, IL: Open Court, 2001), 3.
6 Beauvoir, *Ethics of Ambiguity*, 78.
7 Ibid.
8 Lori J. Marso, "Simone de Beauvoir on Violence and Politics," in *A Companion to Simone de Beauvoir*, ed. Laura Hengehold and Nancy Bauer (Hoboken, NJ: Wiley Blackwell, 2017), 306.
9 Richard D.E. Burton and Fred Reno, eds., *French and West Indian: Martinique, Guadeloupe, and French Guiana Today* (Charlottesville: University Press of Virginia, 1995), 132.
10 Ibid. For example, representing Guadeloupe, Eugene Eboué (Socialist Party) was elected to the constituent Assembly of 1945, followed by Gerty Archimède (Communist Party), who was elected to the National Assembly for 1946–1951. On the other hand, the first Martinican woman elected to the regional council was Madeleine de Grandmaison, and then only in 1983.
11 Emily Musil, *La Marianne Noire: How Gender and Race in the Twentieth Century Atlantic World Reshaped the Debate about Human Rights* (PhD Dissertation, University of California, Los Angeles, 2007), 200.
12 Ibid., 200–202.
13 Burton and Reno, *French and West Indian*, 132.
14 Paulette Nardal, *Beyond Negritude: Essays from Woman in the City*, trans. and intro. T. Denean Sharpley-Whiting (Albany: State University of New York Press, 2009), 6–7.
15 Ibid., 11.
16 Simone de Beauvoir, *The Second Sex*, trans. Constance Borde and Sheila Malovany-Chevallier (New York: Vintage, 2011), 737, 155.
17 Nardal, *Beyond Negritude* 21, 23.
18 Ibid., 21.
19 Robert Bernasconi, *How to Read Sartre* (London: Granta, 2006), 54.

20 Sonia Kruks, "Simone de Beauvoir: Teaching Sartre about Freedom,", in *Feminist Interpretations of Simone de Beauvoir*, ed. Margaret A. Simons (University Park: Pennsylvania State University Press, 1995), 82–83.
21 Bernasconi, *How to Read Sartre*, 54.
22 Ibid.
23 Kruks, "Teaching Sartre about Freedom," 82.
24 Beauvoir, *The Second Sex*, 679–716. What I say here about the lack of freedom among women is shown in Beauvoir's analysis of the political and economic disenfranchisement of women in France, featured in the chapter "The Independent Woman" of *The Second Sex*.
25 Arp, *Bonds of Freedom*, 2.
26 Ibid.
27 Ibid.
28 Ibid., 2–3.
29 Beauvoir, *Ethics of Ambiguity*, 37. To Beauvoir, the situation of the child reflects the "situation of women in many civilizations; they can only submit to the laws, the gods, the customs, and the truths created by the males."
30 Ibid.
31 Arp, *Bonds of Freedom*, 115–16.
32 Beauvoir, *Ethics of Ambiguity*, 38.
33 Arp, *Bonds of Freedom*, 118.
34 Beauvoir, *Ethics of Ambiguity*, 37.
35 Arp, *Bonds of Freedom*, 117–18.
36 Ibid., 118.
37 T. Denean Sharpley-Whiting, "Introduction: On Race, Rights, and Women," in Nardal, *Beyond Negritude*, 18.
38 Ibid., 19.
39 Ibid., 18–19.
40 Beauvoir, *Ethics of Ambiguity*, 37.
41 Sharpley-Whiting, "Introduction," 1.
42 Ibid., 2.
43 Kirkland and Musil, *La Marianne Noire*, 200.
44 Djamila Boupacha, a young Muslim Algerian woman, was accused in 1960 by the French government of attempting to plant a bomb in a cafe in the French quarters in Algiers during the Algerian War. On February 10, Boupacha was arrested, and subsequently tortured by the French colonial administration. Gisèle Halimi, a French-Tunisian lawyer, contacted Beauvoir for assistance. Beauvoir responded and began to author articles on and speak publicly about the problems of detaining Boupacha as a political prisoner. On April 21, 1962, prior to the end of the war, Boupacha was released from jail—all this with the public support of Beauvoir.
45 Beauvoir, *Ethics of Ambiguity*, 37–38.

References

Arp, Kristana. *The Bonds of Freedom: Simone de Beauvoir's Existentialist Ethics*. Chicago/La Salle, IL: Open Court, 2001.
Beauvoir, Simone de. *The Second Sex*. Translated by Constance Borde and Sheila Malovany-Chevallier. New York: Vintage, 2011.
Beauvoir, Simone de. *The Ethics of Ambiguity*. Translated by Bernard Frechtman. New York: Philosophical Library/Open Road, 2015.
Bernasconi, Robert. *How to Read Sartre*. London: Granta, 2006.

Burton, Richard D.E. and Fred Reno, eds. *French and West Indian: Martinique, Guadeloupe, and French Guiana Today*. Charlottesville: University Press of Virginia, 1995.

Kruks, Sonia. "Simone de Beauvoir: Teaching Sartre about Freedom." In *Feminist Interpretations of Simone de Beauvoir*, edited by Margaret A. Simons, 79–96. University Park: Pennsylvania State University Press, 1995.

Marso, Lori J. "Simone de Beauvoir on Violence and Politics." In *A Companion to Simone de Beauvoir*, edited by Laura Hengehold and Nancy Bauer, 299–310. Hoboken, NJ: Wiley Blackwell, 2017.

Morgan, Anne. "Simone de Beauvoir's Ethics of Freedom and Absolute Evil." *Hypatia: A Journal of Feminist Philosophy* 23, no. 4. December 10, 2008.

Musil, Emily, "La Marianne Noire: How Gender and Race in the Twentieth Century Atlantic World Reshaped the Debate about Human Rights." PhD diss., University of California, Los Angeles, 2007.

Nardal, Paulette. *Beyond Negritude: Essays from Woman in the City*. Translated and with introduction by T. Denean Sharpley-Whiting. Albany: State University of New York Press, 2009.

Sharpley-Whiting, T. Denean. "Introduction: On Race, Rights, and Women," in *Beyond Negritude: Essays from Woman in the City*, by Paulette Nardal. Albany: State University of New York Press, 2009.

Simons, Margaret. *Feminist Interpretations of Simone de Beauvoir*. University Park: Pennsylvania State University Press, 1995.

PART III
Situated Experiences

7

OLD AGE AND THE QUESTION OF AUTHENTICITY

Sonia Kruks

One is not born but rather becomes old, and becoming old—like becoming a woman—entails becoming the "Other." Woman, Beauvoir writes in *The Second Sex*, is cast as the "Other," as the object vis-à-vis whom "man" claims to be the "Subject" and the "Absolute."[1] Analogously, she writes in *Old Age* [*La Vieillesse*, 1970] that the old are cast "outside humanity."[2] They are conceived by younger adults as "sub" human (OA 505; V 531) and as "inert objects" (OA 486; V 511). There are, of course, also profound differences, but for both women and the old (of any gender) existence is profoundly shaped by alterity.[3]

Beauvoir had argued in *The Second Sex* that, their alterity notwithstanding, an authentic pursuit of freedom remains possible for women, for "to become a woman" involves a project of active self-making and is not reducible to passively being made one. Although Beauvoir depicts the multitude of constraints within which women must struggle to engage their freedom, she still insists that it is a "moral fault" if they consent to the forms of objectification inflicted on them (TSS 16). However, many women choose to comply in their alterity rather than engage in the anxiety-producing pursuit of freedom. They "flee" their freedom through "bad faith," "complicity," or "the serious": that is, through self-deception, a tacit consent to oppressive "feminine" norms, or the unthinking acceptance of ready-made values. In any (or several) of these ways, a woman can consent to enact the object-like role demanded of her as man's Other. Thus, she may engage, to different degrees and in different ways, in the seemingly paradoxical project of "making herself an object" [*se faire objet*].[4]

In varying forms, Beauvoir writes,

> The traps of bad faith and the mystifications of the serious are lying in wait for both [women and men]; freedom is entire in each. However, because of the fact that in woman this freedom remains abstract and empty, it cannot authentically assume itself except in revolt: this is the only way open to those who have no chance to build anything; *they must refuse the limits of their situation in seeking to open paths to the future; resignation is no more than an abdication and a flight*; for woman there is no other way out than to work for her liberation.
>
> *(TSS 664, emphasis added; TM)*

But what, then, of the old? Can they also seek "to open paths to the future"? Is revolt, or at least resistance, also open to them as an authentic path to freedom? It is of note that *Old Age* has no equivalent to the final part of *The Second Sex* on "the Independent Woman," who, in good faith, struggles to affirm her freedom. Thus, one must ask, does Beauvoir perhaps see old age as a unique situation in which the demands she makes of (younger) women to eschew bad faith and engage in the authentic pursuit of freedom no longer apply? Or could it be that she has radically modified or even abandoned her prior ethics? These are the questions this chapter seeks to address.

Old Age from "Without" and "Within": An Overview[5]

Beauvoir called the second part of *Old Age* "Being-in-the-World" and it is roughly equivalent to the second volume of *The Second Sex*, "Lived Experience." Each offers a phenomenological account, from "within," of the embodied and social experience of becoming the Other. However, becoming a woman has a radically different temporality from becoming old. "Becoming a woman" begins in infancy, and it is both a process to which one is subjected and a project that requires an active engagement. A young girl's "vocation" as a woman is "imperiously breathed into her from the first years of her life," Beauvoir writes (TSS 283), so that it becomes intrinsic to her very existence: for, whether in compliance or resistance, and through the many stages of her life—from puberty to (for most) heterosexual initiation, marriage, motherhood, and, indeed, old age—she must continue to assume this vocation.[6] She must, in one way or another, continuously navigate the tension it poses between the demand that she comply in her alterity and her freedom. However, although we age continuously, "being old" is not similarly integral to our life-span.

To the contrary, Beauvoir argues that old age is, most often, suddenly and unwelcomely thrust upon us from "without." There is an abrupt discovery of our new status as a particular kind of "being-for-others": a shocked realization as we discover we are *seen* (whether it be by particular individuals or through the generalized gaze of society) as "old." It is "through the vision that others have of us" (OA 291 TM; V 309) that we suddenly discover this new and negative status—and it is one that does not align with our inner experience of ourselves. Thus: "Within me, it is the other, that is to say the person I am for others, who is old" (OA 284 TM; V 302); "it is the other within us who is old" (OA 288; V 306).

Initially, we cannot fully grasp this new reality. Beauvoir describes a period when becoming old has the quality of what (using Sartre's notion) she calls an "unrealizable." An unrealizable is an "objective" aspect of my situation that others see but that I do not live as integral to my being-for-myself. Many unrealizables lie, unseen, in the background of our lives, and they do not impinge on us unless our situation changes so that they come into focus as demanding to be addressed. For example, Beauvoir says, when she is in France she does not need to consider what the quality of "being French" means; but when she is in a foreign country this personal characteristic cannot be ignored. She now discovers that she must take up a specific attitude toward her nationality: she must "affirm it, conceal it, forget it, etc." (OA 291; V 309).

To discover that one is old is to make an analogous and disturbing discovery—for that we are now old is an unrealizable, an "objective reality" that conflicts with our "inner certitude" that we are still the same (that is, young, active) person we always were. Thus, she writes, "we must assume a reality which is indubitably one's self even while it reaches us from without and remains ungraspable." For a period, "we can only oscillate" [*nous ne pouvons qu'osciller*]: We swing ambivalently between this new objective reality and our old inner certitude (OA 290 TM; V 308–309).[7] We try to resist our new designation but over time, and as additional aspects of old age impinge, it becomes increasingly difficult to refute. In Chapter 5, "The Discovery and Assumption of Old Age," Beauvoir emphasizes the unrealizability of old age. However, a great many of her examples demonstrate that the reality of old age imposes itself more definitively. In time, the "identity crisis" [*crise de l'identification*] becomes resolved (OA 291. V 310), and old age passes from being an unrealizable to becoming integral to our existence.

There are also practical and material ways that society constitutes the status of the old person as the other from without. Among these, expulsion from valued social activity is of great significance. This expulsion may be gradual, but it often takes place very suddenly at the moment of retirement. Retirement may "fall on the worker like an axe," Beauvoir writes (OA 263; V 281). Even when it is welcomed as an escape from drudgery, its effect is to deny the old recognition as active, human agents—for (drawing here on Sartre's later work, *The Critique of Dialectical Reason* [1960]) Beauvoir argues that relations of "reciprocal recognition" emerge among human beings though work or other practical activities ("praxis"), since this is where we see and grasp each other as purposive existences (OA 216–17; V 231–2).[8] Reciprocal recognition always requires that we recognize the other as an agent who (like oneself) is pursuing transcendent ends (OA 216; V 230). Accordingly, once retired and cut off from visible social activity, it seems that, "apart from some exceptions, the old man doesn't *do* anything. He is defined by an *exis* not a *praxis*: a being and not a doing." Lacking any project through which reciprocity can emerge, the old appear to active adults "as a 'foreign species' in which they do not recognize themselves" (OA 217; V 231). Passive and debilitated, the old are seen by "active adults" as useless, superfluous, and as terrifying harbingers of their own future debility and worthlessness. Here is why this foreign species, which we all know already incipiently dwells within us, incites such aversion. Indeed, says Beauvoir, it "arouses a biological repugnance; in a kind of self-defense one pushes it far away from oneself" (OA 217; V 231). It is no wonder, then, that the old are treated as the Other!

Additionally, old age arrives in more immediate ways—from within. This occurs especially through the body.[9] Indeed, aging bodies themselves often become key sources of alterity and even profound self-alienation. "A woman *is* her body" but her body is "something other than herself," Beauvoir had written in *The Second Sex* (41 TM); but, as old age advances, the body can become a yet more powerful site of alterity. Thus Beauvoir talks of a "biological destiny" (OA 86 TM; V 95) in which the body becomes an "obstacle" instead of being an "instrument" for one's projects (OA 317; V 336). Then, she says, "the coefficient of adversity in things" seems to rise. For example, "stairs are harder to climb, distances longer to cover, streets more dangerous to cross, parcels heavier to carry" (OA 304 TM; V 336).

Yet worse, "Biological decay brings with it the impossibility of transcendence, of becoming passionately involved, it kills projects and in this way it makes death acceptable" (OA 443 TM; V 468). This loss of passion frequently accompanies a loss or diminution of sexual activity. "Sexuality" is "an intentionality lived by the body [… that] takes up its form [*elle s'investit*] in relation to a world which it provides with an erotic dimension." Accordingly, the loss is not one of genital satisfaction alone and it more generally affects "a man's relationship with himself, with others and with the world" (OA 318 TM; V 337). Thus the lives of the old often lack a living warmth. Beauvoir quotes from Rousseau's *Reveries* as an example (cited OA 401):

> "Already my imagination is less vivid, and it no longer glows as it once did at an object that stirs it into life; dreaming is less of an intoxicating rapture […] A lukewarm weariness drains my faculties of all their strength; little by little the spirit of life is going out."

Here, Rousseau also describes another important shift that accompanies old age: our relationship to time changes. Rousseau is looking backwards to a warmer, richer past and also, with sad anticipation, towards a yet more depleted future. The weight of the past grows, Beauvoir says and, since it no longer nourishes new activities, it becomes fixed. It becomes petrified, while the future, the horizon toward which all projects must extend, becomes foreshortened by the approach of death—"a limited future and a frozen past: such is the situation that old people have to confront" (OA 378, TM; V 400). The future then "appears doubly *finished*: it is short and it is closed" (OA 373; V 395). However, it is not only the approach of death that limits the future, for there is also a passing away of one's world. It becomes less peopled as friends and loved ones die; and, especially in a rapidly changing society, as new generations take center stage, the old often find themselves to be out of joint with the values and practices of a new era. They have become governed by a life-time of prior activities and habits that traps them in what, with Sartre, Beauvoir calls the "practico-inert" (OA 372; V 395)[10] and most are condemned to obsolescence (OA 382; V 404).

Throughout *Old Age*, Beauvoir sets out to present what she calls the "constants" (one might perhaps call them structures of existence) that constitute the "being-in-the-world" of those who become old.[11] However, because these constants are always taken up by each individual in a unique synthesis, as it is *lived* old age involves a great "plurality of experiences" (OA 279; V 299). As in *The Second Sex*, Beauvoir employs a method of phenomenological variation, drawing on a multiplicity of examples to show what remains common even as there are stark differences. However, this method exists in a sometimes uneasy tension with her explicit political agenda—for the political thrust of *Old Age* is an attack on the egregious treatment of the working-class old in modern capitalist society, whereas the resources available for her phenomenological inquiry are mostly (although not exclusively) the written reflections of (or about) elite and illustrious European men. Her exemplars are writers, artists, political figures, and so forth. They are most often men of comfortable means, if not considerable wealth, who remain actively engaged in life and enjoy high social status. Beauvoir is aware of this tension, but she sees it as unavoidable since they are the ones "to have the means and leisure to record their evidence" (OA 279; V 299). She admits her dependence on such elite sources is "a drawback" [*un défaut*], but she claims that "the information they provide usually has a significance that goes beyond their own particular cases" (OA 279 TM; V 299).[12]

Many of Beauvoir's examples do, indeed, resonate beyond her particular cases. However, and as she also repeatedly asserts, the vicissitudes of old age do not bear on all equally. Most importantly, although for a privileged few an engaged and meaningful old age remains possible, "it is in the last years of life that the gulf opens most deeply between them and the vast majority of men" (OA 541 TM; V 567). It is to her discussion of this majority that I now turn.

The "Desert" World of Impoverished Old Age and the Question of Bad Faith

In *The Ethics of Ambiguity* (1947), Beauvoir had described the "sub-man" as one who "experiences the desert of the world in his boredom"[13] since he endeavors, in bad faith, to flee his freedom and refuses to commit himself with passion to any projects:

> If we were to try to establish a kind of hierarchy among men, we would put those who are denuded of this living warmth [...] on the lowest rung of the ladder. To exist is *to make oneself* [*se faire*] a lack of being; it is to *cast* oneself [*se jeter*] into the world. Those who occupy themselves in restraining this original movement can be considered as sub-men.
> *(EA 42)*

Apathetic, fearful, lacking desires of his own, the sub-man's acts "are never positive choices, only flights" (EA 43). Strikingly, now, in *Old Age*, Beauvoir also uses the term "sub-man" with reference to the majority of the old—but with a difference: here the sub-man is no longer presented as one who chooses an inauthentic flight from freedom, but as one whose existence is so constituted by deprivations and debilities as to preclude authentic action. "[If] the old person is not the victim of economic and physiological conditions that reduce him to the state of the sub-man [*à l'état de sous-homme*], he remains, throughout the alterations of the aging process, the individual that he has been" (OA 505 TM; V 531)—but few are so fortunate.

For the great majority, especially (but not exclusively) the poor, their final age is, indeed, a desert. However, "if the retired man is rendered hopeless by the lack of meaning [*non-sens*] in his present life, this is because his existence has always been stolen from him" (OA 541–2 TM; V 568). In a profit-oriented, capitalist society, the retired are viewed as an unproductive burden, and are treated accordingly. After a life of alienated labor they are cast aside, regarded merely as "scrap," as "walking corpses" (OA 6; V 12–13). Beauvoir extensively documents the penury that so many were thrown into by the inadequate support of the French pension and welfare systems of the time. She also argues that even those who are not in such acute material need (of whom there are somewhat more nowadays) are condemned to a "dehumanized" old age (OA 7; V 13) since it is the "treatment inflicted on the majority of men during their youth and maturity [that] prefabricates the maimed and wretched state that is theirs when they are old" (OA 542; V 568). Thus, even should better health care, decent housing, and so forth be provided for them, "they cannot be provided with the culture, the interests and the responsibilities that would give their life a meaning" (ibid.). They face a "sterile" future and an "unpeopled" world, and sink into "deathly apathy" [*la sinistre apathie*] (OA 451–2; V 475–6). Then, "Their sadness [...] merges with their consuming boredom, with their bitter and humiliating sense of uselessness, and with their loneliness in the midst of a world that has nothing but indifference for them" (OA 464; V 488).

In *The Ethics of Ambiguity*, as in *The Second Sex*, Beauvoir had criticized those who flee their freedom in strategies of bad faith and self-objectification. But now, in *Old Age*, she portrays with great sympathy a range of attitudes and actions common to many old people that she would once have criticized as instances of such "flight." For many, she argues they are, rather, valid forms of "defense." They are important means through which "the old person tries to defend himself against the objective precariousness of his situation and against his inward anxiety" (OA 466; V 490).

For example, a common defensive strategy that Beauvoir describes sympathetically is to "take refuge in habit" (OA 466; V 490). In *The Second Sex*, Beauvoir critically describes women who throw themselves into compulsive, repetitive routines of housework as a means to evade their freedom. "Housework," she says "in fact permits a woman an indefinite flight from herself" (TSS 478; TM). However, Beauvoir does not similarly depict the, sometimes obsessive, embrace of habits by the old as a flight. Rather, their habits hold out promise of needed protection against the meaninglessness of life. Habit is how

> the old person escapes from the sickening quality of excessive leisure by filling it with tasks and duties that for him take on the form of obligations; and in this way he avoids having to ask himself the dreadful question, "what shall I do?" There is something to be done every moment of the day.
>
> *(OA 467; V 491)*

The rigid habits that many old people adopt foreclose new possibilities,[14] but they also offer a degree of "ontological security": "Because of habit [the old person] knows who he is. It protects him from his generalized anxieties by assuring him that tomorrow will be a repetition of today" (OA 469; V 493).[15]

As well as clinging to habits, the old often cling excessively to their possessions. Indeed, Beauvoir observes, the two traits merge since "the things that belong to us are as it were solidified habits" (OA 469; V 494). Furthermore, ownership itself is also felt to be "a guarantee of ontological security," for, "since it is no longer the old man's role to cause himself to exist by doing, he wishes to *have* in order to be" (OA 470; V 494). Thus self-objectification in things, and especially a self-identification with money (deemed synonymous with power), is a commonly attempted form of defense: "Thanks to his possessions the old person assures himself of an identity against those who see him as nothing but an object" (OA 470; V

494). Objectifying oneself in things in order to protect oneself against social objectification is, once again, a defense that is likely to fail. Indeed, instead of providing the sought-after security, it can give rise to extreme anxiety about losing one's possessions (OA 470; V 494–5). However, Beauvoir does not consider this self-objectification a form of bad faith.

Disrespected, ridiculed, already excluded, many attempt to escape their condition through strategies in which they withdraw yet further from the hostile and threatening world. Some attempt to make this escape by living in a world of past memories, even though their memories cannot "resuscitate the real world from which they emanate" (OA 364; V 386). Against the degradations of old age, they "affirm *a fixed essence* and tirelessly tell themselves how this being that they were lives on inside them [... that] they are forever this ex-serviceman, this worshipped woman, this wonderful mother" (OA 362 TM, emphasis added; V 384). Yet Beauvoir does not criticize such essentializing forms of self-objectification as bad faith.

Yet others assume the disabilities of old age in an unnecessarily exaggerated form to justify excluding themselves from responsibility for action. A frequent device is to turn to hypochondria:

> [The old person] complains of aches and pains to hide from himself the fact that he is suffering from a loss of standing. For many, illness can act as an excuse for the inferiority to which they are now doomed. It can also justify their self-centeredness—henceforth their body requires all their care.
>
> *(OA 302; V 320)*

However, far from being critical, Beauvoir adds that "these forms of behavior are based upon a very real and intense anxiety" (ibid.). Similarly, some exaggerate mild impairments. Having some difficulty walking, they imitate paralysis; others, being a little deaf, stop listening. However, in "playing at being disabled, they become so" (OA 303; V 322). In such ways, they strengthen their exclusion from the world even when this has not yet been fully imposed on them (ibid.). One could say here, as Beauvoir says of many younger individuals, that they are complicit in their oppression; indeed, that they comply in "making themselves an object" [*se faire objet*]. Yet Beauvoir makes no such claim. To the contrary, she sympathetically describes such behavior, especially (but not only) on the part of the impoverished and institutionalized old—for, not only are they "despairing," but they are also "justifiably [*à juste titre*] resentful and demanding" (OA 303; V 322). Some respond to their condition with what Beauvoir calls "attitudes of protest" that may appear bizarre, but they should not be dismissed as mere social deviance. Criticizing a certain Dr. Kuplan, who describes what he calls the "antisocial behavior" of the old as "senile delinquency," she says that he only observes them from without, like an entomologist (OA 481; V 506). Yet "these are men who invent their behavior according to their situation; many of their attitudes are ones of protest because their condition calls for protest" (ibid.).

Sometimes protest takes forms of passive retaliation, of "refusing to take part in the game." Ceasing to comply with social norms, the individual "says anything that comes into his head [...] He no longer governs his impulses, not that he is incapable of control, but because he sees no reason why he should" (OA 480; V 505). Others respond more assertively, but their transgressive behavior remains futile since it cannot fuel effective projects of revolt. For example, they may refuse to conform to social norms of cleanliness and hygiene: "Dirtiness? But they have been tossed on the rubbish-heap, so why should they obey the laws of health and decency?" (OA 481; V 506). Some may refuse to leave their beds; others, like Lear, may strip off their clothes, "using this nakedness as a symbol of the stripping" to which they are subjected (OA 482; V 506). Yet others use incontinence as a revenge, or else they refuse to eat or wander away from a home where, unwanted, they no longer have a role (OA 482; V 506–7).[16] Such so-called "anti-social" ways of behaving are comprehensible: they are meaningful expressions of anger or forms of self-defense against a desperate situation. However, Beauvoir argues, they are counter-productive for they invite tyranny and scorn, and often their effect is but to solidify alterity. Even if they are treated well, such old people are still looked upon "as objects, not as subjects" (OA 479; V 504).

In *The Ethics of Ambiguity*, Beauvoir had written of situations of oppression in which "transcendence is condemned to fall uselessly back upon itself because it is cut off from its goals" (EA 81); but she also argued that such negative or abstract forms of revolt can acquire a positive content. They can become realized as authentic freedom through action—through "escape, political struggle, revolution" (EA 31). Even within severe constraints, there are almost always some means for freedom to assert itself for (younger) women, workers, the colonized.[17] However, it is just such a positive movement of resistance that is precluded from the vain protests of the old. Theirs are intentions that can only fall back uselessly upon themselves, she says, and they fail to become engaged in authentic action. Yet this failure does not make them inauthentic. Thus, we must ask whether, with regard to those in old age: has Beauvoir now abandoned the core distinction between authenticity and inauthenticity that has previously anchored her ethics? Well, yes and no.

Authenticity in "Active" Old Age

Existence in old age is also very variable, and those who are not capable of authentic action (although they are the many) lie only at one end of a spectrum that Beauvoir presents. At the other end, authentic action remains a possibility for those who do not suffer from acute deprivations and who have previously been engaged in meaningful projects. Many of the extended examples Beauvoir offers are of such individuals: they are those who have both the existential and material resources to prolong "active" life. Indeed, some of them may even discover that there are positive benefits to the social exclusions of old age, for sometimes "being cast to the margins of humanity means escaping from the obligations and alienations that are its portion" (OA 487 TM; V 513).[18] George Bernard Shaw, for example, talked of having "an enchanting feeling of freedom, adventure and irresponsibility" after the age of 60 (OA 486; V 512). Others who found a new boldness include Bertrand Russell, who, at considerable physical risk to himself, participated at age 89 in illegal, direct action protest against nuclear weapons (OA 490; V 516), and Benjamin Spock, who risked his great reputation as a pediatrician by engaging in activism against the Vietnam War (OA 490; V 515).

Only a few engage in such radically new departures; but many others (artists, writers, composers, and so forth) enjoy authentic freedom in old age by continuing with their former projects, finally freed from their earlier "fetishes and illusions." Now realizing that "the idea of advancing towards a goal was a delusion" and that (as she cites Sartre) life is "a useless passion" (OA 491; V 517), such individuals can act in ways that "bracket" their earlier personal desires for fame and so forth. Instead, they freely engage in valued activities for their own sake or for the sake of humanity. Indeed:

> Acting, while at the same time "placing one's action in parentheses" is to reach authenticity; it is harder to achieve than falsehood, but once attained one cannot but be happy. The most valuable contribution old age brings is this sweeping away of fetishes and illusions.
>
> *(OA 492 TM; V 517)*

But the opposite can also be the case. For some of the privileged few a prior life of bad faith leads to a meaningless old age since, "when an old person is rich enough to have different possibilities open to him, the way in which he reacts to the disagreeable aspects of age will depend upon the choices he made earlier in life" (OA 305; V 323). As Beauvoir had written in *The Ethics of Ambiguity*, "to will oneself free is to will others free" (EA 73); and, notably, those whose lives have been ones of misanthropy, or who have otherwise sought to flee from human interdependence, may endure an alienated and meaningless old age in spite of their creativity. Thus the misanthropic Jonathan Swift—who, in the portrait of the Yahoos, "ferociously satirized humanity in general" and who, in the Struldbrugs, gave "the cruelest portrait of old age that was ever drawn"—was in his last years, "himself changed into a horrible Struldbrug" (OA 189; V 202). Chateaubriand is another example: his "cantankerous indifference to his century grew worse with the years" and his old age was increasingly bitter (OA 530; V 556). Lamartine too had an "appalling" old age, due in large part to his hypocrisy and especially his bad faith pretense to support liberal politics during the events of 1848 (OA 537–38; V 564). In cases such as these, even for members of the creative elite, their previous bad faith and a refusal to recognize the freedom of others may condemn them to a "desert world" in old age.

However, Beauvoir is more interested in those who, after lives of authentic action, still remain passionately committed to their undertakings as they grow old. For them, she declares, "old age passes, as it were, unnoticed," for they are engaged in projects that "defy time" (OA 492–3; V 518). This is, in my view, rather too optimistic a claim on her part as, de facto, many of the examples of authentic old age she presents contradict her declaration. The tribulations of old age, especially debility and illnesses, catch up with almost all of the eminent individuals she presents, and it is rare that time passes as unnoticed as she proclaims—for, as she also observes, "there is no inherent justice: far from it, sickness and one's social context may wreck the end of an active and generous life" (OA 505 TM; V 531).

It is important to note that, for the active and authentic individuals Beauvoir describes, the initial "discovery and assumption of old age" does *not* come from experiences of alterity or social exclusion. Instead, for this group, the discovery of old age arises through the—increasingly all too "realizable"—alterity of their own bodies. There develops, she says, "a 'fatigability' that spares none" (OA 28; V 34). They too discover that "the coefficient of adversity in things rises" (OA 304 TM; V 336). They too experience "physical weariness, general fatigue and indifference," and they sink into what Flaubert describes as a lack of "alacrity" (OA 400–401; V 424). Verdi is an example. Although he continued to write great music and to receive public acclaim until his very last years, he wrote: "Although the doctors tell me I am not ill, everything tires me [...] I am not living, I vegetate [...] I no longer have anything to do in this world" (cited OA 517 TM; V 543). Similarly, Michelangelo wrote: "I am betrayed" and "if one could die of shame and pain I would no longer be alive" (cited OA 513 TM; V 539). His letters and poems were "dark, disillusioned" yet, at the same time, his work reached its "highest peaks" (OA 515; V 541).

Beauvoir rarely describes illness as fully as she does more general experiences of fatigue and hopelessness. Yet it persistently hovers in many of her examples, as she describes the struggles of individuals who have suffered from heart attacks, severe strokes, cancer, and so forth. For some, the sudden onset of a serious illness or acute pain precipitates a resigned acceptance of old age; but those Beauvoir celebrates are the ones who persist with optimism in their projects in spite of such vicissitudes. Renoir, for example, not only determinedly continued to paint when half-paralyzed but also felt that he was making progress in his art (OA 313; V 332), and Victor Hugo remained creative and enjoyed being publicly celebrated in spite of severe debilities (OA 505 ff.; V 531 ff.). But, more often, illness, debility, and pain induce the decline in alacrity, the loss of passion, the feelings of hopelessness against which Beauvoir insists it is important to struggle. Then, resignation and resistance no longer present themselves as the straightforward alternatives that Beauvoir had declared them to be in *The Second Sex*. They may now exist in an ambiguous tension.

Thus, for example, when severely disabled by a stroke and other ailments, Walt Whitman still remained engaged in the effort to publish his last poems. Yet he also wrote of being "sick and grown old," and of his "ungracious glooms, aches, lethargy, constipation, whimpering *ennui*" (OA 309; V 328).[19] Similarly, Freud—who continued to write while suffering from cancer and living under the shadow of Nazism—wrote: "I cannot accustom myself to the grief and afflictions of old age and I look forward with longing to the journey into the void" (OA 523–4; V 550). Winston Churchill persisted in remaining British prime minister following a stroke, but described himself as "a bundle of old rags" (OA 431; V 455); and Lou Andreas-Salomé (the only woman Beauvoir discusses in the "Examples of Old Age" chapter) remained active during her very last days. She continued narrating her autobiography to a friend although she was suffering from such intense physical pain that she said it was "enough to drive one to despair." Shortly before she died, she remarked: "All my life I have done nothing but work. And when you come to think of it, why?" (OA 519; V 545).

Neither Authenticity nor Bad Faith

Why work all one's life? Why act? Andreas-Salomé's question echoes those Cineas asks of Pyrrhus in Beauvoir's early essay: "What's the use of leaving if it is to return home? What's the point of starting if you must stop?"[20] Beauvoir's answer in *Pyrrhus and Cineas*—and it's one that is reiterated in various keys throughout her oeuvre—is that it is only by engaging in the world through projects that plunge us, transcendent, into an open future together with others that we disclose our freedom: "One only transcends oneself towards an end [...]. One can surpass one project only by realizing another project," she writes, and "I need [the other's] freedom to be available to use and conserve me in surpassing me."[21] While in *The Second Sex* (although she is far more aware here of the constraints on freedom than in her earlier "moral" essay) Beauvoir insists that: "Every subject posits itself as a transcendence concretely, through projects; it accomplishes its freedom only by perpetual surpassing toward other freedoms; *there is no other justification for present existence than its expansion toward an indefinitely open future*" (TSS 16, emphasis added).

Beauvoir continues to affirm such a notion of authentic freedom in her examples of a good old age, and she does so most emphatically in the Conclusion to *Old Age*: "Undergoing age is not an activity. Projects have only to do with our activities," she insists. She continues:

> There is only one solution if old age is not to be an absurd parody of our former life, and that is to go on pursuing ends that give our existence a meaning—devotion to individuals, to groups or to causes, social, political, intellectual or creative work [...] in old age we should wish still to have passions strong enough to prevent us turning in on ourselves. One's life has value so long as one attributes value to the life of others.
> *(OA 540–41; V 566–7)*

The vision of authentic freedom that Beauvoir offers here is presaged on the continuation into old age, albeit somewhat diminished, of the passions and vitality, of the forward temporal thrust and engagement in the world with others that (should) fuel the free, transcendent projects of younger adults. She closes the book by offering the dream of an "ideal society" where these continue throughout late life (OA 543; V 569). In such a society, after enjoying life-long participation in meaningful, collective activity, individuals will remain active and valued social participants during their very last years. They will engage in authentic action until they finally die from a brief illness "without having suffered any degradation" (OA 543; V 569).

Beauvoir's ideal presupposes the overthrow of contemporary capitalist society, and she closes the book with the ringing statement that, "It is the whole system that is at issue and our claim cannot be otherwise than radical—change life itself" (OA 543; V 570). However, as she has shown in extensive detail earlier in the book, old age is far more than an oppressive social condition.[22] Thus, her ideal could also be viewed as expressing an aversive denial on her part of the physical decline and other losses that accompany aging. A conclusion that some critics have drawn is that Beauvoir herself views the old as less than fully human. Martha Nussbaum, for example, angrily accuses Beauvoir of complicity. She claims the book stereotypes and essentializes the old, and she describes it as "an act of collaboration with social stigma and injustice."[23] However, this judgment is not justified.

It is true that Beauvoir herself undeniably shares in the profound terror of old age that pervades modern society. In a well-known passage at the end *Force of Circumstance* she writes that:

> [Old age] has got me now. I often stop, flabbergasted at the sight of this incredible thing that serves me as a face [...]. But when I look [in the mirror], I see my face as it was, attacked by the pox of time for which there is no cure.[24]

However, where she differs from most is that this terror of her own aging does not lead her to flee it by casting the old as Other. To the contrary, her goal is the very opposite: to make us confront old age by disclosing the humanity of the old, by breaking what she calls the "conspiracy of silence" that surrounds them (OA 2; V 8). Her aim, Beauvoir says in the Introduction, is to make the voice of the old heard: "if their voice was heard, one would be forced to acknowledge that this is a *human* voice. I shall force my readers to listen to it" (OA 2 TM, emphasis added; V 8).

In *The Ethics of Ambiguity*, to recall, the sub-man chooses to make his world a desert. His bad faith, his apathy, empties it of passion, of love, and desire, and he "makes his way across a world deprived of meaning toward death" (EA 45). Whether sooner or later, in old age most come to exist in a similarly meaningless desert, but they are not responsible for this situation. For most, ambitious projects of the kind Beauvoir values will become impossible, whether in early old age for the many or later on for a privileged few, and whether initiated by social alterity or/and by increasing physical or cognitive debilities and other losses. This is why Beauvoir does not accuse the old (except for a few privileged misanthropes) of inauthenticity: it is inappropriate to treat their various "defensive strategies," their resignation, their apathy, and so forth as manifestations of bad faith or complicity since they lack the potential for authentic free action.

However, in affirming the humanity of those who no longer can engage in meaningful projects, Beauvoir complicates the distinctions between freedom and flight, between authenticity and inauthenticity, that had long lain at the heart of her ethics. As I have argued in previous work, Beauvoir became increasingly aware of how *la force des choses*, the weight of situations, can constrain freedom, foreclosing projects and even, at times, limiting the possibility of conceiving them.[25] Even so, it is not only in her early "moral essays" of the 1940s but still in works of the 1960s—such as *Les belles images* [1966] and *The Woman Destroyed* [1967]—that her thinking hinges upon the play between the opposing poles of authentic free action and inauthentic flight. Indeed, this antithesis is still operational in *Old Age* itself. She begins the book by denouncing the bad faith embraced by younger people who seek to flee their own immanent old age by objectifying those whom they view as already old. "Let us cease cheating [*cessons de tricher*]," she writes in the Introduction:

> the meaning of our life is in question in the future that awaits us; we do not know who we are if we ignore what we will become. Let us recognize ourselves in this old man, in this old woman. We must do so if we want to take up our human condition in its totality.
>
> *(OA 5 TM; V 11)*

Yet, at the same time, in Beauvoir's portrayal of old age itself there emerges an asymmetry between the "either/or" poles of the antithesis. "Yes," authentic projects do remain possible, at least for the privileged few, until ill-health or other difficulties overtake them. But "no," neither the privileged, when this occurs, nor the majority, whose world has for much longer been a desert, can be accused of inauthenticity since their situation precludes a flight from freedom on their part. *Old Age*, I suggest, thus marks the culmination of a long trajectory in Beauvoir's thinking. Over time, the clear antithesis between authentic action and inauthenticity, which had once shaped her moral universe, had already become increasingly blurred. Now, since the old are also "human," her claim that authentic projects are what give meaning to human existence is put into question.

And What about Freedom? Rethinking "the Project"

Should we then seek for qualities other than authentic freedom, as Beauvoir conceives it, that could give meaning to human existence? And does Beauvoir herself offer any openings towards such alternatives? Some scholars have explored these possibilities. For example, Debra Bergoffen has argued that a "muted voice" also runs throughout Beauvoir's work that affirms not "the ethic of the project" but that of "the disclosure of being"; and Sara Cohen-Shabot has argued that a "crack" in Beauvoir's project-oriented notion of freedom can be found in her treatment of eroticism in *The Second Sex*.[26] Addressing *Old Age* more directly, Kathleen Lennon and Anthony Wilde have argued that, although Beauvoir's phenomenology reveals the meaningful qualities of affect, she cannot develop an ontological structure that adequately accommodates them because she remains too enmeshed in Sartrean binaries.[27]

Such readings, arguing that meaningful human existence does not necessarily lie in the authentic project alone, offer valuable paths of inquiry that should be pursued further. However, I want to conclude by tentatively and briefly exploring a different (although certainly not mutually exclusive) path: by proposing that we could rethink the notion of the project in less demanding terms than Beauvoir's. I shall also suggest that, against the grain of her more explicit and emphatic declarations, Beauvoir herself offers some resources for doing so.

Beauvoir is surely correct (to repeat) that "projects have only to do with our activities [and] undergoing age is not an activity" (OA 540; V 566–7). For Beauvoir, authentic action lies in projects that transcend the given world, opening toward the future and toward others. However, the scope of "action" can be very variable and actions that do not fully meet Beauvoir's ambitious criteria, and that may appear small or even trivial to an external viewer, may be profoundly meaningful to the doer. Think, for example, of a person who is bed-bound and significantly paralyzed after a stroke: for such a person to wish to drink from a glass beside the bed, to struggle to lift it, and then to take it to their lips and drink is, indeed, a project—and a demanding one. Although it may not directly engage with other individuals, it still involves a future-oriented intentionality and the transcendence of a given situation—integral aspects of the project.

Many of Beauvoir's own phenomenological descriptions can also be interpreted more positively, as demonstrating how, within a highly constrained situation, a project remains possible. To recall, she writes that in old age the body can become more an "obstacle" than an "instrument" for our projects (OA 317; V 336). Then, the "coefficient of adversity" in things increases, so that "streets [are] more dangerous to cross, parcels heavier to carry," and so forth (OA 304 TM; V 336). Beauvoir presents such encounters with adversity only negatively: "The world is filled with traps. [...] Every moment difficulties arise, and any mistake is severely punished," she writes (OA 304; V 323). However, such challenges can sometimes (although not always) be met by meaningful, if apparently small-scale, projects. For example, time and space that may appear radically shrunken to an "active" observer may be very differently experienced by one who moves far more slowly, hobbling across a road in the face of approaching traffic. Carefully judging speeds and distances, perhaps signaling to oncoming drivers that they must slow down for you, safely moving one's body across the wide, hazardous space should, indeed, be viewed as a project: an intentional and future-oriented action that transcends a given situation and that constitutes a meaningful achievement for the doer.

Moreover, what Beauvoir describes as futile "attitudes of protest" on the part of the old may also be viewed as projects that seek to engage directly with others: they aim to communicate, calling for—and even demanding—a response from them. The miser, the hypochondriac, the person who refuses to wash or who strips off their clothing is often making demands, be they symbolic and/or practical, for recognition. That such actions may be self-defeating if they elicit a yet-further objectifying response from others is not to say they lack a certain freedom—for, as Beauvoir had argued many years previously in *The Ethics of Ambiguity*, the "element of failure" is a condition of human life itself (EA 157).

Sadly, a time may arrive for some when physical or cognitive impairments become so extreme that anything that could be considered a project, even within my less-ambitious formulation, might appear to be impossible. Yet between Beauvoir's too-ambitious notion of the project and such a condition there lies a wide in-between realm. Here, within many constraints, a certain freedom, neither authentic nor inauthentic, may still be said to persist.

Acknowledgements

Many thanks for their valuable comments and suggestions to Meryl Altman, Sara Cohen Shabot, Charlotte Knowles, Kathleen Lennon, and the editors of this volume, Liesbeth Schoonheim and Karen Vintges.

Notes

1 Simone de Beauvoir, *The Second Sex*, trans. Constance Borde and Sheila Malovany-Chevallier (New York: Knopf, 2010), 6. Referenced in the text hereafter as TSS.
2 Simone de Beauvoir, *Old Age*, trans. Patrick O'Brian (London: André Deutsch and George Weidenfeld and Nicolson, 1972), 6. Referenced in the text hereafter as OA. Simone de Beauvoir, *La Vieillesse* (Paris: Gallimard, 1970), 10. Referenced in the text hereafter as V. Modifications of the English translation of this and other works will be indicated by the abbreviation TM.
3 Beauvoir considers women's old age only briefly in *The Second Sex* (619–637) and even less fully in *Old Age*. As a personal experience, old age is of as much concern to women as men, she says. However, from the perspective of their societal roles and influence on history, "old age is a problem concerning men" (OA 89–90; V 99). Much of what Beauvoir writes in the second part of *Old Age*—"Being-in-the-world," about the lived experience of old age—also pertains to women (and to members of minority ethnic and racial groups in modern Western society). There are, of course, also profound differences that she does not address. However, in what follows, I shall generally bracket the problem of her disregard of women. For an important co-reading of *The Second Sex* and *Old Age*, see Penelope Deutscher, "The Sex of Age and the Age of Sex," in *Simone de Beauvoir's Philosophy of Age: Gender, Ethics and Time*, ed. Silvia Stoller (Berlin: De Gruyter, 2014), 29–42.
4 "Woman is an existent who is asked to make herself an object" (TSS 491); and "for a woman to accomplish her femininity, she is required to make herself an object and to make herself prey; that is, she must renounce her claims as a sovereign subject" (TSS 723). A woman is thus an ontologically divided existent, but she has the freedom to resist or to be complicit in her objectification. For a careful documentation of how Beauvoir frequently uses the notion of "making oneself an object" see Jennifer McWeeny, "The Second Sex of Consciousness: A New Temporality and Ontology for Beauvoir's 'Becoming a Woman'," in *On ne naît pas femme: on le devient: The Life of a Sentence*, ed. Bonnie Mann and Martina Ferrari (New York: Oxford University Press, 2017), 240–45.
5 As Beauvoir says in the Preface, "Every human situation can be viewed from without—seen from the point of view of an outsider—or from within, insofar as the subject assumes and at the same time transcends it" (OA 10; V 16).
6 Transgender individuals may be exceptions here, an issue not discussed by Beauvoir.
7 She expands: "In our society the old person is designated as such by custom, by the behavior of others, by vocabulary itself. This reality must be assumed. There is an infinite number of ways of doing so, but none will enable me myself to coincide with the reality that I assume" (OA 291 TM; V 309). For Sartre's account of unrealizables, on which Beauvoir draws here in an abbreviated form, see Jean-Paul Sartre, *Being and Nothingness*, trans. Sarah Richmond (Abingdon, UK: Routledge, 2018), 684–9.

8 For the passage Beauvoir cites here, see Jean-Paul Sartre, *Critique of Dialectical Reason*, vol. I, trans. Alan Sheridan-Smith (London: New Left Books, 1976), 112–13.
9 Sara Heinämaa has argued that "our own bodies are always given to us in this double way: originally and immediately as systems of sensibility and motility, and secondarily and mediately—via our relations with others—as perceptual and movable objects." See Sara Heinämaa, "Transformations of Old Age: Selfhood Normativity, and Time," in *Simone de Beauvoir's Philosophy of Age: Gender, Ethics, and Time*, ed. Silvia Stoller (Berlin: De Gruyter, 2014), 173. The ambiguities that are entailed in this "double" experience of embodiment are integral to all human existence, but they are experienced particularly acutely in the transition to old age. See also, on this doubling experience in old age, Sarah Clark Miller, "The Lived Experience of Doubling: Simone de Beauvoir's Phenomenology of Old Age," in *The Existential Phenomenology of Simone de Beauvoir*, ed. Wendy O'Brien and Lester Embree (Dordrecht: Kluwer, 2001), 127–47.
10 "I bear from the past all the movements [*les mécanismes*] that my body has accumulated, the cultural tools I use, my knowledge and my ignorance, my relationships with the outside world, my activities, my obligations. Everything that I have ever done has been taken back by the past and has become reified there under the form of what Sartre calls the practico-inert […]. By his praxis every man achieves his objectification in the world and becomes alienated in it [… and] the more advanced in age, the more heavily the pressure of the practico-inert weighs on us" (OA 372–3 TM; V 395).
11 "I shall examine what happens to the individual's relationship with his body and his image during his last years, to his relationship with time, history and his own praxis, and his relationship with others and the outside world" (OA 279; V 300).
12 Beauvoir seeks to address this drawback by describing the lives of retired working people indirectly, by summarizing expert surveys and reports on their conditions. But their voices are presented only in brief snippets taken from survey data (see especially Chapter 4), and they are cited only to illustrate how their condition leads to a vain and futile old age, to "boredom and a feeling of worthlessness" (OA 267 TM; V 285). She also describes her horror when she visited a public assistance institution for the old: "I saw human beings reduced to total abjection," she writes (OA 258 TM; V 276). She reports in detail on their degraded and degrading living conditions—but we do not hear directly from the inmates themselves. Her later participation in the film *A Walk through the Land of Old Age* [1974], in which the voices of the inmates of an institution are directly heard, goes some way toward filling this lacuna. See the transcript by Alexander Hertich, in *Simone de Beauvoir: Political Writings*, ed. Margaret A. Simons and Marybeth Timmermann (Urbana: University of Illinois Press, 2012), 329–63.
13 Simone de Beauvoir, *The Ethics of Ambiguity*, trans. Bernard Frechtman (New York: Citadel, 1967), 45. Referenced in the text hereafter as EA.
14 "The habit of having habits," as Beauvoir nicely puts it, can lead them "to persist in meaningless obsession" (OA 468 TM; V 492) and to refuse new experiences.
15 However, Beauvoir also notes that, although the security sought through habit cannot be fully achieved, still, certain kinds of habit can actually make life richer. There can be, she says, "a poetry to habit" (always taking afternoon tea or walking in one's garden are examples she gives) when "some object, possession or activity acquires the power of revealing the whole world to us." There can be a heightening (she calls it a "crystallization") of experience, in which "the present moment is the past brought to life again, the future anticipated; I experience both together in the for-itself mode—I reach (or I *seem* to reach, for the synthesis is not in fact accomplished) that dimension of being which the existent seeks" (OA

468; V 492–3). Taking afternoon tea or walking in one's garden are not, however, common activities of the impoverished old.

16 Beauvoir's specific examples here come from the most excluded, from those warehoused in care-homes for the impoverished old, or who are in other situations of extreme dependency; however the behaviors she describes are not confined to them alone.

17 Beauvoir argues that there are some "limit-situations" where this "return to the positive" is not possible. In such instance she declares suicide to be "the definitive rejection of the situation" (EA 32). This is a rather formalistic claim on Beauvoir's part; moreover, in extremely dehumanized or debilitated situations old people often lack the means or agency to end their lives.

18 Some women, Beauvoir notes, are able to overthrow conventional feminine roles in old age, now no longer having to care for children or to be subordinate to their husbands (OA 488–9; V 513–14). She had made a similar point in *The Second Sex*, while also saying that very few women were in a position to benefit from their new-found freedom (TSS 626–7).

19 The lines are from *Leaves of Grass*. Beauvoir cites from a French translation and I restore the original English wording here.

20 "Pyrrhus and Cineas," in *Simone de Beauvoir Philosophical Writings*, ed. Margaret A. Simons (Urbana: University of Illinois Press, 2004), 90.

21 Ibid., 140, 137. There is an important point of departure from the early Sartre here, in her insistence that it only through others that an open future is possible for us.

22 In addition, and as earlier chapters of the book that draw on ethnographic and historical material make clear, the social alterity of the old is not a phenomenon of modern market societies alone.

23 Martha C. Nussbaum, "Aging and Control in *King Lear*—and the Dangers of Generalization," in *Aging Thoughtfully: Conversations about Retirement, Romance, Wrinkles, and Regret*, by Martha C. Nussbaum and Saul Levmore (New York: Oxford University Press, 2017), 20.

24 Simone de Beauvoir, *Force of Circumstance*, vol. II, trans. Richard Howard (New York: Paragon, 1992), 378.

25 See Sonia Kruks, *Situation and Human Existence: Freedom, Subjectivity and Society* (London: Unwin Hyman, 1990; reprinted Abingdon, UK: Routledge, 2019), 83–112.

26 Debra Bergoffen, *The Philosophy of Simone de Beauvoir: Gendered Phenomenologies, Erotic Generosities* (Albany: State University of New York Press, 1997); Sara Cohen Shabot, "How Free is Beauvoir's Freedom? Unchaining Beauvoir through the Erotic Body," *Feminist Theory* 17, no. 3 (2016): 269–84.

27 Kathleen Lennon and Anthony Wilde, "Alienation and Affectivity: Beauvoir, Sartre and Levinas on the Ageing Body," *Sartre Studies International*, 25, no. 1 (2019): 35–51.

References

Beauvoir, Simone de. *The Ethics of Ambiguity*. Translated by Bernard Frechtman. New York: Citadel, 1967. [Original French publication 1947]

Beauvoir, Simone de. *La Vieillesse*. Paris: Gallimard, 1970.

Beauvoir, Simone de. *Old Age*. Translated by Patrick O'Brian. London: André Deutsch and George Weidenfeld and Nicolson, 1972. [The US edition is titled *The Coming of Age*]

Beauvoir, Simone de. *Force of Circumstance*, vol. II. Translated by Richard Howard. New York: Paragon, 1992.

Beauvoir, Simone de. "Pyrrhus and Cineas." In *Simone de Beauvoir: Philosophical Writings*, edited by Margaret A. Simons, 77–149. Urbana: University of Illinois Press, 2004. [Original French publication 1944]

Beauvoir, Simone de. *The Second Sex*. Translated by Constance Borde and Sheila Malovany-Chevallier. New York: Knopf, 2010. [Original French publication 1949; 2 vols.]

Beauvoir, Simone de. "A Walk Through the Land of Old Age." In *Simone de Beauvoir: Political Writings*, edited by Margaret Simons and Marybeth Timmermann, 329–363. Urbana: University of Illinois Press, 2012. [Transcript of 1974 film script]

Bergoffen, Debra, *The Philosophy of Simone de Beauvoir: Gendered Phenomenologies, Erotic Generosities*. Albany: State University of New York Press, 1997.

Deutscher, Penelope. "The Sex of Age and the Age of Sex." In *Simone de Beauvoir's Philosophy of Age: Gender, Ethics, and Time*, edited by Silvia Stoller, 29–42. Berlin: De Gruyter, 2014.

Heinämaa, Sara. "Transformations of Old Age: Selfhood Normativity, and Time." In *Simone de Beauvoir's Philosophy of Age: Gender, Ethics, and Time*, edited by Silvia Stoller, 167–189. Berlin: De Gruyter, 2014.

Kruks, Sonia. "Beauvoir: The Weight of Situation." In *Situation and Human Existence: Freedom, Subjectivity and Society*, 83–112. London: Unwin Hyman, 1990; reprinted Abingdon, UK: Routledge, 2019.

Lennon, Kathleen and Anthony Wilde. "Alienation and Affectivity: Beauvoir, Sartre and Levinas on the Ageing Body." *Sartre Studies International*, 25, no. 1 (2019): 35–51.

McWeeny, Jennifer. "The Second Sex of Consciousness: A New Temporality and Ontology for Beauvoir's 'Becoming a Woman'." In *On ne naît pas femme: on le devient: The Life of a Sentence*," edited by Bonnie Mann and Martina Ferrari, 231–273. New York: Oxford University Press, 2017.

Miller, Sarah Clark. "The Lived Experience of Doubling: Simone de Beauvoir's Phenomenology of Old Age." In *The Existential Phenomenology of Simone de Beauvoir*, edited by Wendy O'Brien and Lester Embree, 127–147. Dordrecht: Kluwer, 2001.

Nussbaum, Martha C. "Aging and Control in *King Lear*—and the Dangers of Generalization." In *Aging Thoughtfully: Conversations about Retirement, Romance, Wrinkles, and Regret*, by Martha C. Nussbaum and Saul Levmore, 8–23. New York: Oxford University Press, 2017.

Sartre, Jean-Paul. *Critique of Dialectical Reason*, vol. I. Translated by Alan Sheridan-Smith. London: New Left Books, 1976. [Original French publication 1960]

Sartre, Jean-Paul. *Being and Nothingness*. Translated by Sarah Richmond. Abingdon, UK: Routledge, 2018. [Original French publication 1943]

Shabot, Sara Cohen. "How Free is Beauvoir's Freedom? Unchaining Beauvoir through the Erotic Body." *Feminist Theory* 17, no. 3 (2016): 269–284.

8

EXPECTANT ANXIETY IN *THE SECOND SEX*

Kate Kirkpatrick

In this chapter I argue that Simone de Beauvoir's chapter on 'The Mother' in *The Second Sex* describes but does not name a dimension of the subjective experience of some pregnant persons that I will call 'expectant anxiety.' After some brief comments on Beauvoir's use of the term *l'angoisse* in this chapter, I will situate my analysis in two phenomenological accounts of pregnancy, namely those of Iris Marion Young and Caroline Lundquist.[1] I will then turn to *The Second Sex* and *Old Age* to develop the notion of expectant anxiety and its potential to illuminate the phenomenology of pregnancy and the variety of women's experiences.

In part because of debates about the metaphysical status of the foetus and the morality or legality of abortion, many philosophical discussions of pregnancy (e.g. those of Young and Lundquist) are framed in terms of a given pregnancy's being 'chosen' or 'unchosen.' The concept I call 'expectant anxiety' problematizes the polarizing rhetoric of 'choice' by attending to the subjective experience of pregnancy, which includes multiple metamorphoses: whether or not a pregnancy is carried to term, each pregnancy occurs in a particular human situation and includes bodily transformation, navigating social expectations, considerations of material conditions, and facing a range of radically different (unknown and, in many cases, unknowable) concrete possibilities for one's own life and those of a possible human other. I draw on contemporary cultural and literary representations of pregnancy, abortion, and miscarriage to illustrate this concept. These include the Japanese Buddhist practice of *mizuko kuyō* and two novelistic depictions of infertility and abortion—Ayobami Adebayo's *Stay With Me* [2017] and Britt Bennett's *The Mothers* [2016].

To give some indication of the urgency of the ethical, political, and medical contexts in which this concept may be needed, contemporary data show that death in childbirth is nearly six times more likely than death by intimate partner violence;[2] there is a global maternal mental health crisis; and the leading cause of death in the year after childbirth in many high-income countries is suicide. As such, I take it that providing conceptual resources for social interpretation remains a much-needed feminist intervention.

Anxiety: Lost in Translation?

It is well established that the first English translator of *The Second Sex*, H. M. Parshley, cut Beauvoir's text extensively and did not translate her philosophical terminology accurately or consistently.[3] The chapter on 'The Mother' (*La Mère*), and the concept of *l'angoisse* in it, is an interesting case in point. 'Anxiety' is a core concept in the philosophical anthropologies of Kierkegaard, Heidegger, and Sartre; *l'angoisse* is its common French translation. However Parshley rendered both the French words *l'angoisse* and *l'anxiété* as the English 'anxiety,' and cut large swathes of Beauvoir's citations of women and several instances of *l'angoisse*, altering the tone and content of her presentation of pregnancy. In the cases that remained, Parshley's sentences (on my reading) present women's experience of gestational or maternal anxiety as psychological or even pathological phenomena that are unworthy of philosophical reflection.[4] In Beauvoir's French, although she employs the terms relatively infrequently, she uses the term *l'angoisse* when she is discussing the subjective experience of pregnancy, and *l'anxiété* to speak of maternal experiences once the child is *ex utero*. Whether or not this indicates intent on her part to make a philosophical distinction between the two, her discussion of *l'angoisse* describes a phenomenon experienced by many pregnant persons that is distinctive from *l'angoisse* of Kierkegaard and Sartre. Moreover, naming it may usefully contribute to discussions of the variety of women's experiences in the phenomenology of pregnancy and to ameliorating the care of pregnant people.[5] To explain why I think it has this potential, I will begin with two influential phenomenological accounts of pregnant embodiment.

Two Phenomenologies of Pregnant Embodiment

In Iris Marion Young's essay "Pregnant Embodiment: Subjectivity and Alienation," first published in 1983, she seeks to redress the problematic absence of women's experience in the discourse on pregnancy by "considering some of the experiences of pregnancy from the pregnant subject's viewpoint." She confines the scope of her argument to "women in technologically sophisticated Western societies," and states a presupposition that "pregnancy can be experienced for its own sake, noticed, and savoured"—in other words, that it can be "chosen by the woman."[6]

With respect to this scope, Young's analysis has been "problematized and supplemented" by Caroline Lundquist, who wishes to develop a phenomenology of pregnancy that is inclusive of the experiences of women whose pregnancies are not *chosen*.[7] Lundquist's 2008 article "Being Torn: Toward a Phenomenology of Unwanted Pregnancy," explores the phenomena of rejected and denied pregnancy in order to "challenge the assumption that there is a narrow range of pregnancy experience that can be captured in a single, totalizing account, while acknowledging the value of expanding theoretical discourse on pregnancy via tentative descriptive categories of pregnancy experience."[8]

Young's article analyses "bodily experiences unique to pregnancy," and suggests that the pregnant subject is "decentered, split, or doubled" in several ways that challenge the phenomenological approaches to the body taken by Merleau-Ponty and others. These thinkers, Young suggests, retain a dualist idiom in speaking of the body experienced as subject or experienced as object, and "implicitly assume a unified subject and sharp distinction between transcendence and immanence."[9] Young draws on the work of Kristeva in claiming that "Reflection on the experience of pregnancy reveals a body that is decentered, myself in the mode of not being myself"[10] —and offers a phenomenological description of this (as she calls it) "revelation."

On Lundquist's view, however, Young's account needs to be supplemented by a recognition that, "For the pregnant subject who never positively accepts her pregnancy, the sense of splitting subjectivity can be radically unlike the experiential mother-child differentiation of chosen pregnancy Young describes."[11] Lundquist explores several types of rejected and denied pregnancies, including cases which end in maternal neonaticide or infanticide, noting that researchers face a significant difficulty in exploring such marginal experiences: namely, that women rarely speak about them. She writes that it is hardly surprising that:

> women who radically reject or conceal their pregnancies are loathe to speak openly about their pregnancy experiences [...]; more striking is that women seem reluctant even to express ambivalence regarding their pregnancies, despite the fact that ambivalent feelings are an ordinary part of most women's pregnancy experience.[12]

In what follows, therefore, I offer a conceptual tool which is intended to accommodate the reputedly too-positive account Young offers, and the overwhelmingly negative, 'marginalized' cases of pregnancy highlighted by Lundquist, but which contests the paradigm of choice on which both rely. In order to develop this notion of 'expectant anxiety' we will now turn to Beauvoir's account of pregnancy in *The Second Sex*.[13]

The Second Sex

Beauvoir's writing on pregnancy and motherhood went through a period of being rejected on the basis that she reduces pregnancy to a "uniformly and inevitably negative experience" where biology is "inherently oppressive for all women, thereby ignoring differences between women, as well as the complex interaction between corporeality, psychology, and culture."[14] Literal readings of Beauvoir's negative language—which either do not consider or dismiss the possibility that she is reporting or parroting patriarchal evaluations of pregnancy rather than endorsing them—have led some feminist readers to characterize her account as "a process without a subject"[15] or to question whether Beauvoir's "own inexperience and prejudice in this area make her treat maternity in an altogether too idiosyncratic way" to be of use today.[16]

I have argued elsewhere that this is not the full story, drawing on *Old Age* to claim that Beauvoir's account is more nuanced than it is widely credited to be.[17] It is significant that Beauvoir's account does not mask the dark side of pregnancy or motherhood under patriarchy and inadequate material conditions. Not being a mother herself (insofar as we define that as someone who has carried a pregnancy to term and birthed a child), she drew on other women's voices to show that "Pregnancy and motherhood are lived in very different ways depending on whether they take place in revolt, resignation, satisfaction, or enthusiasm" (TSS 546 TM; DS II 339). Her explicit intent was to banish "dangerous misconceptions" (TSS 579) about motherhood; and, consequently, she did not censor the ambivalence that Lundquist and others rightly point out as having been lacking in women's discourse on the subject.[18]

On Beauvoir's account, pregnancy, like any bodily metamorphosis, "can only be understood as a whole: [as] not only a biological, but also a cultural fact."[19] It is experienced differently by different women, both physiologically and psychologically. In *The Second Sex* Beauvoir notes that some women feel creative power during childbirth—they feel "they truly accomplished a voluntary and productive piece of work"; she also notes that "many others feel passive, a suffering and tortured instrument" (TSS 563). Both the 'chosen' and 'unchosen' (or 'active' and 'passive') aspects feature, to use the language of Young and Lundquist, because both are present in the lived experience of pregnant embodiment—sometimes in a single pregnancy.[20] But these lived experiences cannot be analysed without an account of a woman's *situation*, because every individual is conditioned by the theoretical and practical attitudes of her society and her concrete material circumstances.

In *Old Age* Beauvoir rejects Cicero's dictum that "everything that is natural must be considered good." Every metamorphosis, she writes "has something frightening about it."[21] In the metamorphosis of ageing, the experience of temporality is "profoundly altered"[22] for the reason (among others) that death draws nearer. "For human reality," Beauvoir writes, "existing means existing in time: in the present we look towards the future by means of plans that go beyond our past, in which our activities fall lifeless, frozen, and loaded with passive demands." Age changes our relationship with time, our horizon of possibilities, and our being-for-others; as the years go by "our future shortens, while our past grows heavier."[23] In one sense we are always being-towards-death, but, in another, that term must be understood contextually.

To return to *The Second Sex*, Sara Heinämaa argues that Beauvoir's main idea is not that the feminine body is invalid, but that it is experienced differently to the masculine body. As Beauvoir writes, "Woman, like man, *is* her body; but her body is something else than she is."[24] In particular, Heinämaa argues that there is a difference in the "temporal structures" of masculine and feminine experience.[25]

Expectant Anxiety

If one takes seriously Heinämaa's suggestion that embodied experiences of temporality differ, then pregnancy—as a 'temporal structure' of some embodied experience which we might call being-towards-birth (although not in Heidegger's or Arendt's senses)—arguably brings with it a distinct variety of anxiety—expectant anxiety—that contests the scope or normativity of the concept of anxiety as used in Beauvoir's phenomenological and existentialist predecessors. So let us turn to that concept before examining Beauvoir's contestation of it.

The term *l'angoisse* was in use in the 1940s in physiological and metaphysical senses, and I will read Beauvoir's use of it in light of both. *L'angoisse* was used in the 1930s to translate the work by Kierkegaard known in English as *The Concept of Anxiety* (three separate translations of which appeared in France in 1935) and in Sartre's discussion of *l'angoisse* in his *War Diaries* and *Being and Nothingness*. However, contemporary studies such as Juliette Favez-Boutonnier's 1945 *L'angoisse* show that this concept was the subject of extended discussion and debate in French philosophy and psychology in the late 19th and early 20th centuries prior to Kierkegaard's (or Heidegger's) reception—when, for example, Pierre Janet claimed that *l'angoisse* was "fear without an object."[26]

We know Beauvoir was familiar with the concept of *l'angoisse* of her philosophical predecessors (and later existentialist cliché) and that she sent Sartre his first Kierkegaard, writing to Sartre that she herself had "heaps of books by him" as well as Jean Wahl's essays.[27] Bearing this in mind, let us recall Beauvoir's statement about the difference between male and female embodiment—"Woman, like man, *is* her body; but her body is something else than she is";[28] and also Young's statement that: "Reflection on the experience of pregnancy reveals a body that is decentered, myself in the mode of not being myself."[29] And now let us turn to the section of *Being and Nothingness* in which Sartre describes the anxiety of existing in time:

> I *am* not the self which I will be. First I am not that self because time separates me from it. Secondly, I am not that self because what I am is not the foundation of what I will be. Finally I am not that self because no actual existent can determine strictly what I am going to be. Yet as I am already what I will be (otherwise I would not be interested in any one being more than another), *I am the self which I will be, in the mode of not being it.*[30]

On the surface, at least, Beauvoir's and Young's definitions of pregnant female embodiment bear a striking (indeed, almost verbatim!) resemblance to this Sartrean formulation of *l'angoisse*.

For Sartre and for Kierkegaard, anxiety is the reflective apprehension of freedom; and it must not be confused with fear, which is provoked by an empirical object: "fear is fear of beings in the world whereas [anxiety] is [anxiety] before myself," Sartre writes—"[a] situation provokes fear if there is a possibility of my life being changed from without; my being provokes [anxiety] to the extent that I distrust myself and my own reactions in that situation."[31] Anxiety does not correspond to an object encountered in the world, but rather to my own freedom in it.

For Beauvoir too anxiety is *revelatory*, and the content of its revelation is freedom's possibility: *l'angoisse* is my consciousness of *my* concrete possibilities, and is not, like fear, determined by foreign causes. In the context of pregnancy, however, a question immediately arises: what, for an expectant person, is a 'foreign cause'? When I reflectively apprehend my freedom, for *whose possibilities* am I anxious—my own or those of this freedom *in potentia* within me? How recognizable as *mine*, after birth, will my possibilities be? Beauvoir writes that:

> Pregnancy is above all a drama playing itself out in the woman between her and herself [*entre soi et soi*]. She experiences it both as an enrichment and a mutilation; the fetus is part of her body, and it is a parasite exploiting her; she possesses it, and she is possessed by it.
>
> (*TSS 551–552; DS II 345*)

Whether or not Beauvoir endorses what contemporary metaphysicians call the foetal container model of pregnancy, through the literary strategies of example and direct citation she illustrates that women's subjective experience of the foetus varies: it is not always lived as something 'in' the woman's body; for some, the foetus *is* part of the woman's body or its processes. Moreover, for many the way the pregnant body is experienced subjectively changes during the process of pregnancy.

Beauvoir describes 'early,' 'middle,' and 'late' stages of pregnancy in terms that map roughly on to common temporal expectations of the first, second, and third trimesters. The early stages are characterised by "a mixture of desire and anguish" (TSS 555). Many women desire pregnancy and motherhood—whether because they have chosen to value this intersubjective possibility for themselves or because they have been encouraged to see it as their biological destiny or a source of social glory. But in the early stages of pregnancy its physical outcome is not given and its moral meaning is undecided. The possibilities of miscarriage and, for some, abortion are live.[32] Beauvoir describes variations in women's experience at this stage, but they are variations on a theme: *l'angoisse*. Some women deliberate about abortion in "anguish and fear" (TSS 543); some experience "anguish that they will not carry their pregnancy to term" (TSS 549); and for some anguish is so intense that Beauvoir takes it to cause miscarriage (TSS 548). I take it that expectant anxiety accompanies pregnancy whether it is aborted, miscarried, or 'kept'; its only condition is that the person is conscious of being pregnant and aware that the possibilities of pregnancy are neither merely natural nor entirely within the control of her will.

Beauvoir's chapter on motherhood famously begins with a discussion of abortion; and it is no concession to conservatives, in my view, that she so clearly distinguishes abortion from contraception. While she rejects the view that abortion is 'an assassination,' she claims that it cannot be assimilated to the category 'contraception' because "an event has happened" which is the beginning of a development that can be stopped. Moreover, without condemnation, she acknowledges that some women who have had abortions are haunted by the memory of the child that was not.[33]

Men, Beauvoir writes—*les hommes*, in the masculine universal, so it is unclear whether she means only males or *human beings*—have a tendency to take abortion too lightly, to see it as something to which nature has doomed women. We are mistaken to do so, she argues, because 'nature' is not responsible for individual conceptions or for all of the material and social conditions of women's lives: those who take abortion lightly fail to take into account the values that are engaged (TSS 545; DS II 337). Could it be that, for Beauvoir, pregnancy is not just a singular experience of female bodies on account of a difference of "temporal structures," as Heinämaa argues, but that it is also a singular axiological experience?

The values engaged in any deliberation about pregnancy and abortion will depend on the natural history of the woman in question. They may concern her material or social circumstances, not wanting to have a child or be a mother, feeling incapable of providing for a child's needs, foetal malformation, health risks to herself, and many more possibilities besides. She may desire motherhood but not yet; she may fear that when—or if—she is ready her body will no longer be able. What Beauvoir calls "the moral aspect of the drama" of pregnancy "is more or less intensely felt depending on the circumstances" (TSS 544).

Beauvoir's use of direct citation shows some of the variation of women's experiences and evaluations of abortion; nearly three-quarters of a century later we have more, and more diverse, testimony on which to draw. Consider the Japanese practice of *mizuko kuyō*: a memorial service (*kuyō*) for the unborn dead (*mizuko*), whether miscarried, stillborn, or aborted. The practice has roots in Japanese Buddhism, but over recent centuries it has changed in response to women's material conditions and reproductive legislation.[34] In the Edo period, for example, famine sometimes led to infanticide and abortion, and the practice was expanded to cover deaths of these kinds. In the middle of the twentieth century, Japan had a population crisis: in 1946, 10 million people were at risk of starvation, and in the half decade between 1945 and 1950, the population increased by 11 million. In 1948, Japan became one of the first countries to legalize abortion; the pill, by contrast, would not be legalized there until 1999.[35] Alongside abortion, in the second half of the twentieth century the practice of *mizuko kuyō* became particularly visible.

Specific elements of the ceremony vary, but it is common for temples to offer the mourner a statue representing Jizō—the bodhisattva who is believed to protect children—which is then displayed in the temple garden.

At the very least, I take it that modern 'Gardens of Unborn Children' are potent material reminders that the 'choice' to terminate a pregnancy does not preclude grief—not necessarily for the action itself, but for a situation of

FIGURE 8.1 Jizō statues at Zōjō-ji Temple, Japan. Gorgo/Public Domain

foreclosed possibilities, for so few alternatives when "for the human species nature can never be separated from artifice" (TSS 561).

In cases where pregnancy is 'carried to term,' Beauvoir writes that, as the pregnancy proceeds, "the relation between the mother and foetus changes. It is solidly settled in the maternal womb, the two organisms adapt to each other and there are biological exchanges between them allowing the woman to regain her balance" (TSS 557). Later, the separation between mother and child begins:

> Women experience his first movement differently, his kick knocking at the doors of the world, knocking against the wall of the womb that encloses him away from the world. Some women marvel at this signal announcing the presence of an autonomous life; others think of themselves with repugnance as the receptacle of a foreign individual.
>
> (TSS 560)

In juxtaposing an unexpected teenage pregnancy with a wanted mature one, Britt Bennett's novel 2016 novel *The Mothers* offers a contemporary American illustration of the axiological complexity of pregnancy and the hypocrisy many women experience between the values professed about motherhood and the actions expected of women—in this case, in an African American Christian community. As the novel's protagonist, Nadia, puts it—after years of concealed pain: "Magic you wanted was a miracle, magic you didn't want was a haunting."[36]

Beauvoir herself employs language of the miraculous and religious in this chapter—seemingly without irony or the other techniques of authorial distance that she employs so liberally elsewhere in *The Second Sex*. It is a "strange miracle" (TSS 563) to hold a being formed in and coming out of oneself. In one sense, Beauvoir claims,

> the mystery of incarnation is repeated in each woman; every child who is born is a god who becomes man; he could not realize himself as consciousness and freedom if he did not come into the world; the mother lends herself to this mystery, but she does not control it; the supreme truth of this being taking shape in her womb escapes her.
>
> (TSS 553)

At times, Beauvoir writes, the pregnant person may feel like neither subject nor object: "[She] is no longer an object subjugated by a subject; nor is she any longer a subject *anguished by her freedom*, she is this equivocal reality: life."[37] But this, Beauvoir says, is an illusion (TSS 553). Some women feel justified by the feeling that they are 'life'; but on Beauvoir's view it is bad faith—and not all women succeed in believing it. In contexts where women are encouraged to see maternity as destiny, it is a pervasive temptation. But, rather than flee freedom and the ambivalence that accompanies ambiguity, on Beauvoir's view authenticity requires that we assume it. No woman is merely life or pure object; she is a free existent, a subject—but in pregnancy she lives a singular subjective experience that many human beings do not share: her freedom is transcended by her body (TSS 552, 554) and the emergence of another. Some experience this bodily transcendence as immanence: "Alienated in her body and her social dignity, the mother has the pacifying illusion of feeling that she is a being *in itself*, a ready-made *value*" (TSS 553; italics original). But not all do: the dancer Isadora Duncan is cited as a counterexemplary case—a woman whose pregnancy was lived 'in anguish' (TSS 562, TM; DS II 358).

In 1949, Beauvoir seems optimistic that birth control and legal abortion would allow women to control their pregnancies freely, that motherhood can be "freely chosen" (TSS 776). But a problem with this idea of 'free control' or, to use the language of Young and Lundquist, 'choice,' is that to choose pregnancy is to choose the unknown. Even if one leaves aside the situation in which the choice to become or remain pregnant is made—the importance of which Beauvoir and Lundquist rightly highlight—one is still left with many contingent and (possibly) unchosen outcomes. And though these outcomes—individually—can be the object of fear, collectively their possibility may provoke expectant anxiety. To 'choose' to carry a child is *always* to choose the unknown, initiating a process that will affect one's body, one's self, and one's social relations in ways that cannot be determined in advance. These three dimensions of experience are interrelated and together constitute the *situation* of an expectant person, but for ease of discussion I will distinguish briefly between them here.

In bodily terms, to give a non-exhaustive list for illustrative purposes, here are some potential consequences of choosing to be pregnant:

- Miscarriage: the UK National Health Service (NHS) estimates that 1 in 8 pregnancies miscarries; however, including miscarriages that take place before the pregnancy is known, some estimates are as high as 1 in 3.[38]
- Feeling sick: 75–88 percent of pregnant women experience some nausea in the early months.[39]
- Complications: examples include pregnancy-related pelvic girdle pain (PGP), which makes it very painful to do things like walk, go up stairs, stand on one leg, or turn over in bed.[40]
- Tearing in childbirth: according to the Royal College of Obstetricians and Gynaecologists, up to 9 in 10 will experience a perineal tear in childbirth.[41]
- Dying in childbirth: 8.8 women die per 100,000 live births in the UK—but maternal mortality rates are four times higher for black women than for white women, and twice as high for Asian women.[42]

As one contemporary memoirist put it: "Pregnant women used to be menaced by jealous spirits and malevolent gods; now they are frightened by statistics."[43] But for some, those statistics are more than ink on paper. They are lived experiences: sometimes pain in the flesh, and sometimes losses that haunt them in mind and body. A cramp may merely be a lengthening ligament, stretching to accommodate new life; but it may also be the first spasm of my body's rejection of it.

This leads us to the level of the self. At this point it is pertinent to note that in medicalized or pathologized form anxiety *is* treated in medical literature about pregnant women—it proliferates in accounts of the 'view from without' because it is linked with undesirable 'foetal outcomes,' as the literature puts it, such as lower birth weight and decreased gestation periods.[44] But it is ill-defined and difficult to 'diagnose,' for behind each piece of statistical data given above there are many pregnant subjects who have had to live 'unchosen' consequences of their 'choices'—here freedom's possibilities are far from freedom's control. The mind may be undivided in positive valence towards an end, but the means—the embodied experience that leads to a child's life—may result in negative valence or ambivalence. Any sense of negative valence towards a wanted pregnancy may be suppressed out of fear that the inevitable outcome is negative valence toward the child. As Susan Hoang has shown, for those women whose notion of feminine (or other) identity is tied to 'successful mothering' or parenting, beginning with a healthy and optimistically undertaken pregnancy, their physical pain may be amplified by the anxiety that accompanies it.[45]

This is closely linked, of course, to the social and political expectations of those who bear children. Economically, in the UK, becoming a mother renders one statistically likely to earn *half*, over one's lifetime, of what one would have earned had one remained childless. Professionally, women who have children are taken to be less committed to their work than women who do not, or men who do. Socially, a woman's relationships with her friends, family, and (where relevant) partner will alter as a result of her becoming a mother—or not. In some contexts, as Ayobami Adebayo's novel *Stay With Me* illustrates so well, infertility can lead to phantom pregnancies, ostracism, deception, and familial pressure to adopt polygamy.[46]

On the interpersonal level, there is a further factor: the baby, the person to be. As I read Beauvoir, the pregnant woman is aware that, while she may "have *her* reasons for wanting *a* child," "she cannot give to *this* other" his own *raisons d'être* (TSS 553). Her anxiety is not the reflective apprehension of her freedom alone, but in authentic motherhood also involves recognition of the responsibility that accompanies bringing a new freedom into the world—for this child is my child and, though he has his own possibilities, they are intricately intertwined with mine. Eventually her body and mine will part, but I feel her movement in my body from within—not as double sensation, but as flesh within flesh.

Empirical research shows that in the first year after a mother gives birth she may suffer not only from feelings of physical incongruity with her former self but also from feelings of loss and disorientation. According to some estimates, women in the first year of being a mother are five times more likely to suffer mental illness than at any time in their life, and 16 times more likely to develop a serious, psychotic illness.[47] In the UK, 1 in 5 women suffers perinatal depression;[48] and, as I've already mentioned, according to the World Health Organization, in "developed countries" (including the UK) suicide is the leading cause of maternal death in the year following delivery.[49]

Beauvoir's account of women as *situated* subjects shows that any 'phenomenology of pregnancy' must tread carefully because women "live their bodies differently":[50] "The mother's attitude is defined by her total situation and by the way she accepts it. It is, as we have seen, extremely variable" (TSS 567). However, shared structures of this embodied experience can be identified: the temporality of the process; the indeterminacy of its outcome, in which my freedom's concrete possibilities (*mes possibles*) are ambiguously mixed with the possibilities of another incipient freedom; and the situatedness of each expectant subject. The physical aspects of pregnancy and birth may seem unchangeable, but they are, as Beauvoir wrote and contemporary medical research confirms,[51] experienced differently "depending on whether they take place in revolt, resignation, satisfaction, or enthusiasm" (TSS 546). And that 'resignation' or 'enthusiasm' cannot be separated from the material conditions of the expectant person, the way her pregnancy is received in her body, intimate relationships, and work; her country's policies about parental leave, her society's expectations about parenting, and other women's honesty about the weight— sometimes euphorically light, sometimes lethally heavy—of bearing new life.

Conclusion: Ethical, Political, and Medical Ends

In the conclusion of Lundquist's "Being Torn," she writes that:

> Contemporary discourse on pregnancy, with its attentiveness to the positive aspects of pregnancy to the exclusion of all else, continues to silence women who cannot describe their experience in unambiguously positive terms. Until women have the vocabulary with which to express ambivalent and even negative feelings regarding pregnancies, especially unwanted pregnancies, they will continue to suffer in silence.[52]

Drawing on Beauvoir, in sketching the notion of expectant anxiety I have attempted to provide a conceptual tool with which to speak into this silence—not only of 'unwanted' pregnancies but also of the ambiguous possibility of all pregnancies where 'choice' does not preclude the unknown and the unchosen. I take it that this concept can serve ethical, political, and medical ends. Although the concrete shape of these ends must be attentive to particular situations, I hope that thinking with Beauvoir in this way may illuminate our relations with others and inform our treatment of those experiencing the pregnant temporality that is being-towards-birth.

Notes

1 Iris Marion Young, "Pregnant Embodiment: Subjectivity and Alienation," in *Throwing Like a Girl and Other Essays* (Oxford: Oxford University Press, 2005), 46–62; Caroline Lundquist, "Being Torn: Toward a Phenomenology of Unwanted Pregnancy," *Hypatia* 23 no. 3 (2008): 136–155.
2 Recent reports indicate that each day 810 people die in childbirth, while 137 women die daily of intimate partner violence, according to the World Health Organization (WHO) and the World Economic Forum (WEF) respectively. See https://www.who.int/news-room/fact-sheets/detail/maternal-mortality and https://www.weforum.org/agenda/2020/11/violence-against-women-femicide-census/.
3 For the pioneering work in this area see Margaret Simons, "The Silencing of Simone de Beauvoir: Guess What's Missing from *The Second Sex*," *Women's Studies International Forum* 6 no. 5 (1983): 559–564; Toril Moi "While We Wait: The English Translation of *The Second Sex*," *Signs* 27 no. 4 (2002): 1005–1035.
4 Fortunately for this generation of Beauvoir's readers in English, the second translation by Borde and Malovany-Chevallier more consistently renders *l'angoisse* anguish and *l'anxiété* anxiety.
5 In what follows I will sometimes speak of 'women' and 'mothers' to follow Beauvoir's language and save time; but I do not think the explanatory power of this concept is limited to those pregnant people who identify in these terms, so I will also speak of 'pregnant persons' and 'parents.'
6 Young, "Pregnant Embodiment," 46, 47.
7 Lundquist, "Being Torn," 136–137.
8 Ibid., 137.
9 Young, "Pregnant Embodiment," 47–49.
10 Ibid., 49.
11 Lundquist, "Being Torn," 141.
12 Ibid.
13 References to Beauvoir's *The Second Sex* are to *The Second Sex*, trans. Constance Borde and Sheila Malovany-Chevallier (London: Jonathan Cape, 2009) and preceded by the abbreviation TSS. When I modified the translation, I indicate this with TM. References to the original French text are to Beauvoir, *Le Deuxième Sexe*, 2 vols. (Paris: Gallimard, 1949), and cited as DS I/DS II.
14 Emily Jeremiah, "Motherhood to Mothering and Beyond: Maternity in Recent Feminist Thought," *Journal of the Association for Research on Mothering* 8 no. 1–2 (2006): 21–33, 23.
15 See Linda Zerilli, "A Process without a Subject: Simone de Beauvoir and Julia Kristeva on Maternity," *Signs* 18 no. 1 (1992): 111–135.
16 Anne Whitmarsh, *Simone de Beauvoir and the Limits of Commitment* (Cambridge: Cambridge University Press, 1981), 147.
17 Beauvoir also describes holding a being that came from oneself as a "strange miracle" (TSS 563); writes that in the right circumstances "the mother will find herself enriched by a child" (TSS 567); and, as I have argued elsewhere, includes an ethical dimension that assigns an uncommon respect to the child. See Kate

Kirkpatrick, "Past Her Prime? Simone de Beauvoir on Motherhood and Old Age," *Sophia* 53 no. 2 (2014): 275–287.
18 See, e.g., Susan Maushart's *The Mask of Motherhood* (London: Penguin, 2000). As is the case with many topics in feminist theory, discourses concerning motherhood have proliferated since the turn of the century; whether those discourses have ameliorated the experience of mothers is another question.
19 Simone de Beauvoir, *Old Age*, trans. Patrick O'Brien (London: Penguin, 1977), 20.
20 Indeed, Beauvoir herself includes mention of extreme cases of unchosenness, including maternal infanticide: "it also happens that a small strangled corpse is found in the bushes, in a ditch, or in an outhouse." See TSS 543.
21 Beauvoir, *Old Age*, 11.
22 Ibid., 484.
23 Ibid., 402.
24 Sara Heinämaa, *Toward a Phenomenology of Sexual Difference* (Lanham, MD: Rowman & Littlefield, 2003), 71, citing Beauvoir, DS I, 67/TSS 61.
25 Heinämaa, *Toward a Phenomenology*, 72.
26 Pierre Janet, *De l'angoisse à l'extase*, vol. II (Paris: Alcan, 1928), 308. In 1937 René Lacroze wrote that *l'angoisse* "indulges in a metaphysical intuition which, historically, has taken the most diverse forms: the vertigo of Pascal's infinity, the feeling of the useless becoming of things in Schopenhauer, the myth of the 'eternal return' in Nietzsche, Baudelaire's taste for nothingness, etc." See René Lacroze, *L'angoisse et l'émotion* (Paris: Boivin, 1937).
27 *The Concept of Anxiety* was published in France as *Le Concept de l'angoisse* in 1935, six years after the first of Kierkegaard's works appeared in French—the "Seducer's Diary" of *Either/Or*—and eight years before the publication of Sartre's *Being and Nothingness*. In a letter dated 1 December 1939, Sartre requested a copy of *Le Concept de l'Angoisse* from Beauvoir to read while on military service. See Jean-Paul Sartre, *Witness to My Life: The Letters of Jean-Paul Sartre to Simone de Beauvoir, 1926–39*, trans. Lee Fahnestock and Norman MacAfee (London: Hamish Hamilton, 1992), 378. In the same month Sartre read it carefully, making many notes in his diary. Later that December, in a letter to Beauvoir, he writes that he "found a theory of nothingness while reading Kierkegaard" (ibid., 421). The next year Beauvoir's own letters express that she has "heaps of books by Kierkegaard" and Jean Wahl's essays on him, which "really interest me." See Simone de Beauvoir, *Letters to Sartre*, trans. Quentin Hoare (London: Vintage, 1991), 355–7.
28 Heinämaa, *Toward a Phenomenology*, 71, citing Beauvoir, DS I 67/TSS 61.
29 Young, "Pregnant Embodiment," 49.
30 Jean-Paul Sartre, *Being and Nothingness*, trans. Hazel Barnes (London: Routledge, 2003), 56.
31 Ibid., 53.
32 The term 'live possibility' is borrowed from William James, according to whom a possibility is live if it is actually considered by the subject—if it is "among the mind's possibilities." See William James, *The Will to Believe and Other Essays in Popular Philosophy, and Human Immortality* (Overland Park, KS: Digireads.com, 2010), 9–10.
33 "Car s'il n'est pas vrai que l'avortement soit un assassinat, il ne saurait non plus être assimilé à une simple pratique anticonceptionnelle; un événement a eu lieu qui est un commencement absolu et dont on arrête le développement. Certaines femmes seront hantées par la mémoire de cet enfant qui n'a pas été" (DS II 336).
34 Bardwell Smith, *Buddhism and Abortion in Contemporary Japan: Mizuko Kuyō and the Confrontation with Death* (Albany: State University of New York Press, 1992).

35 See Tiana Norgren, *Abortion before Birth Control: The Politics of Reproduction in Postwar Japan* (Princeton, NJ: Princeton University Press, 2001).
36 Britt Bennett, *The Mothers* (London: Dialogue, 2016), 267.
37 TSS 552; emphasis added and translation modified (*equivoque* was translated 'ambivalent').
38 See https://www.nhs.uk/conditions/miscarriage/; Allen J. Wilcox, Clarice R. Weinberg, John F. O'Connor et al., "Incidence of Early Loss of Pregnancy," *New England Journal of Medicine* 319 no. 4 (1988): 189–194.
39 See Young, "Pregnant Embodiment," 56.
40 http://www.nhs.uk/conditions/pregnancy-and-baby/pages/pelvic-pain-pregnant-spd.aspx.
41 https://www.rcog.org.uk/for-the-public/perineal-tears-and-episiotomies-in-childbirth/perineal-tears-during-childbirth/.
42 Marian Knight, Kathryn Bunch, Derek Tuffnell, Judy Shakespeare, Rohit Kotnis, Sara Kenyon, and Jennifer J. Kurinczuk (eds.) on behalf of MBRRACE-UK, *Saving Lives, Improving Mothers' Care: Lessons Learned to Inform Maternity Care from the UK and Ireland Confidential Enquiries into Maternal Deaths and Morbidity 2017–19*. Oxford: National Perinatal Epidemiology Unit, University of Oxford 2021.
43 Joanne Limburg, *The Woman Who Thought Too Much: A Memoir of Obsession and Compulsion* (New York: Atlantic, 2011), 232.
44 See Susan Hoang, "Pregnancy and Anxiety," *International Journal of Childbirth Education*, 29 no. 1 (January 2014): 67–70; Lori E. Ross and Linda M. McLean, "Anxiety Disorders during Pregnancy and the Postpartum Period: A Systematic Review," *Journal of Clinical Psychiatry* 67 no. 8 (2006): 1285–1298.
45 See Hoang, "Pregnancy and Anxiety."
46 Ayobami Adebayo, *Stay With Me* (Edinburgh: Canongate, 2017). Set in the political turmoil of 1980s Nigeria, this novel tells the story of a couple's desire for a child, discovery of infertility, and the desperate lengths to which they go to fulfill the weight of their families' expectations.
47 These figures are cited in Sheila Kitzinger's *The Experience of Childbirth* (London: Penguin, 1987), 13. For more recent statistics (which reveal that the rate of change is not encouraging), see Louise M. Howard and Hind Khalifeh, "Perinatal Mental Health: A Review of Progress and Challenges," *World Psychiatry* 19 no. 3 (2020): 313–327.
48 Annette Bauer, Michael Parsonage, Martin Knapp et al., *The Costs of Perinatal Mental Health Problems* (London: Centre for Mental Health, 2014). https://www.centreformentalhealth.org.uk/publications/costs-perinatal-mental-health-problems.
49 https://maternalmentalhealthalliance.org/news/maternal-suicide-still-the-leading-cause-of-death-in-first-postnatal-year/; http://www.who.int/mental_health/prevention/suicide/MaternalMH/en/.
50 Heinämaa, "Toward a Phenomenology," 111.
51 See Hoang, "Pregnancy and Anxiety."
52 Lundquist, "Being Torn," 51.

References

Adebayo, Ayobami. *Stay With Me*. Edinburgh: Canongate, 2017.
Bauer, Annette, Michael Parsonage, Martin Knapp, Valentina Iemmi, and Bayo Adelaja. *The Costs of Perinatal Mental Health Problems*. London: Centre for Mental Health, 2014. https://www.centreformentalhealth.org.uk/publications/costs-perinatal-mental-health-problems.

Beauvoir, Simone de. *Le Deuxième Sexe*. 2 vols. Paris: Gallimard, 1949.
Beauvoir, Simone de. *Old Age*. Translated by Patrick O'Brien. London: Penguin, 1977.
Beauvoir, Simone de, *Letters to Sartre*. Translated by Quentin Hoare. London: Vintage, 1991.
Beauvoir, Simone de. *The Second Sex*. Translated by Constance Borde and Sheila Malovany-Chevallier. London: Jonathan Cape, 2009.
Bennett, Britt. *The Mothers*. London: Dialogue, 2016.
Heinämaa, Sara. *Toward a Phenomenology of Sexual Difference*. Lanham, MD: Rowman & Littlefield, 2003.
Hoang, Susan, "Pregnancy and Anxiety." *International Journal of Childbirth Education* 29 no. 1 (2014): 67–70.
Howard, Louise M., Hind Khalifeh "Perinatal Mental Health: A Review of Progress and Challenges." *World Psychiatry* 19 no. 3 (2020): 313–327.
James, William. *The Will to Believe and Other Essays in Popular Philosophy, and Human Immortality*. Overland Park, KS: Digireads.com, 2010.
Janet, Pierre. *De l'angoisse à l'extase*. Paris: Alcan, 1928.
Jeremiah, Emily. "Motherhood to Mothering and Beyond: Maternity in Recent Feminist Thought." *Journal of the Association for Research on Mothering* 8 no. 1–2 (2006): 21–33.
Kirkpatrick, Kate. "Past Her Prime? Simone de Beauvoir on Motherhood and Old Age." *Sophia* 53 no. 2 (2014): 275–287.
Kitzinger, Sheila. *The Experience of Childbirth*. London: Penguin, 1987.
Knight, Marian, Kathryn Bunch, Derek Tuffnell, Judy Shakespeare, Rohit Kotnis, Sara Kenyon, and Jennifer J. Kurinczuk (eds.) on behalf of MBRRACE-UK. *Saving Lives, Improving Mothers' Care: Lessons Learned To Inform Maternity Care from the UK and Ireland Confidential Enquiries into Maternal Deaths and Morbidity 2017–19*. Oxford: National Perinatal Epidemiology Unit, 2021.
Lacroze, René. *L'angoisse et l'émotion*. Paris: Boivin, 1937.
Limburg, Joanne. *The Woman Who Thought Too Much: A Memoir of Obsession and Compulsion*. New York: Atlantic, 2011.
Lundquist, Caroline. "Being Torn: Toward a Phenomenology of Unwanted Pregnancy." *Hypatia* 23 no. 3 (2008): 136–155.
Maushart, Susan. *The Mask of Motherhood*. London: Penguin, 2000.
Moi, Toril. "While We Wait: The English Translation of *The Second Sex*." *Signs* 27 no. 4 (2002): 1005–1035.
Norgren, Tiana. *Abortion before Birth Control: The Politics of Reproduction in Postwar Japan*. Princeton, NJ: Princeton University Press, 2001.
Ross, Lori E. and McLean, Linda M. "Anxiety Disorders During Pregnancy and the Postpartum Period: A Systematic Review." *Journal of Clinical Psychiatry* 67 no. 8 (2006): 1285–1298.
Sartre, Jean-Paul. *Witness to My Life: The Letters of Jean-Paul Sartre to Simone de Beauvoir, 1926–39*. Translated by Lee Fahnestock and Norman MacAfee, London: Hamish Hamilton, 1992.
Sartre, Jean-Paul. *Being and Nothingness*. Translated by Hazel Barnes. London: Routledge, 2003.
Simons, Margaret. "*The Silencing of Simone de Beauvoir: Guess What's Missing from The Second Sex*." *Women's Studies International Forum* 6 no. 5 (1983): 559–564.

Smith, Bardwell. *Buddhism and Abortion in Contemporary Japan: Mizuko Kuyō and the Confrontation with Death*. Albany: State University of New York Press, 1992.

Young, Iris Marion. "Pregnant Embodiment: Subjectivity and Alienation." In *Throwing Like a Girl and Other Essays*. Oxford: Oxford University Press, 2005.

Whitmarsh, Anne. *Simone de Beauvoir and the Limits of Commitment*. Cambridge: Cambridge University Press, 1981.

Wilcox, Allen J., Clarice R. Weinberg, John F. O'Connor, Donna D. Baird, John P. Schlatterer, Robert E. Canfield, E. Glenn Armstrong, and Bruce C. Nisula. "Incidence of Early Loss of Pregnancy." *New England Journal of Medicine* 319 no. 4 (1988): 189–194.

Zerilli, Linda. "A Process without a Subject: Simone de Beauvoir and Julia Kristeva on Maternity." *Signs* 18 no. 1 (1992): 111–135.

PART IV
Fighting Back

9

'MUSCULAR REVOLT'

Resisting Gender Oppression through Counter-Violence

Dianna Taylor

Simone de Beauvoir endorsed the use of counter-violence to oppose oppressive systems, such as fascism and colonialism, that are grounded in and reproduced through violence. Although her own analysis of women's situation illustrates that normative gender functions as an oppressive system, *The Second Sex* [1949] does not address, let alone advocate for, women's use of counter-violence. Given that, as Beauvoir shows, violence against women is not simply an effect or expression but rather constitutive of normative gender, in this chapter I argue that counter-violence needs to be part of feminist efforts to oppose women's oppression and restore conditions for the possibility of their freedom. My references to 'women' in this chapter are inclusive of cisgender and trans women, and it is important to note that the latter are disproportionately subjected to all forms of sexual violence.[1]

I begin by providing an overview of colonialism through the work of Beauvoir and Frantz Fanon in order to identify key characteristics of oppressive systems. Next, I show that women's situation as Beauvoir describes it in *The Second Sex* possesses these same characteristics and draw upon contemporary feminist analyses that reinforce the perspective she provides. The chapter proceeds by offering an account of counter-violence which delineates its effectiveness in opposing oppressive violence and undermining oppressive systems, and shows that Beauvoir came to support its use for opposing the sexual violence that defines gender oppression. Arguing for the inclusion of counter-violence as a component of broader feminist resistance is not to claim that counter-violence is appropriate or effective in every situation, or that all women can or should exercise it. My point, rather, is that counter-violence can be effective for some women in some situations, and that feminists should therefore not reject it out of hand on the grounds that it can only function in the service of oppression. I conclude by presenting the 2020 film *Promising Young Woman* as a site that reflects and in turn promotes feminist critical reflection on counter-violence and its effects.

Oppression, Oppressive Violence, and Oppressive Systems

In *The Ethics of Ambiguity* [1947], Beauvoir describes oppression as an exercise of "freedom which is interested only in denying" the freedom of others.[2] Freedom is understood as human beings' ability to generate meaning and shape (but not determine) their conditions of existence (to, that is, create and further their own projects), and it defines human existence. Being denied freedom (being oppressed) entails having one's conditions of existence defined externally, and thus being relegated to a less than fully human situation.[3] Although objects may deny or curtail freedom, only human beings *aim* to do so, making oppression a distinctively human phenomenon. "Only man can be an enemy for man," Beauvoir writes. "Only he can rob him of the meaning of his acts and his life because it also belongs only to him alone to confirm it in its existence, to recognize it in actual fact as a freedom."[4] Like freedom, oppression emerges from the interconnected nature of human existence. The relation of self to self is not distinct from relations to others and world; my projects require the assistance of others who are in turn free to foster, inhibit, or destroy them.[5]

Both individual actions and human-created structures and systems may facilitate, impede, or deny freedom. While structures and systems can therefore be construed as oppressive, I do not consider them to be violent. Structures and systems rather produce, and are themselves reproduced and enforced, by way of generating, legitimizing, and proliferating violent acts—through, in other words, generating conditions under which the human potentiality or capacity for violence may be actualized. Like all human capacities, violence is an effect of the interconnected nature of our existence. Mutually dependent projects inevitably come into conflict with one another, and this conflict always has the potential to escalate. Insofar as humans are embodied beings, this conflict, escalation, and resulting violence are themselves embodied. Violence is, then, an embodied violation. It is an imposition or intrusion, and thus by definition not only unwelcome but also harmful in the sense that it harms the body against which it is inflicted. This harm takes the form of not only bruises or broken bones, but also self-blame and guilt—effects which may be experienced by those upon whom violence is inflicted as well as by those who exercise it.

Beauvoir sees the "torture, humiliation, servitude, [and] assassination" perpetrated by the Nazi and French colonial regimes as paradigms of oppressive violence.[6] As Fanon's analysis of colonialism clearly illustrates, such acts emerge from, reproduce, and bolster oppressive systems. Colonialism originates in and reproduces itself through violence. Colonizers create and enforce the system, and they maintain their dominance through imposing a combination of material deprivation, political and economic disenfranchisement, and institutions such as the police and the military that surveil and regularly invade (using "rifle butts and napalm") colonized spaces and lives.[7] These structural conditions and institutions in turn open onto and legitimize violent acts on the part of individual colonizers against individual colonized persons. Fanon shows that colonialism also simultaneously normalizes its oppressive violence (in part by casting it as not violence at all but rather, for example "peacekeeping") and pathologizes the violence of the colonized. The system (re)produces the identities of 'colonizer' and 'colonized,' which are in turn central to its functioning. The colonizer, Fanon writes, has "*fabricated* and *continues to fabricate* the colonized subject."[8] Imposing an identity, and thus a mode of self-understanding, on another human being denies their freedom, and the characteristics of colonized identity and self-understanding reinforce this denial. Casting colonized persons as primitive, inherently lacking in rational capacities, and inherently violent appears to justify violent colonial rule. Algerian 'primitivism' was presented as fundamentally biological and therefore inevitable and fixed. On the premise that they are incapable of comprehending and therefore responding to reason, the colonist asserts that Algerians must be managed by means of force. "There is therefore no mystery nor paradox," Fanon quotes a white physician as saying. "The colonizer's reluctance to entrust the native with any kind of responsibility does not stem from racism or paternalism but quite simply from a scientific assessment of the colonized's limited biological possibilities."[9]

Since human beings constitute our relationship to ourselves both through our relationships with other people and in terms of prevailing norms, the oppressed will internalize, to at least some degree, oppressors' perspectives. As Judith Butler shows, normative, socially generated identity categories "guarantee social existence."[10] The identity 'colonized person' affords intelligibility, but the inferior status implicit in that identity also becomes constitutive of how colonized people understand and relate to themselves; intelligibility comes at the expense of freedom. Fanon describes experiencing himself as being "*fixed*" in immanence by a white gaze that reduces him to his merely physical and raced body and, in doing so, also "objectively cut[s]" away "sections of [his] reality."[11] Being made to experience himself through the lens of white racism in turn deeply constrains Fanon's freedom. "I arrive slowly in the world," he writes. "I crawl along. The white gaze, the only valid one, is already dissecting me."[12] Because oppressed identities are framed as inherent and therefore natural, moreover, the oppressed (again, to at least some extent) come to see their truncated freedom and circumscribed existence as deserved. Beauvoir's observation that "relentless" degrading portrayals of the oppressed instill within them "disgust [...] in regard to themselves" is apparent in Fanon's experience of "shame [...] self-contempt [...] and nausea."[13]

A primary target of this self-directed negative affect is colonized persons' own ostensibly merely destructive capacity for violence. Fostering a mode of oppressed self-relation in which this is the case serves the oppressive colonial system in at least three ways. First, and perhaps most fundamentally, framing their situation as an effect of who they are rather than of an oppressive system may make resistance appear useless or simply impossible. "[A]fter all," Beauvoir writes, "one cannot revolt against nature."[14] Second, as Fanon discusses, colonized individuals come to view not only themselves but also those who share their situation as worthy of disgust, shame, and nausea. Resentment, aggression, and violence that can and need to be directed against the oppressive regime are (at least initially) subsequently redirected back against the colonized themselves: they "train [the] aggressiveness sedimented in [their] muscles against [their] own people."[15] Third, to the extent that colonized people see their violence as posing an indiscriminate threat, they may come to believe that it should never be actualized, not even to defend themselves against or pre-empt oppressive violence and promote their own freedom.

Normative Gender as an Oppressive System: Women's Situation in *The Second Sex*

Beauvoir's analysis of women's situation in *The Second Sex* shows that normative gender is an oppressive system. I understand normative gender in terms of what Judith Butler refers to as the "compulsory order of sex/gender/desire": gendered relations of power that assume and reproduce binary constructions of sex and gender which in turn generate cis- and heteronormativity.[16] Like colonialism, normative gender brings into existence the identities (female/male, woman/man) and corresponding modes of self-relation upon which it relies and which, because of this reliance, it duly posits and reproduces precisely as natural. As Beauvoir shows, this normative gendered order of things casts women as men's "inessential Others" specifically on the basis of their sexed and sexualized embodiment. "Woman," she writes, "is nothing other than what man decides; she is thus called 'the sex,' meaning that the male sees her essentially as a sexed being; for him she is sex, so she is it in the absolute."[17] Insofar as women's ostensible inferiority is sexed and sexualized, their oppression, as Debra Bergoffen argues, will be most effectively enforced through sexualized violence that "targets the sexed body *qua* sexed,"[18] while all oppression is enforced through violence—in other words, a specifically sexualized form of violence is needed to enforce women's oppression.

Beauvoir's account of the transitions from childhood to adolescence, adolescence to sexual initiation, and sexual initiation to marriage reveals feminization as a sexually violent process. Following Jennifer McWeeny, I characterize feminization in terms of the development of a particular mode of self-relation that Beauvoir refers to as *se faire objet*: to make oneself into an object.[19] As described by Beauvoir, female children have not been initiated into the norms of femininity; they have not yet developed the self-relation of *se faire objet*. Like boys, girls experience the world as autonomous beings; they "exist for themselves."[20] The physical differences between girls and boys have not yet been transformed into *sexual* difference—markers of inferiority and superiority, submission and dominance. "For girls *and* boys," Beauvoir explains, "the body is first the radiation of a subjectivity, the instrument that brings about the comprehension of the world: they apprehend the universe through their eyes and hands, and not through their sexual parts."[21]

All of this changes with the onset of puberty. "It is a strange experience," Beauvoir reflects,

> for an individual recognizing himself as subject, autonomy, and transcendence, as an absolute, to discover inferiority—as a given essence—in his self: it is a strange experience for one who posits himself for himself as One to be revealed to himself as alterity. That is what happens to the little girl when, learning about the world, she grasps herself as a woman in it.[22]

Adolescence ushers in the sexualization of the female human body and, hence, the feminization of women's relationship to themselves. Adolescent girls are made aware that their bodies as well as their sexual, affective, and physical (i.e., domestic labor, childrearing) embodied capacities—their very selves, in other words—exist primarily for others, and especially for men. Beauvoir writes:

> For the girl, erotic transcendence consists in making herself prey in order to make a catch. She becomes an object; and she grasps in herself an object [...] it seems to her that she has been doubled; instead of coinciding exactly with her self, here she is existing *outside* of her self.[23]

Beauvoir's description of *se faire objet* points to how, as a mode of self-relation, it is bound up with sexual violence. Becoming a woman entails making oneself into a specifically *sexual* object for others and experiencing oneself in this way. Women, Beauvoir writes, do not "dream of taking, pressing, violating"; they experience their sexuality in terms of *being taken*.[24] There is nothing inherently oppressive about giving oneself over sexually to another person. But it is oppressive to have one's sexuality, one's sexual self, externally defined exclusively in terms of, and thus reduced to, a singular mode of sexual expression and experience, especially one defined by vulnerability to sexual violation. To make oneself another's sexual prey is to constitute oneself as a being for whom sexuality and this vulnerability, and hence by extension actual violation, are interconnected. Understanding oneself as a being who can only be taken sexually, in other words, is inextricably linked with being defined as a being who can be taken *forcibly*.

Beauvoir describes heterosex generally and heterosexual intercourse more specifically in terms of this oppressive dynamic in which men exercise their freedom at the expense of women. She asserts that late in childhood girls come to understand, and as young women subsequently experience, (hetero) sexual intercourse as a violation. "[T]he most obvious and detestable symbol of physical possession," Beauvoir writes, "is penetration by the male sex organ."[25] She argues that girls view penetration in this way because it can be "*inflicted*"; the invasive nature of penetration, in other words, is the source of its "obscene and humiliating meaning."[26] Beauvoir is not saying here (as she makes clear in later work) that all heterosexual intercourse is rape.[27] Her point is rather that, within the context of oppressive gendered relations of power, being sexually penetrated by men connotes women's subordination, and that women therefore experience, or at least have a sense of, being penetrated as being dominated. If, as McWeeny argues is the case, heterosexual intercourse definitively marks the transition from female human being to woman, this experience will be most acute within the context of (hetero)sexual initiation and then subsequently normalized within the context of marriage.[28] "[T]he love act," Beauvoir writes, "is a service" wives "*render*" and from which their husbands "[*take*] pleasure."[29] Marriage solidifies *se faire objet* and, by extension, heterosex; it enforces femininity and the inferior status it imposes. Hence, then, the deep ambivalence Beauvoir describes adolescent girls expressing with respect to becoming sexually mature women.

At the same time that it is characterized by and thus reproduces vulnerability to sexual violence, *se faire objet* generates within women ambivalence relative to their own capacity for violence. Beauvoir observes that adolescent boys undergo "a veritable apprenticeship in violence."[30] When they confront one another through aggressive sports that involve bodily contact (i.e., football, wrestling) as well as through fighting, boys assert themselves as autonomous beings. Precisely because it serves this function, violence is discouraged and even prohibited among girls. Their adolescence is spent preparing themselves for a lifetime of embodied feminine submission. Young women are "banned from exploring, daring, pushing back the limits of the possible."[31] They may express disagreement but not actually engage in the more physical act of confrontation, an encounter between "two freedoms" through which the capacity of "defiance," upon which acts of resistance at least in part depend, is developed.[32] "To lose confidence in one's body," Beauvoir writes, "is to lose confidence in oneself."[33] Women learn not to trust their bodies as a source of strength, and therefore cease to have an empowering experience of their embodied self-relation. Norming violence as unfeminine reinforces the 'timidity' that characterizes *se faire objet*. Femininity fosters conciliation, complacency, or (polite) withdrawal in the face of conflict; freezing is a common response to confrontational and violent situations.

Internalization and self-constitution in terms of natural passivity both suppresses women's capacity for violence and generates negative self-judgment (shame, nausea, disgust) concerning violent acts they do commit against others. Women's ambivalent relationship to their capacity for violence thus stems less from experiencing it as an indiscriminate threat than as a threat to the femininity that affords them intelligibility. As with other oppressed groups, violence that women cannot externalize gets turned back against them. Echoing Fanon's description of his own process of self-constitution, Beauvoir describes becoming intelligible as a woman as requiring a kind of excision. *Se faire objet* cuts away and cuts women off from other possible modes of self-relation, rendering them unintelligible and thus requiring their disavowal. For girls, this disavowal is violent and corporeal: "The girl gashes her thigh with a razor, burns herself with cigarettes, cuts and scratches herself."[34] Girls literally inscribe loss—of autonomy, of alternatives—into their bodies, permanently marking themselves with what they have been forced to excise.

Expanding Beauvoir's Analysis: Women's Situation in Structural and Institutional Context

Recent work by Catharine MacKinnon and Claudia Card expands Beauvoir's elucidation of normative gender as an oppressive system by analyzing the structural and institutional context within which women's situation is located, and which in turn shapes it. Carefully unpacking the September 11, 2001 attacks on the United States, both thinkers illustrate the harm sexual violence inflicts by illustrating the extent to which it approximates acts defined as terrorism. They then expose the hypocrisy of a society that can mobilize massive resources in the case of the latter but frames the former as simply inevitable, and therefore fails to act in the face of it.

MacKinnon identifies the following defining characteristics of the 9/11 attacks: they were premeditated rather than spontaneous; ideologically and politically rather than criminally motivated; directed against civilians (i.e., noncombatants); and carried out by nonstate actors but nonetheless legitimated by states.[35] The 9/11 attacks were also highly gendered, in that they were carried out solely by men. All of this, MacKinnon observes, holds true for sexual violence. Drugging women in nightclubs; upskirting; stalking, and other forms of harassment; sexual assault and rape, as well as "gang rapes and serial murders [...] a lot of pornography production," and "most sex trafficking" are also carried out (almost exclusively) by men, and usually with some level of forethought.[36] These unprovoked sexual violations are ideologically and politically driven insofar as they are grounded in and reinforce sexism and misogyny generally, and entitlement to women's sexual capacities more specifically. State and broader social legitimation of sexual violence is apparent in the fact that "acts of violence against women are regarded not as exceptional but inevitable, even banal."[37] In MacKinnon's view, this characterization of sexual violence as a normal (if, perhaps, unfortunate) part of society stems in large part from the fact that it occurs within what is considered to be the "unexceptional" context of daily life. If, in contrast, the violence that defines women's "peacetime" situation were to occur within the exceptional context of "a war among men" (which, like terrorism, is characterized by "armed conflict") it would be considered a violation of international law, and the women against whom it was being perpetrated would be entitled to protection under Common Article III of the Geneva Conventions.[38]

In light of these points of intersection between acts defined as terrorism and sexual violence against women, both MacKinnon and Card draw attention to a series of paradoxes. Women are systematically subjected to violence strongly resembling that which characterizes armed conflicts, yet the framing of this violence as 'normal' (simply an inevitable part of what it means to live as a woman) gives the state and society license to do little to counter it. While they are therefore effectively held responsible for their own protection, women are nonetheless deeply constrained in their ability to do so because of the normative repression of their capacity for violence. Card illustrates the multiple pernicious effects of normalization of sexual violence and repression of women's counter-violence by juxtaposing pre-emptive actions taken by Francine Hughes (1977) and Inez Garcia (1974) with those taken by the U.S. following the 9/11 attacks.[39] Hughes killed her abusive husband by setting him on fire while he was asleep and "heavily intoxicated." Garcia shot and killed a man who, "just minutes before," had raped her and threatened her life should she tell anyone.[40]

While Card admits that comparing the actions of individual members of a disempowered group with those of an incredibly powerful nation may seem "outrageous," in her view it is precisely in its ostensible outrageousness that the comparison is instructive.[41] Through her own elucidation of shared characteristics between sexual violence and acts defined as terrorism, Card shows that, like the U.S. after 9/11, Hughes and Garcia believed with good reason that the parties threatening them were neither being nor going to be "*restrained*"; nor were they going to be "*held accountable by anyone else or by the law.*"[42] Like the U.S. after 9/11, Hughes and Garcia engaged in what can be seen as pre-emptive strikes to defend themselves against future harm. The U.S., Hughes, and Garcia all "stepped outside of existing law" in response to being attacked. Yet while the U.S. response was deemed legitimate and necessary (or at least tolerated), both Hughes and Garcia were charged with murder, and Garcia was subsequently convicted.[43]

This deeply contradictory normative framing of what is essentially the same response to the same threat is instructive, in part because it shows in dramatic fashion that there is nothing banal or unexceptional about sexual violence. If sexual violence is akin to *systemic* terrorism, whereas the 9/11 attacks were a singular event, doesn't that fact alone make such violence exceptional? Is it not therefore apparent that sexual violence poses an at least equivalent threat which warrants the same degree of mobilization and expressions of moral outrage?[44] Why is a single attack on an incredibly powerful nation with the resources available to defend and protect itself considered more serious than pervasive violence inflicted against women, a disempowered group? In short, if sexual violence is in no way unexceptional, why is it framed as such? One answer to this question is apparent in MacKinnon's and Card's accounts of why women's counter-violence is necessarily repressed, in part through being criminalized and thus pathologized. Neither the state nor society more broadly can (at least not easily) acknowledge that its own constitutive elements (including law enforcement, courts, and social services that function as primary resources for victims/ survivors) are simultaneously fundamental and destructive. Insofar as society in its current oppressive iteration relies on systemic sexual violence to sustain itself, mobilizing against sexual violence in the way that the U.S. mobilized against the 9/11 attacks would require the state to mobilize against its foundational institutions and prevailing relations of power— against, in other words, itself and its own interests. What MacKinnon and Card thus make quite clear is that structures and institutions can at best deal with (at the present time, mostly ineffectively) oppressive sexual violence after the fact; they do virtually nothing to prevent it.

Counter-Violence

Normative gender is a violent system. Grounded in and reproduced through (especially sexual) violence, normative gender represses women's capacity for violence; and the ambivalent relationship to that capacity it generates within women undermines their ability to use violence when necessary. Given that violence emerges from conditions of human existence, all human beings therefore possess the capacity for it. Denying some the ability to actualize this capacity, especially in the service of their own emancipation, is therefore dehumanizing.⁴⁵ It "stifles the voice of revolt" that asserts freedom.⁴⁶ Beauvoir writes:

> Violence is the authentic test of every person's attachment to himself, his passions, and his own will; to radically reject it is to reject all objective truth, it is to isolate one's self in an abstract subjectivity; an anger or a revolt that does not exert itself through the muscles remains imaginary.⁴⁷

The muscular, embodied violence of revolt, directed against oppression with the aim of undermining and ultimately eradicating it, is what I refer to as counter-violence. Oppressive systems are inherently unequal. The fabricated identities of 'oppressor' and 'oppressed' in whatever form ('colonizer/colonized,' 'man/woman') confront one another on grounds that are permanently skewed in favor of those who are already dominant. By restoring the humanity of the oppressed, counter-violence evens the playing field; through it, the oppressed relate to and assert themselves, and confront their oppressors, as fully human. It is this ability to restore conditions for the possibility of freedom that, from Beauvoir's perspective, endows counter-violence with ethical potential.

Counter-violence and oppressive violence thus differ in fundamental ways. Through confronting, identifying, and redirecting oppressive violence, counter-violence disrupts and may prevent the actualization of the violence upon which oppressive systems rely. Confronting oppressive violence involves adopting an embodied stance in which one puts oneself in its way and, in doing so, commits oneself to striking back; it therefore necessarily involves putting oneself at risk. Confrontation intervenes in, circumvents, or (at least temporarily) disables oppressive violence. Because it positions counter-violence specifically as a response, confrontation further points to the existence of an external source of provocation, thereby distinguishing itself from oppressive violence. Identifying oppressive violence as this source, and potentially marking publicly the bodies of oppressors, redirects the effects of oppressive violence back toward oppressive systems and actions. This redirection counteracts internalization of oppression's harmful effects by the oppressed. It undermines modes of embodied self-relation that reflect and reproduce the purported inherent inferiority that oppression inscribes onto oppressed bodies; in doing so, it opens onto new and potentially empowering experiences of one's embodied self-relation. Finally, by exposing oppressive violence for what it is, especially when undertaken collectively, counter-violence can disrupt the reproduction of oppressive conditions more broadly, as well as foster solidarity among the oppressed.

Through her involvement in the French Women's Liberation Movement (MLF), Beauvoir both came to see economic independence alone as insufficient for emancipating women and to support women's use of counter-violence to oppose the violence of gender oppression. "[C]hanging the relations of production is not sufficient to really change society," she observes in 1972.[48] Her call to eliminate the institutions of both marriage and the (nuclear) family reflects her view that oppression, and by extension oppressive violence, pervades fundamental aspects of women's situation as well as (given that they function as broader modes of social organization) society as a whole. Beauvoir argues, in fact, that eliminating marriage and the family must *precede* economic transformation. It was also through her involvement in the MLF that Beauvoir came to support the use of counter-violence to oppose women's oppression. Echoing her position vis-à-vis fascist and colonial violence, Beauvoir asserts that sexual violence must be confronted by means of counter-violence. "Men use violence against women in their language as well as in their gestures," she observes. "They assault women: they rape them, insult them, and certain looks are aggressions. Women must equally defend themselves with violence."[49] Beauvoir specifically mentions self-defense training as a means for creating the reciprocity that allows women to confront men as equals, as well as for transforming women's experience of their embodiment and, therefore, of themselves. Self-defense fosters an experience of the embodied self-relation not as timid, inhibited, and vulnerable, but instead as a powerful resource that can be deployed when it is needed. "Some women learn karate or other forms of combat. I am in complete agreement," Beauvoir asserts. "This way they will be much more comfortable with their bodies and in the world than if they feel unarmed when faced with male aggressions."[50] More broadly, women conducting themselves in empowered ways, and more specifically in ways that disrupt and potentially prevent the execution of oppressive violence, subverts the seamless reproduction of gender norms and, therefore, gender oppression.

At the time that Beauvoir made these remarks, the anti-rape contingent of the U.S. Women's Liberation Movement (WLM) was also overtly advocating for women's use of counter-violence to oppose rape and sexual assault. Such opposition included but was not limited to individual women physically defending themselves against individual attackers. In some cities, women formed groups, referred to as 'rape squads,' that patrolled the streets and intervened on behalf of women in need, took pre-emptive action, and also identified and sometimes publicly exposed violent men.[51] Organized, broad-based, collective anti-sexual violence feminist action involving counter-violence does not exist in the contemporary U.S. A contemporary instance of it does exist, however, in the form of the Gulabi Gang in India. Sampat Pal Devi founded the organization in 2006 in response to systemic violence against women (especially in rural areas) and the failure of police to respond effectively (or at all). The initial aim of the Gulabi Gang was:

to punish oppressive husbands, fathers and brothers, and combat domestic violence and desertion [...] more serious offenders were publicly shamed when they refused to listen or relent. Sometimes the women resorted to their lathis [heavy bamboo rods], if the men resorted to use of force.[52]

While it is beyond the scope of this chapter to examine why collective feminist counter-violence in the U.S. fell out of practice, two possible reasons are worth mentioning. The first is the institutionalization of the anti-rape movement, in part through replacing grassroots feminist staffing of rape crisis centers and domestic violence shelters with trained professionals.[53] The second is the prevailing perspective among feminists that all violence is oppressive, or at least has oppressive potential, and should therefore be used only defensively as a last resort. I see this perspective reflecting women's ambivalent relationship to their capacity for violence—a relationship which, as I have shown, is an expression of oppressive gendered relations of power. In that view, then, it therefore seems important for feminists to begin critically analyzing how (by some women in some situations) counter-violence might be effectively incorporated into feminist anti-sexual violence.

Feminist Counter-Violence in Contemporary Culture: *Promising Young Woman*

The 2020 film *Promising Young Woman* grapples with questions concerning the use of counter-violence against the systemic sexual violence that characterizes gender oppression.[54] The film's protagonist is Cassie, a thirty-something coffee shop employee. The film's backstory is that Cassie's best friend, Nina, was raped at a party and subsequently dropped out of medical school. Cassie also dropped out in order to provide support for Nina, who nonetheless died by suicide. Cassie expresses her grief and rage one night a week by frequenting a nightclub, pretending to be seriously impaired by alcohol ("I act like I'm too drunk to stand"), and going home with a man who sexually assaults and clearly intends to rape her. Cassie prevents these assaults from escalating, however, by revealing that she is quite in control of her faculties and confronting the men about their actions. After learning from another former classmate—now practicing pediatrician and budding romantic love interest, Ryan—that the former classmate who raped Nina has moved back to the U.S. from London and is engaged to be married, Cassie turns her attention to everyone implicated in Nina's violation and death, especially the rapist, Al Monroe.

Promising Young Woman conveys the need for counter-violence through its unsparing portrayal of women's systematic subjection to sexual violence, and therefore of normative gender as an oppressive system. The accumulation of tick marks in the notebook where Cassie records her weekly nightclub encounters serves as a testament to not only the number of men she has challenged about their behavior, but also the number of men who have readily sexually violated her. As Cassie tells one of the men during a confrontation, her ruse never fails: every week a man picks her up, takes her home with him, and assaults her. The predictability of these events reflects the extent to which, as Beauvoir shows, vulnerability to and actual sexual violation define normative femininity. Watching Cassie prepare for her weekly club outing (in one scene she applies garish makeup while watching a YouTube tutorial on how to create 'blowjob lips') we see a woman making herself into prey. The nature of the 'catch' Cassie intends to make, however, decontextualizes and thus de-normalizes this feminine ritual, exposing the trappings of femininity as fabricated, oppressive expressions of *se faire objet*. The extent to which normative femininity is bound up with (vulnerability to) sexual violation is also expressed through the film's depiction of men's normative attitudes and actions toward women. Through exposing how the 'normal' behavior of 'nice men' (as those who assault and intend to rape Cassie often refer to themselves) reduces women to 'the sex,' the film illustrates how vulnerability to sexual violence and the victimization onto which it opens are constitutive of the normative femininity, masculinity, heterosexuality, and heterosex that, as Beauvoir shows, structure society.

Viewers never actually see Cassie commit acts of counter-violence, but it is clear that she does.[55] In the scene following the initial depiction of her being picked up in a club and assaulted, Cassie is walking home the next morning. She is barefoot, carrying her shoes in one hand and a burger in the other. Red liquid runs down the arm of the hand holding the burger; her blouse is spattered with red liquid; there's also a splotch on her leg. The obvious interpretation here is that the liquid is ketchup; but the fact that some of the tick marks in Cassie's notebook (including the one she records later that morning) appear in red pen suggests that she has spilled the blood of some of the men she encounters.

Cassie intends to spill the blood of Al Monroe. Near the end of the film, she crashes his bachelor party by pretending to be a stripper. After spiking the drinks of, and thereby disabling, Al's guests, Cassie takes Al upstairs, handcuffs him to a bed, confronts him about Nina, and tells him to confess to raping her. Extracting a scalpel from the medical bag that is part of her sexy nurse stripper costume, she informs Al that she is going to make sure he is never able to forget Nina's name, just as she was never able to forget his. Cassie's intention to inscribe Al's sexual violation of Nina into his flesh, to corporeally re-establish equality between oppressor and oppressed, is especially significant given Fanon's and Beauvoir's respective references to incision in their descriptions of how the bodies of the oppressed are marked when their capacity for violence is turned back against them, reconstituting them as inherently inferior bodies. Consistent with counter-violence as I understand it, Cassie aims to disrupt that reconstitution, to perform a second redirection back against Al, permanently and corporeally marking him as an oppressor.

The fact that Cassie is not only unable to fulfill her intentions but also killed in the process seems to affirm feminist skepticism about and overt rejection of counter-violence on the grounds that it is not worth the risk it poses to women. Feminist friends with whom I viewed and discussed *Promising Young Woman* found the film's ending deeply dissatisfying: they, understandably, wanted Cassie to prevail. In light of the institutional failures MacKinnon and Card identify, moreover, even though Al is ultimately arrested, my friends saw the fact that his fate and those of the other men involved is left in the hands of a system that rarely prosecutes let alone convicts rapists as akin to one more violation. I want to suggest, however, that *Promising Young Woman* concludes on a more ambivalent and, surprisingly within the context of a film that eschews realism in so many ways, a therefore more realistic note. Men mostly do get away with the acts of sexual violence they commit. The cases of Francine Hughes and Inez Garcia show that even when they don't, a woman has still been violated. Women's fates usually are left in the hands of institutions constituted in and through the same norms that give rise to sexual violence in the first place.

Promising Young Woman doesn't allow viewers to lose sight of this reality; but it also doesn't take the perspective that women have to resign themselves to it. In fact, the film illustrates the subversive potential of the characteristic of counter-violence that most gives feminists pause: the fact that exercising it entails putting oneself in the way of oppressive violence. Because Nina's violation and death both propel the film's narrative and consume Cassie, it is possible for viewers to lose sight of the fact that Cassie's counter-violence is inextricably bound up with her own weekly sexual violation. Retaliation requires a violation, which means the violation has to occur. While there is much to unpack in this aspect of the film, I do not see here either a kind of self-sacrifice or self-effacement in which Cassie surrenders her body and merely allows herself to be violated or an expression of the bad faith Beauvoir attributes to adolescent girls whose self-harm ultimately reflects their acceptance of their situation.[56] Cassie's actions are not portrayed as pathological. Rather, by confronting viewers with how feminine sexuality is reduced to 'being taken'—with how conciliation, compliance, and passivity (the timidity of *se faire objet*) are women's expected sexual 'responses'—Cassie's actions expose the pathological character of normative feminine sexuality. That men are sexually aroused by Cassie when they believe her to be barely conscious and see her as a 'psycho' when she is fully alert graphically depicts the extent to which normative feminine sexuality is interconnected with and thus reproduces (vulnerability to) sexual violation. A similar subversive exposure and reversal characterize Cassie's confrontation with Al. Forcing him to confront the fact that he is a rapist, Cassie redirects Al's oppressive violence back against him, identifying him as an oppressor. When Al admits that he is afraid of Cassie, she confronts him as an equal; and in that seemingly unlikely moment of the film the ethical potential of counter-violence is revealed.

Perhaps part of the reason feminist viewers may find *Promising Young Woman* unsatisfying is because the film depicts so clearly the normative and systemic character of oppressive violence and why it remains a fixture of women's existence but does not offer clear-cut solutions. If the 'solutions' we seek are strategies of resistance we know in advance will be effective and which are devoid of risk, then real-world solutions are not forthcoming either. Counter-violence is a real-world strategy; it does not offer guarantees and it does not come without risks. Especially in light of institutional complicity, limitations, and failures, counter-violence does have an important role to play within overall feminist efforts to combat the oppressive violence upon which gender oppression relies. Its empowering, self-transformative effects undermine and disrupt the seamless reproduction of the very constructions of normative femininity that encourage women to see its actualization as merely and always (too) dangerous, and to therefore discourage them from exploring its emancipator potential. Self- and social transformation is never without risk. Women need to be able to determine for themselves, from within the context of their own situations and ideally in feminist solidarity with other women, how they wish to (individually and collectively) engage in the work of transformation and, therefore, whether, when, and how the risks associated with incorporating counter-violence as part of those projects are worth taking.

Notes

1 Jennifer L. Truman and Rachel E. Morgan, "Violent Victimization by Sexual Orientation and Gender Identity: 2017–2020," U.S. Bureau of Justice Statistics, https://bjs.ojp.gov/content/pub/pdf/vvsogi1720.pdf. It is also important to note that women of color, and trans women of color in particular, disproportionately experience sexual violence.
2 Simone de Beauvoir, *The Ethics of Ambiguity*, trans. Bernard Frechtman (New York: Citadel, 1976), 91.
3 Oppression undermines transcendence, "cutting it off from its goals," so that it is "condemned to fall uselessly back upon itself." Beauvoir, *The Ethics of Ambiguity*, 81.
4 Ibid., 82.
5 "As we have seen, my freedom, in order to fulfill itself, requires that it emerge into an open future: it is other men who open the future to me, it is they who, setting up the world of tomorrow, define my future; but if, instead of allowing me to participate in this constructive movement, they oblige me to consume my

transcendence in vain, if they keep me below the level which they have conquered and on the basis of which new conquests will be achieved, then they are cutting me off from the future, they are changing me into a thing." Beauvoir, *The Ethics of Ambiguity*, 82.
6 Beauvoir, *The Ethics of Ambiguity*, 102.
7 Frantz Fanon, *The Wretched of the Earth*, trans. Richard Philcox (New York: Grove, 2004), 4.
8 Ibid., 2; original emphasis.
9 Ibid.
10 Judith Butler, "Bodies and Power Revisited" in *Feminism and the Final Foucault*, ed. Dianna Taylor and Karen Vintges (Urbana: University of Illinois Press, 2004), 191.
11 Frantz Fanon, *Black Skin/White Masks,* trans. Richard Philcox (New York: Grove, 2008), 95; original emphasis.
12 Ibid.
13 Beauvoir, *The Ethics of Ambiguity*, 101; Fanon, *Black Skin/White Masks*, 96.
14 Beauvoir, *The Ethics of Ambiguity*, 83.
15 Fanon, *The Wretched of the Earth*, 15. Fanon makes clear that once the colonized become organized politically they cease to direct violence toward one another.
16 Judith Butler, *Gender Trouble* (New York: Routledge, 1990).
17 Simone de Beauvoir, *The Second Sex*, trans. Constance Borde and Sheila Malovany-Chevallier (New York: Vintage, 2011), 6.
18 Debra B. Bergoffen, "Why Rape? Lessons from *The Second Sex*," in *The Blackwell Companion to Simone de Beauvoir*, ed. Laura Hengehold and Nancy Bauer (Hoboken, NJ: Wiley Blackwell, 2017), 313.
19 See Jennifer McWeeny, "Varieties of Consciousness under Oppression: False Consciousness, Bad Faith, Double Consciousness, and *Se Faire Objet*," in *Phenomenology and the Political*, ed. S. West Gurley and Geoff Pfeifer (New York: Rowman & Littlefield, 2016), 149–163 and "The Second Sex of Consciousness: A New Temporality and Ontology for Beauvoir's 'Becoming Woman,'" in *On ne naît pas femme: on le devient: The Life of a Sentence*, ed. Bonnie Mann and Martina Ferrari (New York: Oxford University Press, 2017), 231–273.
20 Beauvoir, *The Second Sex*, 283.
21 Ibid.; my emphasis.
22 Ibid., 311.
23 Ibid., 349. As McWeeny puts it, "[a] woman achieves *se faire objet* by placing herself in a space where she can realize her body as a conduit for another's subjectivity" ("Varieties of Consciousness under Oppression," 159).
24 Beauvoir, *The Second Sex*, 334.
25 Ibid., 335.
26 Ibid.; original emphasis.
27 Claiming that all heterosex is rape "would mean that the man's sexual organ is a sword, a weapon," whereas in her view feminists should aim to "[invent] new sexual relations that are not oppressive." See Simone de Beauvoir, "The Rebellious Woman: An Interview by Alice Schwartzer," trans. Marybeth Timmermann, in *Feminist Writings*, ed. Margaret A. Simons and Marybeth Timmermann (Urbana: University of Illinois Press, 2021), 197.
28 See McWeeny, "Varieties of Consciousness under Oppression" and "The Second Sex of Consciousness."
29 Beauvoir, *The Second Sex*, 444; my emphasis.
30 Ibid., 341.
31 Ibid., 343.

32 Ibid.
33 Ibid., 344.
34 Ibid., 366.
35 Catharine A. MacKinnon, *Are Women Human? And Other International Dialogues* (Cambridge, MA: Harvard University Press, 2006), 264.
36 Ibid. Most U.S. agencies that collect data on crime provide information on the gender of victims but not perpetrators of sexual violence. Ian A. Elliott and Alexandra Bailey, based on a 2005 international study by Cortoni and Hansen, state that "approximately 4–5% of adult sexual offenders are women." Their data include child molestation and other violations I do not consider in my definition of sexual violence. See Ian A. Elliott and Alexandra Bailey, "Female Sex Offenders: Gender and Risk Perception," in *Responding to Sex Offending: Perceptions, Risk Management, and Public Protection*, ed. Kieran McCartan (New York: Palgrave Macmillan, 2014).
37 MacKinnon, *Are Women Human?*, 261.
38 Ibid., 261–263.
39 Claudia Card, *Confronting Evils: Terrorism, Torture, Genocide* (New York: Cambridge University Press, 2010).
40 Ibid., 143.
41 Ibid., 145.
42 Ibid., 145; original emphasis.
43 Ibid. Hughes was found not guilty by reason of temporary insanity. Garcia was initially convicted but exonerated on appeal when she was represented by feminist attorney Susan Jordan.
44 Neither MacKinnon nor Card calls for the same *kind* of response to violence against women as that which was taken after 9/11. Their aim is not to demand the sort of punitive juridical measures that expand the carceral system, but rather to show that it is quite possible to garner strong state and societal responses to "massive nonstate violence against civilians," and therefore to call into question the prevailing view that insurmountable obstacles exist to mobilization *on the same scale* in the face of systemic sexual violence. MacKinnon, *Are Women Human?*, 260.
45 Hannah Arendt makes the same point: "[R]age and the violence that sometimes […] goes with it belong among the 'natural' *human* emotions, and to cure man of them would mean nothing less than to dehumanize […] him." See Arendt, *On Violence* (New York: Harvest Books, 1970), 64; original emphasis.
46 Beauvoir, *The Ethics of Ambiguity*, 101.
47 Beauvoir, *The Second Sex*, 343.
48 Beauvoir, "The Rebellious Woman," 194.
49 Ibid., 204.
50 Ibid. These remarks resonate with the work of contemporary feminist scholars, such as Ann Cahill and Martha McCaughey, who reject the view that promoting self-defense simply reinforces the neo-liberal perspective that women are responsible for protecting themselves, and therefore blameworthy if they fail to do so. See Ann Cahill, "In Defense of Self-defense," *Philosophical Papers* 38, no. 3 (2009): 363–380 and Martha McCaughey, *Real Knockouts: The Physical Feminism of Women's Self-Defense* (New York: New York University Press, 1997).
51 For examples of various forms of feminist resistance, including actions by rape squads, see Pam McAllister, "Feminist Law-Challenging Actions," in *Fight Back! Feminist Resistance to Male Violence*, ed. Frédérique Delacoste and Felice Newman (Minneapolis: Cleis, 1981), 212–221.
52 The Gulabi Gang has expanded its scope to empower women more broadly by fostering women's independence (especially economically). This enables them to

reshape or cut ties with men in ways that reduce vulnerability to some forms of men's violence. https://gulabigang.in.
53 See Ann Pride, "To Respectability and Back: A Ten Year View of the Anti-Rape Movement," in Delacoste and Newman, *Fight Back!*, 114–118.
54 *Promising Young Woman*, dir. Emerald Fennell (Universal Pictures, 2020).
55 *Promising Young Woman* has been categorized as a 'rape-revenge' narrative, the vengeful violence of which is sometimes condemned for being merely destructive and even oppressive. There is, however, nothing in my own definition that disqualifies the violence of revenge from functioning as a form of counter-violence. Beauvoir's early work illustrates, moreover, that it is not easy to draw, and even more difficult to maintain in practice, a clear distinction between vengeful and counter-violence. See Simone de Beauvoir, "An Eye for An Eye," trans. Kristana Arp, in *Philosophical Writings*, ed. Margaret A. Simons, Marybeth Timmermann and Mary Beth Mader (Urbana: University of Illinois Press, 2004), 257. Beauvoir asserts in *The Ethics of Ambiguity*, that this punishment entails oppressors being treated "like things, with violence" (97).
56 "Sadomasochistic crazes imply a fundamental bad faith: if the girl indulges in them, it means she accepts, through her rejections, her future as a woman." Beauvoir, *The Second Sex*, 367.

References

Arendt, Hannah. *On Violence.* New York: Harvest, 1970.
Beauvoir, Simone de. *The Ethics of Ambiguity.* Translated by Bernard Frechtman. New York: Citadel, 1976.
Beauvoir, Simone de. "An Eye For An Eye." In *Philosophical Writings*, edited by Margaret A. Simons, Marybeth Timmermann, and Mary Beth Mader, translated by Kristana Arp, 245–260. Urbana: University of Illinois Press, 2004.
Beauvoir, Simone de. *The Second Sex.* Translated by Constance Borde and Sheila Malovany-Chevallier. New York: Vintage, 2011.
Beauvoir, Simone de. "The Rebellious Woman: An Interview by Alice Schwartzer." In *Feminist Writings*, edited by Margaret A. Simons and Marybeth Timmermann, translated by Marybeth Timmermann, 192–208. Urbana: University of Illinois Press, 2021.
Bergoffen, Debra B. "Why Rape? Lessons from The Second Sex." In *The Blackwell Companion to Simone de Beauvoir*, edited by Laura Hengehold and Nancy Bauer, 311–324. Hoboken, NJ: Wiley Blackwell, 2017.
Butler, Judith. *Gender Trouble.* New York: Routledge, 1990.
Butler, Judith. "Bodies and Power Revisited." In *Feminism and the Final Foucault*, edited by Dianna Taylor and Karen Vintges, 183–194. Urbana: University of Illinois Press, 2004.
Cahill, Ann. "In Defense of Self-defense." *Philosophical Papers* 38, no. 3 (2009): 363–380.
Card, Claudia. *Confronting Evils: Terrorism, Torture, Genocide.* New York: Cambridge University Press, 2010.
Elliott, Ian A. and Alexandra Bailey. "Female Sex Offenders: Gender and Risk Perception." In *Responding to Sex Offending: Perceptions, Risk Management, and Public Protection*, edited by Kieran McCartan, 48–71. New York: Palgrave Macmillan, 2014.
Fanon, Frantz. *The Wretched of the Earth.* Translated by Richard Philcox. New York: Grove, 2004.

Fanon, Frantz. *Black Skin/White Masks*. Translated by Richard Philcox. New York: Grove, 2008.
Fennell, Emerald, dir. *Promising Young Woman*. Universal Pictures, 2020.
MacKinnon, Catharine A. *Are Women Human? And Other International Dialogues*. Cambridge, MA: Harvard University Press, 2006.
McAllister, Pam. "Feminist Law-Challenging Actions." In *Fight Back! Feminist Resistance to Male Violence*, edited by Frédérique Delacoste and Felice Newman, 212–221. Minneapolis: Cleis, 1981.
McCaughey, Martha. *Real Knockouts: The Physical Feminism of Women's Self-Defense*. New York: New York University Press, 1997.
McWeeny, Jennifer. "Varieties of Consciousness under Oppression: False Consciousness, Bad Faith, Double Consciousness, and *Se Faire Objet*." In *Phenomenology and the Political*, edited by S. West Gurley and Geoff Pfeifer, 149–163. New York: Rowman & Littlefield, 2016.
McWeeny, Jennifer. "The Second Sex of Consciousness: A New Temporality and Ontology for Beauvoir's 'Becoming Woman.'" In *On ne naît pas femme: on le devient: The Life of a Sentence*, edited by Bonnie Mann and Martina Ferrari, 231–274. New York: Oxford University Press, 2017.
Pride, Ann. "To Respectability and Back: A Ten Year View of the Anti-Rape Movement." In *Fight Back! Feminist Resistance to Male Violence*, edited by Frédérique Delacoste and Felice Newman, 114–118. Minneapolis: Cleis, 1981.
Truman, Jennifer L. and Rachel E. Morgan. "Violent Victimization by Sexual Orientation and Gender Identity: 2017–2020." U.S. Bureau of Justice Statistics, June 2022. https://bjs.ojp.gov/content/pub/pdf/vvsogi1720.pdf.

10

"I DIDN'T ASK FOR IT"

Balkan Women vs. the Invisibility of Rape

Ana Maskalan

The online initiative "I Didn't Ask for It" (#nisamtrazila) was launched in January 2021, motivated by a young Serbian actress's public disclosure of being raped by a well-known Belgrade drama teacher.[1] She was soon joined by other female colleagues, and a portal was opened where thousands of women of the former Yugoslavia took the opportunity to describe and report the various forms of sexual abuse to which they had been exposed during their childhood, education, and employment—perpetrated by people they often knew and looked up to. As a belated Balkan version of the "Me Too" movement, the "I Didn't Ask for It" initiative inherited a number of the former's attributes while displaying some new ones, depending on the specific socio-cultural and political context and heritage of the region. The latter is, in my opinion, grounded in the complex permeation of socialist attitudes to women's rights and sexual violence, the unresolved traumas of mass wartime rapes, and the contemporary experience of the threat to Balkan masculinity.

"I Didn't Ask for It" not only called for solidarity in the fight against gender-based violence but, by its very name, also suggested the need to address the epistemic (testimonial and hermeneutical) injustice to which victims of sexual violence are exposed given the individual's inability to understand their own experiences and adversities, the institutional lack of confidence in the truth of their claims, and the wider social entrenchment in conservatism and patriarchy. The women behind the initiative thus correctly assumed that the ensuing public backlash would be based on the accusation that women victims themselves were responsible and willing participants in acts of sexual violence—making their struggle to raise awareness of the phenomenon of sexual violence, a struggle unprecedented in the former Yugoslav context, all the more important.

DOI: 10.4324/9781003366089-15

In this chapter I will offer a feminist analysis of the evolution of the above-mentioned initiative (followed by a silencing backlash) and of the socio-cultural and political context that made it unique. I will concentrate in more detail on several aspects that seem characteristic of "I Didn't Ask for It" that I consider to be consequences of the socio-cultural and political context of the region. These are the victims' *resignation* and need for *anonymity*, as well as the fierce *backlash* (response) of sections of the public to the actions of the initiative itself and to its leaders. Although I am aware that resignation, anonymity, and backlash can be recognized in the "Me Too" movement as well, I do not consider them to be its dominant features; nor do I understand them to be connected to the same social phenomena. As a theoretical point of departure, I will utilize Simone de Beauvoir's theoretical framework, especially her understanding of the myth of femininity and the ideas of complicity, solidarity, violence, and of sex and sexual autonomy. Beauvoir's elaboration of the concept of the Other serves here as an ontological foundation of the epistemic problem of not recognizing another's experience, discussed through Miranda Fricker's theory of epistemic injustice,[2] as well as an explanation of why victimization in the case of rape victims does not stop at the sole act of rape.

When using the term 'Balkans' I primarily refer to the five ex-Yugoslav countries—Slovenia, Croatia, and Serbia, Bosnia and Herzegovina, and Montenegro—where, in my opinion, the "I Didn't Ask for It" movement echoed the loudest. I am aware that the term 'Balkans' is often disputed, especially from the perspective of the citizens of the aforementioned countries who, aware of its pejorative meaning, do not always appreciate being called Balkan people.[3] Nevertheless, I chose this name for the geographical area and the people who inhabit it not so much because of brevity but to try to escape the notion of its perpetual negative connotations of primitive, tribal, warrior, wild, and conservative. Although I am aware that, in the context of the debate on rape, any attempt to rehabilitate the term 'Balkans' is potentially doomed to failure, it is precisely in "I Didn't Ask for It" that I find elements on the basis of which it is possible to observe the term, the people, and the geographical area it describes with fresh, less judgmental eyes.

Guilt and Otherness

As outlined above, the "I Didn't Ask for It" or *Nisam tražila* Facebook page was launched in January 2021. It was initiated by four female ex-students of the Academy of Performing Arts in Sarajevo, Bosnia (Ana Tikvić, Nadine Mičić, Matea Mavrak, and Asja Krsmanović) after hearing the shocking testimony of Serbian actress Milena Radulović.[4] Milena and several other women reported to the police that they had been sexually harassed and raped, some of them for years, by Miroslav Mika Aleksić, the influential drama teacher and owner of the acting school in Belgrade they attended. In this prestigious school, called the "Matter of the Heart," one acting lesson cost up to 60 euros, which is a very high price in a country where the average monthly net salary in 2021 was 540 euros.[5] But the parents of Aleksić's pupils accepted the price as they felt that the 'right values' were being passed on in his school. For example, the girls had to wear skirts and the boys formal shoes; their hair and nails had to be neat; students had to read one book a week; they went to the theatre regularly, and every lesson began with the Lord's Prayer. When the female pupils complained about Aleksić's inappropriate remarks and behaviour, their parents usually responded that his abusive methods served to strengthen and prepare them for the cruel world of (primarily male) directors and producers. Mika Aleksić was eventually charged with nine offenses involving rape and sexual abuse against seven women, including one minor.[6] He denied all the charges and claimed to 'feel not guilty.'

As an integral component of conscience, guilt is an emotion caused by belief in one's own wrongdoing. Feeling guilty means taking responsibility for another person's negative state or for harming another person;[7] and, while feeling guilty does not necessarily imply being truly responsible, it is also true that responsibility does not necessarily lead to a feeling of guilt. In other words, not all guilty people *feel* guilty. Research shows that sex offenders are more prone to distorting accounts of their offenses, justifying their crimes or denying them as such.[8] Although I am aware that denial does not necessarily imply a lack of feeling of guilt, some authors have noticed that it is not unusual for sex offenders as a group to express a lack of guilt for their crimes and fail to show compassion for their victims.[9] Paradoxically, sexual assault is probably the only crime in which considerable guilt is expressed not by the perpetrators but by their (female) victims. It is also a crime for which victims, in comparison to their offenders, are often blamed to the same extent (and sometimes even more)—by their partners, families, law enforcement, and the wider public. To put it simply, the sad irony of rape is that it makes the guilty feel innocent and the innocent feel guilty.

The belief that no wrong has been done—whether based on the attitude that there was no sexual assault or that there is nothing wrong with sexual assault as such—has its foundation in the social understanding of women and of femininity. That is, it is based on the specific ontology of gender, described by Simone de Beauvoir. In her book *The Second Sex* [1949], becoming a woman is described as a constant lifelong process of alienation or of *othering* imposed on women by men (and, sometimes, by other women through acts of complicity), with violence as a frighteningly effective way of keeping the process alive.[10] Othering is an integral part of defining oneself through identifying what oneself is not; and, as such, it is not reserved just for relationships between men and women:

Village people view anyone not belonging to the village as suspicious 'others.' For the native of a country inhabitants of other countries are viewed as 'foreigners'; Jews are the 'others' for anti-Semites, blacks for racist Americans, indigenous people for colonists, proletarians for the propertied classes.[11]

By its very nature, othering is the establishment, not only of a difference but also of a hierarchy between 'the One' and 'the Other,' where the Other is always understood as a lower ontological category, the bearer of weaker values, *the object, the inessential*. Influenced by Hegel and by the anthropological findings of Lévi-Strauss on the emergence of human culture through the establishment of contrasts, dualities, and oppositions, Beauvoir concluded that human society does not rest on friendship and solidarity: "a fundamental hostility to any other consciousness is found in consciousness itself; the subject posits itself only in opposition; it asserts itself as the essential and sets up the other as inessential, as the object."[12]

The process of making a person Other is in most cases reciprocal, resting on a kind of dialectic of relations in which those who dominate become dominated, and vice versa. Even if there is no real reciprocity, those being dominated can often separate, move away, or escape—building their strength in separation, solidarity, a common culture, and mutual experience. But not women! Women are the only Others, claimed Beauvoir, who remember nothing but oppression, their Otherness being from the beginning of time immutable, *absolute*.[13] She concluded that women are historically incapable of changing their social status and imposed ontology, being passive and complicit. She reasoned that:

> [Women] lack the concrete means to organize themselves into a unit that could posit itself in opposition. They have no past, no history, no religion of their own; and unlike the proletariat, they have no solidarity of labor or interests.[14]

Although she criticized women's resignation, while writing *The Second Sex*, Beauvoir couldn't help being resigned herself.[15] She did not see a real opportunity for rebellion in women's condition, believing that change was possible only if it suited men's interests.[16] Even her early views on feminism were based on the understanding that it is not an autonomous movement, but an instrument in the hands of (male) politicians.[17]

Making a person (or a group) Other is not just a matter of proclamation but of action as well, with violence being the most convincing way of making others Others—"because violence done to another is the clearest affirmation of another's alterity."[18] The mechanism of othering through sexual violence is perhaps best explained by Dianna Taylor, who refers to the phenomenon of sexual humiliation "as a manifestation of the relationship one has to oneself."[19] Influenced by the work of philosopher Avishai Margalit, Taylor concludes that humiliation comes as a deliberate consequence of violence, making victims see and understand themselves through the eyes of the perpetrator. Sexual violence is, hence, a humiliating behaviour that violates self-respect and denies the freedom of becoming in the future something other than what one currently is.

> Humiliating behaviors and conditions deny this capacity to become otherwise specifically by treating humans as nonhuman—as not worthy of freedom—while seeing them as subhuman; by extension then, being humiliated is the experience of being treated and seen in these ways.[20]

The tragedy of humiliation is not just in treating a human as a non-human; in a way it also makes that particular human see and treat themselves as non-human as a consequence.

The use of violence becomes a tool not only for acquiring and maintaining a dominant position, but also for proving who deserves to be higher on the human scale, who becomes a subject and who remains something less than a subject, who deserves to be human, and who is reduced to the *not (yet) human*.[21] This masculinist ontology is followed by a masculinist epistemology implying the interpretation of reality in such a way that it serves to maintain existing gender power relations. Or, in the words of Beauvoir: "The representation of the world as the world itself is the work of men; they describe it from a point of view that is their own and that they confound with the absolute truth."[22] In such a world, women, because of their many alleged defects and inadequacies, should be dominated, ruled, exploited, and, when unruly, punished. Such an epistemology, at the same time, blocks the vision of men who, as a consequence, do not question the origin of their privilege. On the other hand, it often silences women, making them complicit, devoid of solidarity with other women, and slow to recognize the need for social change, the need for revolution.

An example of this patriarchal representation of the world is rape culture, an environment in which sexual violence is tolerated, normalized, even glorified—where victims are blamed and men feel the need to confirm their masculinity through sexually aggressive behaviour. In such an environment even when violence is recognized as such it is individualized and reduced to the pathology of both perpetrator and victim. In other words, at the wider social level violence against women, especially sexual violence, is still not recognized as a systemic, structural, and all-pervading problem—and sometimes it is still not recognized as a problem at all. The consequences of this are also evident in the usual understanding of the act of rape: that, to be considered as such, it must include force and active resistance. This not only undervalues the right and capacity of women to say 'no' but also ignores all the intricacies of the power relations between men and women that render physical violence unnecessary for rape to happen.[23] In other words, in contemporary patriarchal societies—where men more often than women hold financial, political, and social power—women do not need to literally be held at gunpoint to feel pressured, coerced, and forced against their will. Not recognizing that fact is the worst form of cynicism.

In Balkan languages, the word for rape usually contains the term *sila*, meaning 'force'—signifying that sexual intercourse in which there is no use or threat of physical force cannot be considered rape. Consequently, in Bosnia and Herzegovina,[24] Montenegro,[25] and Serbia[26] rape is still limited to sexual violence under coercion and direct threat of assault on the victim or another person, which deviates from the definition given by the Istanbul Convention—namely, absence of consent.[27] The distinction between rape and sexual intercourse without consent was abolished in Croatia in 2019[28] and in Slovenia two years later.[29]

Resistance and Resignation

Two days after Milena Radulović went public, on January 18, the Facebook page "I Didn't Ask for It" opened with the hashtag #*Nisi sama*—"You Are Not Alone." The four administrators invited women to anonymously share similar traumatic stories to draw attention to what they had experienced, and thus change the atmosphere in a society where any form of violence against women is enveloped by prejudice and tacitly approved, supported, and encouraged. Although at the beginning among the first to speak were actresses and women working in the public eye—journalists, musicians, and politicians—over the course of 24 hours the site became a place of testimony of many, uniting women from once war-torn countries. What happened next was described by the media and the initiators of the Facebook page themselves as opening Pandora's box.[30] In just two days the site published a large number of shocking testimonies of sexual harassment and rape. The victims were mostly girls and women; the perpetrators were usually men in positions of power; and the violence often took place during high school or college years, sometimes even in educational institutions, and it was often an open secret. Everybody knew about it, but nobody did anything.

As discussed so far, "I Didn't Ask for It" is more or less an extension of the global "Me Too" movement, sharing the characteristics of an online platform and certain spokespersons, as well as substantial media support and sympathy, and culminating in institutional changes and law reform. But it also displays some traits specific to the region's socio-cultural and political context and heritage that are grounded in the complex permeation of socialist attitudes to women's rights and sexual violence, unresolved traumas of mass wartime rapes, and contemporary experience of the threat to Balkan masculinity. Three specific features that I will discuss in more detail are *resignation, anonymity*, and *backlash*.

The first distinctive feature of the "I Didn't Ask for It" movement, especially at the beginning, was the pervasive feeling of resignation. Many women sharing their stories could not help but feel resigned to the situation they were in. In Beauvoir's opinion, resignation naturally follows women's life path and their historical situation of profound powerlessness.[31] Women on "I Didn't Ask for It" often told their stories not as a form of rebellion but as a form of emotional discharge, a confession or even a tired lament. Their pervading attitude was that nothing could or would be done; they just needed to voice their trauma and to be heard by somebody who understands.[32]

Although resignation could be understood as universal to all women under patriarchy, there is a form of resignation in the Balkans that has a precise socio-historical rationale. I believe it comes as a consequence of failed expectations following initial enthusiasm after major social changes. It should be borne in mind that the Balkan area is historically marked by many political upheavals and ethnic conflicts, among the most shocking of which took place in the 1990s, when socialist Yugoslavia disintegrated and independent nation states were established. From its very beginning in 1945, ideologues of socialist Yugoslavia (the Socialist Federal Republic of Yugoslavia), led by Josip Broz Tito and inspired by the texts of Friedrich Engels (especially *Origin of the Family* from 1884),[33] emphasized the role of women in building a new supra-nation.[34] Prominent in the fighting ranks of the People's Liberation Army and organized into the powerful Women's Antifascist Front (WAF), women represented a group whose support was of crucial importance for the political and social establishment of Yugoslavia. That is why Tito, in his speech at the First WAF Conference in 1942, said that:

> [The women] here today, once and for all, have a right to establish one fact: that this struggle must bear fruit for the women of Yugoslav nations and that no one will ever be able to snatch this expensive fruit from their hands again![35]

In the years that followed, Yugoslavia made a huge leap in the fight for women's rights, granting them equality in the 1974 Constitution of the Socialist Federal Republic of Yugoslavia.[36] This also included provisions guaranteeing equal pay for equal work, employment protection, and protection of the interests of mothers and children (article 24). The right to abortion was also included in this Constitution (article 191), just one year after the notable decision of the Supreme Court to include the same right in the U.S. Constitution. In 1953 WAF was dissolved, and Tito's speeches little by little shifted its members' focus from being warriors and heroines to being mothers and wives, locking Yugoslav women within the sacred walls of the family. In the decades that followed, women's calls for more substantial social transformations were silenced by the endless postponement of solving women's issues in the name of dealing with those related to class.[37]

Although initially favouring socialism, Beauvoir eventually realized that, to change their condition, women did indeed need a separate feminist movement. Of course, the rejection of the socialist solution did not push her toward accepting the capitalist system, which she believed did not allow for true gender equality:

> Once inside the class struggle, women understood that the class struggle did not eliminate the sex struggle. It's at that point that I myself became aware of what I have just said. Before that I was convinced that equality of the sexes can only be possible once capitalism is destroyed and therefore—and it's this "therefore" which is the fallacy—we must first fight the class struggle. It is true that equality of the sexes is impossible under capitalism. [...] However, just look at Soviet Russia or Czechoslovakia, where (even if we are willing to call those countries "socialist", which I am not) there is a profound confusion between emancipation of the proletariat and emancipation of women. Somehow, the proletariat always end up being made up of men. The patriarchal values have remained intact there as well as here. And that—this consciousness among women that the class struggle does not embody the sex struggle—is what is new. Yet most women in the struggle know that now. That's the greatest achievement of the feminist movement. It's one which will alter history in the years to come.[38]

Blaženka Despot, a leading Croatian feminist philosopher, spoke in a similar vein, believing that the basis of socialism is the constant postponement of solving the 'women's question'—always being placed on the historical timeline behind the resolution of the class question.[39] What some critics also noticed is that socialist states often lacked the very ideology on which they supposedly rested—the socialist one. Another Croatian feminist philosopher, Gordana Bosanac, understood the Yugoslav political system as paradoxical, defining its main feature to be the forced proclamation or inauguration of something that did not yet exist.[40] In other words, socialism in Yugoslavia never truly existed; it was aggressively proclaimed before it was realized, which is why real socialism, as understood and described by Karl Marx and Friedrich Engels, never existed in Yugoslavia. The final solution to women's issues was thus not in socialism, let alone in its propaganda illusion. Gender equality itself was an instrument of that illusion. Socialist Yugoslavia promised gender equality, proclaimed it (although it was not implemented or lived in the true sense of the word), and then gave up on it—especially on gender equality in the intimate, private sphere. Unlike socialist philosophers such as Fourier or Engels, and unlike Beauvoir, Yugoslav ideologues refused to recognize that the battlefield for women was also within the family. This can be seen in the fact that, for example, in Yugoslavia marital rape was never actually considered rape.

Despite the above, it should be pointed out that socialist Yugoslavia introduced important changes in the lives of women, primarily concerning their education and employment. Unfortunately, these interventions proved to be rather unimportant during the country's disintegration in the 1990s. It is difficult to say with certainty whether, at that particular time, women forgot about Yugoslavia's contribution to changing their social position or whether it was more important for them to side with men in the fight for national freedom. What I remember from those times is deep disappointment with Yugoslavia and keen expectation of promised times of political and economic freedom carried on the wings of national identity. Although what followed brought positive trends, it also brought negative ones; or, in the words of Slovenian scholar Mitja Velikonja:

> However, notwithstanding its many unquestionably positive developments, the post-socialist transition also opened a Pandora's box of unexpected troubles. On one hand, the transition resulted in the long anticipated pluralization of societies in all respects—social, political, economic, and cultural. On the other hand, this was inevitably accompanied by a series of negative processes and events, including the demolition of [the] welfare state, the introduction of what might be called *turbo-capitalism*, the rise of social injustices, repatriarchalization, retraditionalization, clericalization, and nationalist conflicts. Not one post-socialist country, not even the most successful, was spared such negative consequences, their malign effects varying only in intensity.[41]

Unfortunately, the economic transition—marked by crime and the return and restoration of traditional values that threatened to stop the modernization processes started in Yugoslavia, especially in the war-stricken countries—caused disappointment and resignation among a large part of the population.[42] It seemed as if nothing had changed or that matters had even got worse. Women of the "I Didn't Ask for it" movement still cannot count on the institutions that should provide help and protection against sex crimes, such as legal entities and social welfare centers.

Anonymity and Epistemic Injustice

Most of the women sharing their stories did not want to identify themselves or the perpetrators, sending their testimonies to the Facebook page administrators through private channels. They claimed anonymity provided them with a safe space for communication, protecting them from public judgment. It also allowed them to reveal the deep shame they felt and the helplessness they suffered, feelings that are caused by the sexual assaults but also dependent on the cultural determinants of femininity so vividly described by Beauvoir.

Through publishing their testimonies, "I Didn't Ask for It" helped the women understand their trauma. In other words, women chose anonymity not only as a shield against public mistrust but also in a way against mistrust in themselves and their capacity to understand and describe what happened to them. Many women did not initially believe that they were actually raped, which is not surprising considering that they lived in a culture in which rape was surrounded by misconceptions and silence. What contributed to their confusion was not only the cultural understanding of rape but also the social understanding of the rapist himself.

Like "Me Too," "I Didn't Ask for It" questioned at least two widespread misconceptions about the perpetrators of sexual violence. The first is that they are mostly strangers lurking in dark corridors and alleys, crazed predators, and hardened criminals. Even though statistics show that sexual assault is usually perpetrated by someone known to the victim, the pervasive belief about unknown rapists negatively affects how women understand and describe their own experiences of sexual assault.[43] It also allows perpetrators to deny guilt for what they have done (believing that it was not rape but, for example, seduction), and the public to blame the victim instead of condemning the culprit. The second misconception is that sexual abusers are always people from the margins of life, lonely and unloved individuals lacking erotic or any other capital. "I Didn't Ask for It" revealed that the truth is often diametrically opposite—exposing not a lack but often an abuser's surplus of charm, and not impotence but an excess of social power, often accompanied by undeserved privilege and assumption of rights over other human beings. Women who dare to stand up to such men, both during the act itself and during a potential trial, are faced not only with this excess of power but also with their own lack of it, manifested in the tendency of the police and the judges to disregard their opinion and experience.

Here I would like to recall Miranda Fricker's useful notion of epistemic injustice, referring to those forms of unfair treatment that "relate to issues of knowledge, understanding, and participation in communicative practices." Among the forms of unfair treatment mentioned are exclusion, marginalization, distrust, systematic distortion, and misrepresentation of somebody's accounts, meanings, and opinions.[44] Epistemic injustice means silencing women—rendering them invisible, inaudible, or less authoritative in communicative practices.

In her book, Fricker differentiated between hermeneutical injustice and testimonial injustice, claiming that testimonial injustice occurs when a hearer attributes lesser credibility to someone's testimony due to prejudices on the basis of the speaker's gender, race, or sexuality.[45] Although testimonial injustice is manifested in numerous aspects of public and private life, it acquires its most harmful qualities precisely in the courts. In the Balkans, as in the rest of the world, victims of sexual assault are forced to defend and justify themselves in and out of court more often than victims of other crimes. Testimonies by women are also frequently dismissed on the basis of common misconceptions about women's nature, such as: they are born to be sexually dominated; or, when they say 'no,' they actually mean 'yes.'

For many Balkan women, anonymous speech was the first cautious step after years of silence. And, when they finally made it, they were painfully aware that many would not believe them and that the violence would go unpunished since the bearers of injustice were not only the sexual abusers but also the police, judges, family members, social welfare centers—all those who engage in victim-blaming instead of with crime. Furthermore, in a world where rapists are portrayed as unknown monsters from the margins of society, for women the criminal actions of teachers, mentors, and idols are not only difficult to explain to the police and lawyers but also to themselves. And this is where hermeneutic injustice comes into play.

According to Fricker, hermeneutical injustice occurs when a "gap in collective interpretive resources puts someone at an unfair disadvantage when it comes to making sense of their social experiences."[46] In other words, hermeneutical injustice pertains to obscuring or marginalizing certain experiences, making them difficult to understand or explain for those who experienced them.[47] Denial of epistemic authority and interpretative resources as a crucial element of systemic discrimination that women suffer is most obvious in cases of sexual violence and abuse. In her book, Fricker gave the example of Carmita Wood, a woman who quit her job in the seventies because of the sexual harassment she endured from her work colleague, physicist and director of the Laboratory of Nuclear Studies at Cornell University, Boyce McDaniel. At a time when the term 'sexual harassment' was not publicly acknowledged, Carmita had difficulty explaining the reasons for her resignation, deeming them personal; and, as a result, was denied unemployment benefits.[48] After many years of being tormented by shame and discomfort, she had the same problem in describing and interpreting her own experience, which can still be seen in many women of the "I Didn't Ask for It" movement. Most of them told their story years after their violent experience, deeply horrified by the growing public attacks on Milena Radulović for not reporting 'on time.' The fight to have one's own marginalized experience acknowledged thus becomes a provocation of the dominant group's experience; or, in the words of philosopher Charles W. Mills:

> It is not a matter of an innocent misunderstanding or gap, but of a misrepresentation generated organically, materially, from the male perspective on the world, motivated by their group interests and phenomenologically supported by their group experience. And depending on how pivotal this misrepresentation or non-representation is to the preservation of the status quo, its reformist naming or renaming will be vigorously resisted by the system's male beneficiaries.[49]

Silencing and marginalization of women's experiences took a particularly dark turn in the Balkans during the wars of the 1990s, when mass war rapes took place. During that period the female body became a battlefield over which biological tactics of warfare, nationalist retaliation, and misogyny were applied.[50] In Bosnia alone between 25,000 and 50,000 people—mostly women—were exposed to sexual abuse and rape.[51] Because of the war and the events that followed, Balkan women know that in this part of the world rape goes unpunished and that victims are often rejected by their families and forced into silence by their country. War rapes did not just victimize women; they also provoked a strong patriarchal sense of shame that awakens when something considered property was being defiled. In this same patriarchal sense, nations were ashamed as well—especially in the cases of rape camps, where women were held until the late stage of any pregnancy so the children would inherit their father's ethnicity.[52]

During the war and in its aftermath, Balkan women were forced—some of them in suicidal acts of complicity and at the cost of their humanity and sanity—to hide their triple or quadruple victimization or their multiple othering. They were victimized as girls and women living in a world that disparages their experiences and imposes on them distorted views of their reality; victimized as casualties of war when they were raped, mutilated, and killed; victimized after the war when they received almost no institutional help; victimized when, because they were raped, their families turned their backs on them; and victimized because, in the end, they were forced to remain silent so as not to embarrass their country. In the meantime, their voices were taken over by their nation states, usually for the political purpose of gaining power and leverage. This is why many women do not trust those who pretend to speak in their name and why, to this very day, many women choose to stay anonymous when they speak.

Backlash and Balkan Masculinity

A few days after it was launched, the "I Didn't Ask for It" Facebook page was falsely reported and blocked, which is why the "I Didn't Ask for It"

Facebook group and web page were opened, providing women with new areas of testimony.[53] By that time the social media backlash had strengthened considerably, dominated by intimidating, vulgar, and misogynistic attacks. The first of these attacks appeared immediately after the public testimony of Milena Radulović, and came down to the infamous, infinitely repeated sentence that rape victims are often faced with: 'You asked for it!'[54] Also, due to frequent criticism of women for not reporting their attackers, at the end of 2021 the Twitter initiative "I Didn't Report" started, resulting in 15,000 posts in the first two days alone.

There were also clickbait headlines describing a rape as a 'sex scandal' or 'affair' and articles problematizing the personal history of women who spoke about sexual violence or writing complete fabrications, as well as fake news and conspiracy theories aimed at discrediting the victims. And this is where again Simone de Beauvoir comes to mind, especially regarding the trial of Algerian war rape victim Djamila Boupacha. Beauvoir described the case in her *Le Monde* article starting with a famous sentence: "The most scandalous thing about a scandal is that you get used to it."[55]

In her article on this young Algerian woman, who was tortured and raped by members of the French army in 1960 to force a confession about her activities within the Algerian National Liberation Front, Beauvoir suggested the idea that rape is a punishment for women's claim to legitimacy. Sexual violence again becomes a tool directed against all those women who do not agree to be just flesh and reduces them to that same flesh. Those who dare to engage in public affairs, who dare to be seen—actresses, politicians, and journalists—are especially detested since they call into question the gender norms and myths of masculinity and femininity as strictly separated.

The idea of the impropriety of women's work and activities in the public space is well reflected in several notable Croatian dictionaries of foreign words, where 'public woman' and 'prostitute' are regularly defined as synonymous.[56] In this context, actresses are particularly interesting. Simone de Beauvoir considers actresses to be women who are eternally exposed to moral reproach but who, freed from dependence on men, manage to realize their humanity through their profession. "By realizing themselves as human beings, they accomplish themselves as women."[57] Perhaps that is precisely why the initial online attack by many (mostly anonymous men but also women) on Milena Radulović was so vicious, jumping to conclusions about the innate promiscuity of actresses, their hunger for attention and money, and the rejection of men (in this case Mika Aleksić) when no longer having any use for them.

In the essay *Brigitte Bardot and the Lolita Syndrome* [1959], Beauvoir tried to explain why the French public disliked the beautiful and talented actress. Here, as in the Djamila Boupacha story, Beauvoir identified the collapse of the myth of femininity understood as a force of nature, sexual and instinctive, childish and capricious and, at the same time, submissive to the patriarchal morality and power. That collapse happened primarily in the movies of director Roger Vadim, where Bardot is shown rejecting those "safe values, vain hopes and irksome constraint."[58] There she refused passivity, immobility, and complicity—in short, she refused access to male desire. As a consequence, in real life Brigitte Bardot was forced to face hate and boycott, and her public image had to be beautified with stories of her purity, honesty, and love for her country. Balkan actresses face a similar destiny, but with a reversed image. It is not the movies that make them despised but their public personas, which are fundamentally different from the angel-devil-prostitute characters played in the Balkan movies. Balkan actresses are young, emancipated, and educated women—often looking, living, and thinking in unconventional ways, not asking permission for their choices. In a culture where an actress is still sometimes considered to be just one step away from a prostitute, women who choose that career choose not to go with the flow, not to be passive, complicit, and accessible. And that is what irritates many.

The strong backlash against the women of "I Didn't Ask for It" should also be put in the context of the strengthening of nationalism and religious extremism accompanied by the aforementioned renewal of tradition and patriarchy in gender relations after the fall of Yugoslavia. The result was the emergence of a specific patriarchal capitalism in the European semi-periphery. The re-patriarchalization of gender relations since the early 1990s has brought again the enthronement of family values, serving as a justification for severe sanctions against those women who do not want to live by the rules. Again, we should recall Beauvoir's claim: "Because man is sovereign in this world, he claims the violence of his desires as a sign of his sovereignty."[59]

Women finding their voice on "I Didn't Ask for It" threatened some of these freshly restored myths, thus provoking a backlash. One target was the myth of the family as a sacred community headed by a righteous father whose function and power are then transformed into the professions of priest, doctor, and teacher. The idea that perpetrators of sexual violence were men playing the role of holy fathers has shaken not just the established understanding of sexual violence but the established justification of power over others by the alleged moral superiority of those holding the power.

Another development took place that we can characterize as a crisis of the myth of Balkan masculinity. It is true that Balkan masculinity was historically deeply connected to nationalism, militarism, and sexism; but it is also true that, in the words of Serbian sociologist Marina Blagojević:

> "Transition" has produced a situation in which the largest number of men are those who do not enjoy patriarchal dividends, or enjoy them to a small extent. Both men and women have been largely instrumentalized in the "war transition" project and represent the "losers of the transition." There is a gap between hegemonic masculinities, the models of

masculinity that dominate the media and that are key to re-patri-archalization and re-traditionalization, and the real life of the vast majority of men.[60]

Blagojević claims that in the Balkans today there is a gap between the dominant hegemonic masculinity (as described above) and the real life of men, which is not characterized by privilege or power. In other words, Balkan men have been othered as well. Ironically, their othered status did not make them necessarily sympathetic to women, especially not to those educated, privileged, and socially networked women who were the only ones who dared to tell their stories without anonymity. The attitudes of many men are reminiscent of the old socialist criticism of feminism as too Western and bourgeois, distant from the problems and struggles of the working class (women).[61] That is why, just by the very fact of similarity with "Me Too," "I Didn't Ask for It" provokes negative sentiments which bring to mind the socialist intolerance of the feminist struggle but also represent the spiteful resistance of the 'European backward periphery' to the rich and privileged West and its values.

By Way of Conclusion

When Simone de Beauvoir wrote *The Second Sex*, as already indicated, she was not fully convinced of the strength of the women's movement and women's solidarity, believing that the history of otherness—the history of observing oneself through other people's critical and negative eyes—stood in the way of sisterhood. Her attitude is not surprising as *The Second Sex* appeared immediately after the Second World War, when the voice of the suffragettes had long been forgotten and the new feminist wave had not even begun. Paradoxically, it was her book that gave impetus to new women and new articulations of injustices that affect women, among other things—injustices that take place in the private and intimate sphere of existence. This is precisely why she wrote so enthusiastically about feminists in the seventies, describing them as those who should and could change the world for the better, giving feminism priority over all other political theories that promised to change women's social position.

The justification of her faith in female collective strength was shown by the "Me Too" and subsequent "I Didn't Ask for It" movements. Of course, their creation and maintenance were certainly facilitated by the new technologies of communication and social engagement, enabling the connection of the traditionally disconnected—women confined to the domestic sphere. When it comes to the Balkans, women have not only crossed the borders of their households, but also the barbed borders of their national states, where intolerance and hatred reigned until recently. What "I Didn't Ask for It" made possible was that women, recounting their own experiences and their pain, no longer viewed themselves through men's eyes but through women's eyes, identifying with other women and finding togetherness, solidarity, and strength in that.

In the meantime, "I Didn't Ask for It" attracted much institutional and individual attention on a transnational level, gaining substantial support from many. For example, the Bosnian Agency for Gender Equality announced that crisis centers for victims of rape and sexual violence would open in major cities in 2021;[62] and academies and colleges in Balkan countries formed various platforms for students to report abuse or harassment. In just a few days initial reports were made naming abusers, and by the end of January there were hundreds of them. Public campaigns, lectures, and educational videos were launched, and blogs, open letters to governments, and thousands of newspaper articles were written. Balkan women are now at a time when the burden of action has shifted from women's groups to law enforcement; and conventional political and legal institutions—institutions that are traditionally slow and patriarchal—are taking concrete steps to eliminate or alleviate the problems of sexual violence in the Balkans.

Despite the unfavourable odds, "I Didn't Ask for It" made a giant step by successfully connecting women from countries that are still healing the wounds of war. It was through social networks that they found a way not only to connect with others but also to give meaning to their painful experiences through mutual support and understanding.[63] Today, their voices are no longer sad but angry, calling for changes to the petrified and unjust patterns in the patriarchal Balkan societies. At the same time, they also reveal a certain level of maturity that the aforementioned societies have reached, which is also reflected in the readiness of institutions to implement certain changes, however small and insignificant they may seem at times, as well as in the open support of many men. What should also be noted is that, like "Me Too," the "I Didn't Ask for It" movement in one way or another spills over into all pores of society, which is thereby changed and renewed.

Although there is still a lot to be done in the Balkans, it is promising that the movement's ideas are slowly spreading, encouraging women's testimonies not only in the area of sexual violence but also regarding reproductive rights, domestic violence, unpaid work, and the like. By finding their voice through solidarity and compassion, Balkan women not only freed themselves from their trauma but also from their ontological otherness, *becoming women* this time on their own terms.

Notes

1 https://www.facebook.com/NisamTrazila/. For additional information see: Samira Trešnjo, "Nisam Tražila: Four Girls Who Fought against Gender-Based Violence," *Balkan Diskurs*, January 12, 2022, https://balkandiskurs.com/en/2022/01/12/nisam

-trazila-initiative/; Aida Sofic Salihbegovic, "The Balkans Face Their #Metoo Moment," *Deutsche Welle*, February 7, 2021, https://www.dw.com/en/the-balkans-face-their-metoo-moment/a-56469884; Đurđa Radulović, "How Facebook Became the New Feminist Battleground for #MeToo in the Western Balkans," *The Calvert Journal*, June 21, 2021, https://www.calvertjournal.com/features/show/12875/feminist-facebook-groups-fighting-change-memes-western-balkans; Lepa Mlađenović, Milena Milojević, and Mina Damjanović, "Balkan Women Uprising against Sexual Violence," *CSSP Civil Society Strengthening Platform*, February 1, 2021, https://cssplatform.org/balkan-women-uprising-against-sexual-violence; Dolores Cviticanin, "#NisiSama: The Constructive Role of Social Media in Supporting the Ex-Yugoslav #MeToo Movement," *International Public Policy Review*, February 27, 2021, https://ippr-journal.com/2021/02/27/nisisama-the-constructive-role-of-social-media-in-supporting-the-ex-yugoslav-metoo-movement/; Marion Dautry, "'You Are Not Alone': Balkan Women Seize #Metoo Moment," *France 24*, January 27, 2021, https://www.france24.com/en/live-news/20210127-you-are-not-alone-balkan-women-seize-metoo-moment; Ivan Fischer, "Serbian Rape Testimonies Spark Regional Women's Movements," *Brussels Morning*, February 5, 2021, https://brusselsmorning.com/serbian-rape-testimonies-spark-regional-womens-movements/10463/.

2 Miranda Fricker, *Epistemic Injustice: Power and the Ethics of Knowing* (Oxford: Oxford University Press, 2007).

3 The specific centuries-old Western-European imagery of the Balkans as a backward periphery inhabited by fratricidal tribes, due to which it could never be anything other than 'not-quite-Europe,' has been discussed by numerous authors, among whom the work of Maria Todorova deserves perhaps the greatest attention. See for example: Maria Todorova, *Imagining the Balkans* (Oxford: Oxford University Press, 2009), 1–37, and "The Balkans: From Discovery to Invention," *Slavic Review* 53, no. 2 (1994): 453–482. Consequently, such a perception of the region has had a negative impact on its inhabitants, who refuse to identify themselves as Balkan. See for example: Robert Bideleux and Ian Jeffries, *The Balkans: A Post-Communist History* (London: Routledge, 2007), 16, who claim that they "are fully aware that the words 'Balkan' and 'the Balkans' are heavily laden with multiple cultural meanings, connotations and stereotypical images, that some of these meanings and images are quite rightly considered to be demeaning, condescending, derogatory or at best ambiguous, and that the terms 'Balkan' and 'the Balkans' are therefore by no means fully accepted by this peninsula's inhabitants."

4 Milena Radulović described her terrifying experiences in an interview with journalist Ivana Mastilović Jasnić, who published parts of it in a Serbian daily newspaper. See Ivana Mastilović Jasnić, "Poznata mlada glumica Milena Radulović: 'Silovao me učitelj glume Miroslav Mika Aleksić kad sam imala 17 godina,'", *Blic*, January 16, 2021, https://www.blic.rs/vesti/hronika/milena-radulovic-miroslav-mika-aleksic-optuzbe-silovanje-seksualno-zlostavljanje/5fj8cjv.

5 Statistical Office of the Republic of Serbia, "Statistical Release: Average Salaries and Wages per Employee, January 2021" (April 26, 2021), https://publikacije.stat.gov.rs/G2021/HtmlE/G20211080.html.

6 Milica Stojanović, "Renowned Serbian Acting Teacher Detained over Rape Claims," *Balkan Insight*, January 19, 2021, https://balkaninsight.com/2021/01/18/custody-urged-for-serbian-acting-teacher-accused-of-rape/.

7 Mica Estrada-Hollenbeck and Todd F. Heatherton, "Avoiding and Alleviating Guilt through Prosocial Behavior," in *Guilt and Children*, ed. Jane Bybee (San Diego: Academic Press, 1998), 216.

8 See for example: Harry G. Kennedy and Donald H. Grubin, "Patterns of Denial in Sex Offenders," *Psychological Medicine* 22, no. 1 (1992): 191; Chris Jackson

and Brian A. Thomas-Peter, "Denial in Sex Offenders: Workers' Perceptions," *Criminal Behaviour and Mental Health* 4, no. 1 (1994): 21–23; Jill S. Levenson, "'But I Didn't Do It!,'" *Sexual Abuse* 23, no. 3 (2010): 346–364.

9 See for example: Lorenne M. Clark and Debra J. Lewis, *Rape: The Price of Coercive Sexuality* (Toronto: Women's Press, 1977), 105; Madhumita Pandey, "'My Mother Is a Goddess', 'I Am an Inmate Here': Male Prisoners' Attitudes towards Women and Their Perceptions of Culpability from Delhi Prison" (doctoral thesis, Anglia Ruskin University, 2018), 219–225.

10 Simone de Beauvoir, *The Second Sex*, trans. Constance Borde and Sheila Malovany-Chevallier (New York: Vintage, 2011).

11 Ibid., 6–7.

12 Ibid., 7.

13 Ibid., cf. 8.

14 Ibid., 8.

15 Simone de Beauvoir wrote *The Second Sex* in 1949, just four years after the Second World War and 14 before Betty Friedan's famous book *The Feminine Mystique* that breathed new life into the American and then the global feminist movement. The historical moment in which she wrote her book was marked by the recovery of a post-apocalyptic world in which the struggle for women's rights was almost forgotten, or at least postponed. Later, in the 1970s and on the wings of the second wave of feminism, Beauvoir relinquished her resignation, believing instead in the importance and power of the feminist movement and giving it priority over other political forms of struggle for women's rights. See for example: Filosofi för Gymnasiet, "Simone de Beauvoir 'Why I'm a Feminist', 1975," YouTube video, *49:42*. November 5, 2021. https://www.youtube.com/watch?v=g6eDMaDWquI.

16 Beauvoir, *The Second Sex*, cf. 151. See, also, for example, the subsequent section: "For the most part, women resign themselves to their lot without attempting any action; those who did try to change attempted to overcome their singularity and not to confine themselves in it triumphantly. When they intervened in world affairs, it was in concert with men and from a masculine point of view." Ibid.

17 Ibid.

18 Ibid., 85.

19 Dianna Taylor, "Humiliation as a Harm of Sexual Violence: Feminist versus Neoliberal Perspectives," *Hypatia* 33, no. 3 (2018): 438.

20 Ibid.

21 Here I am referring to the Western philosophical tradition—starting with Aristotle, then Thomas Aquinas, Spinoza, Rousseau, Kant, Hegel, Schopenhauer, Nietzsche, Heidegger, Wittgenstein, and all the way to Otto Weininger—that considers women to be morally and intellectually inferior to men while reserving only for them the full status of a human being. Of course, historically, not only women were condemned to such a fate since large numbers of people were not considered human in the true sense of the word, thus justifying the need to manage and exploit them.

22 Beauvoir, *The Second Sex*, 166.

23 Of course, it should be kept in mind that this specific form of violence should not be viewed exclusively through the lens of male perpetrators and female victims. In addition to women, the victims of patriarchal violence are often other men (boys, queer men, men who do not conform to the strict framework of hegemonic masculinity, etc.), and the perpetrators of violence can be both men and women. However for the purposes of this work, while not intending to minimize or deny other forms of violence, I concentrated on male sexual violence against women as this was the reason behind the "I Didn't Ask for It" movement in the first place.

24 Vladana Vasić, "Krivična djela seksualnog nasilja u pravnom sistemu Bosne i Hercegovine [Criminal Acts of Sexual Violence in the Legal System of Bosnia and Herzegovina]," in *Krivična djela silovanja i ostalog seksualnog nasilja u Bosni i Hercegovini*, ed. Vesna Pirija (Sarajevo: Sarajevo Open Centre, 2017), 29; Amnesty International, "Criminalization and Prosecution of Rape in Bosnia and Herzegovina: Submission to the UN Special Rapporteur on Violence against Women, Its Causes and Consequences," https://www.amnesty.org/en/wp-content/uploads/2021/05/EUR6324572020ENGLISH.pdf.
25 OECD, "Social Institutions & Gender Index 2019: Montenegro," https://www.genderindex.org/wp-content/uploads/files/datasheets/2019/ME.pdf. The same document claims that, although spousal rape is recognized under article 212 of the Civil Code of Montenegro, marital rape is not subject to *ex officio* prosecution but only to private litigation.
26 Dušan Dakić, "Silovanje bez prinude? [Rape without Coercion?]," *Otvorena vrata pravosuđa*, January 17, 2022, https://www.otvorenavratapravosudja.rs/teme/krivicno-pravo/silovanje-bez-prinude.
27 Recognizing social context and power relations that allow for the possibility of sexual violence without the use of coercion or threat as well as a possibility of victimhood without active physical resistance, the Istanbul Convention requires only the absence of consent for an act to be considered rape. See: "The Council of Europe Convention on Preventing and Combating Violence against Women and Domestic Violence," May 5, 2011, https://rm.coe.int/168008482e.
28 Anja Vladisavljevic, "Croatia Toughens Penalties for Domestic and Sexual Violence," *Balkan Insight*, November 5, 2019, https://balkaninsight.com/2019/10/25/croatia-toughens-penalties-for-domestic-and-sexual-violence/.
29 STA, "Slovenia Redefines Rape to Focus on Consent, Not Violence," *Total Slovenia News*, May 6, 2021, https://www.total-slovenia-news.com/politics/8233-slovenia-redefines-rape-to-focus-on-consent-not-violence.
30 The opening of Pandora's box is a formulation that runs through numerous articles, where the evils that came out of the mythological box refer not just to the testimonies of abuse but also to the response of sections of the audience to those testimonies, exposing deep social misogyny and sexism. See for example: Tamara Zablocki, "Žene koje su otvorile Pandorinu kutiju [The Women Who Opened Pandora's Box]," *Urban Magazin*, September 2, 2021, https://www.urbanmagazin.ba/ispovijesti-prezivjelih-zene-koje-su-otvorile-pandorinu-kutiju/; or Klix, "Ukazuje li pokret 'Nisam tražila' na općeprihvaćenu mizoginiju u našem društvu? [Does the 'I Didn't Ask For It' Movement Point to Generally Accepted Misogyny in Our Society?]," *Klix.ba*, January 21, 2021, https://www.klix.ba/magazin/ukazuje-li-pokret-nisam-trazila-na-opceprihvacenu-mizoginiju-u-nasem-drustvu/210121127, with the caption: "The page 'I Didn't Ask For It' was launched on January 18. Then Pandora's box was opened and every day there are more and more posts on this platform in which women and girls anonymously talk about the sexual violence they have experienced—both verbally and physically."
31 "One of their typical features is resignation. When the ashes of Pompeii's statues were dug out, it was observed that the men were caught in movements of revolt, defying the sky or trying to flee, while the women were bent, withdrawn into themselves, turning their faces toward the earth. They know they are powerless against things: volcanoes, policemen, employers, or men. 'Women are made to suffer,' they say; That's life; nothing can be done about it.'" Beauvoir, *The Second Sex*, 657.
32 Here are several examples from the movement's web page: "Why am I writing all this? To make it easier for me [to do it] anonymously. And I would like to tell you that there is no adequate punishment for abusers. And if they were sentenced to

thousands of years in prison, if they rolled over in their graves for hundreds of years, it wouldn't be enough. Nothing will compensate for my mutilation. [...] Who and in what way will pay for my lost, cut, mutilated, painful heart? Who will give me back my years and in what way? To erase horrors? Make me normal again? The system makes fun of us with funny stories how sometimes abusers are punished. And society [...] society stones us as much as the abuser. A neverending circle" (https://www.nisamtrazila.org/svjedocanstva/nisamtrazila-pria-531). "In short, I feel emotionally disabled because I try to forget everything ugly, and in that way I miss so many beautiful things. I feel guilty because he is still working and probably has another victim. I feel helpless because I already tried to tell someone twice, but both the teacher and my mother turned a deaf ear to my words. I'm just not brave enough and capable enough to report him myself. Even if I report him, I would be to blame before the system, he would get away with it because after eight years I have no evidence, and even if he ended up in prison, thanks to the system, he would get out before he was locked up" (nisam trazila@org/svjedocanstva/nisamtrazila-pria-546).
33 See: Friedrich Engels, *The Origin of the Family, Private Property and the State* (Chippendale, NSW: Resistance Books, 2004).
34 Ana Maskalan, "Place of Women's Rights in Supra-Nation-Building: Comparison of Socialist Yugoslavia and the European Union," *Croatian Political Science Review* 59, no. 2 (2022): 43–49.
35 As cited in Vladimir Čerkez, *Bosanski Petrovac u NOB: zbornik sjećanja*, volume 4 (Bosanski Petrovac: Opštinski odbor SUBNOR-a, 1974), 7.
36 https://www.worldstatesmen.org/Yugoslavia-Constitution1974.pdf.
37 It is worth noting that, in the 1980s, the weakened political commitment to women's human rights was replaced by an activist one as various feminist groups became involved in Yugoslavia at that time. In 1982, 33 years after publication of the original book, a translation of Beauvoir's *The Second Sex* was published in Serbia; unfortunately, the Croatian version appeared much later. For the Serbian version see: Simone de Beauvoir, *Drugi pol*, trans. Zorica Milosavljević and Mirjana Vukmirović (Belgrade: Beogradski izdavačko-grafički zavod, 1982); and for the Croatian version, *Drugi spol*, trans. Mirna Šimat (Zagreb: Naklada Ljevak, 2016).
38 Simone de Beauvoir, "Interview with Simone de Beauvoir: The Second Sex 25 Years Later," by John Gerassi, *Society*, Jan–Feb 1976, https://www.marxists.org/reference/subject/ethics/de-beauvoir/1976/interview.htm.
39 "Dogmatic and Stalinist Marxism carried out a vulgar reduction of the 'women's question' to a class question. With this reductionism, the 'women's question' is not even raised, because the problem of women's equality is viewed from the point of view of what is 'now' possible and 'later', that is, its complete solution in a classless society." Blaženka Despot, *Žensko pitanje i socijalističko samoupravljanje* (Zagreb: Cekade, 1987), 109.
40 She called this phenomenon *inaugural paradox*. See: Gordana Bosanac, "Još jednom o nazivlju političkog iluzionizma: inauguralni paradoks," *Philosophical Investigations* 38, no. 1 (2018): 186–187, https://doi.org/10.21464/fi38114.
41 Mitja Velikonja, "Lost in Transition," *East European Politics and Societies* 23, no. 4 (2009): 537, https://doi.org/10.1177/0888325409345140.
42 It should be taken into account that the phenomena described here are not absolutely identical in all the Balkan countries discussed in this chapter. After the breakup of Yugoslavia, each country went its own way, and it cannot be claimed that the transition processes were equally (un)favourable everywhere. Also, while Croatia, Serbia, and Bosnia and Herzegovina were actively at war, Slovenia and Montenegro suffered the consequences of wars and war casualties to a

significantly lesser extent. Despite this, common political and economic heritage and culture and similar languages, as well as mutual population fluctuations, make certain comparisons and conclusions applicable to the "I Didn't Ask for It" phenomenon.
43 Stephanie L. Schmid, "Date Rape/Acquaintance Rape," in *Encyclopaedia of Rape*, ed. Merril D. Smith (Westport, CT: Greenwood, 2004), 54–56.
44 Ian James Kidd, Jose Medina, and Gaile Pohlhaus, Jr., "Introduction to *The Routledge Handbook of Epistemic Injustice*," in *The Routledge Handbook of Epistemic Injustice*, ed. Ian James Kidd, José Medina, and Gaile Pohlhaus, Jr. (London: Routledge, 2019), 1.
45 Fricker, *Epistemic Injustice*, 91.
46 Ibid., 1.
47 Consider the following post published on the Twitter page #*Nisam Prijavila* (I Didn't Report): "Neither groping nor grasping at school #I Didn't Report because I didn't know how to talk about it, what the problem really is, how I really feel and what needs to happen to stop it. The story about those things was solved by parents with books about how babies are born, but it was not discussed at school." Milica Jovanović (@PlaceSoft), 26 December 2012, 9:52 a.m., https://twitter.com/PlaceSoft.
48 Fricker, *Epistemic Injustice*, 150.
49 Charles W. Mills, "Ideology," in *The Routledge Handbook of Epistemic Injustice*, ed. Ian James Kidd, José Medina, and Gaile Pohlhaus, Jr. (London: Routledge, 2019), 105.
50 Here I deliberately do not distinguish between the usual interpretations of the reasons for war rapes, and am more focused on their consequences. For an interesting discussion on the reasons see: Jonathan Gottschall, "Explaining Wartime Rape," *Journal of Sex Research* 41, no. 2 (2004): 129–136.
51 Cindy S. Snyder, Wesley J. Gabbard, J. Dean May, and Nihada Zulcic, "On the Battleground of Women's Bodies," *Affilia* 21, no. 2 (2006): 189.
52 Ibid., 190.
53 https://www.facebook.com/groups/httpswww.nisamtrazila.org/; https://www.nisamtrazila.org/.
54 Here are some of the comments following the original article from January 2021 on Milena Radulović's case (Mastilović Jasnić, "Poznata mlada glumica"): "Rape is rape only if it is reported on the same day or the next day at the latest. It is now fashionable that almost all actresses were raped, but once upon a time, that is something completely different. You are not going to get a role—he raped me. No money—he raped me"; "Careful with that. After all, these are professional actresses."; "So why have you been silent until now? For eight years, you gave him the opportunity to abuse other girls as well"; "The girl chose to become famous in this way. Rape can be once, but not more. Stupidity!"; "Now, this is not paedophilia, the girls were older than 14, and rape requires force or a serious threat […] This (if it's true) looks more like an old man taking advantage of the fact that he is smarter and more experienced than young girls"; "If someone had stolen her cell phone, she would have reported it, for rape she was silent. Or else the parents played the main role in keeping quiet in order to get a shortcut to success, i.e. the price of success."
55 Simone de Beauvoir, "Pour Djamila," *Le Monde*, June 1, 1960, https://www.lemonde.fr/archives/article/1960/06/02/pour-djamila-boupacha_2092987_1819218.html.
56 See for example: Bratoljub Klaić, "Prostitucija [prostitution]," in *Rječnik stranih riječi A–Z* (Zagreb: Nakladni zavod Matice Hrvatske, 1986), 1102; Želimir Domović, Šime Anić, and Nikola Klaić, "Prostituirati se [to prostitute]," in *Rječnik stranih riječi: tuđice, posuđenice, izrazi, kratice i fraze* (Zagreb: Sani-Plus, 2002), 1176.

57 Beauvoir, *The Second Sex*, 757.
58 Simone de Beauvoir, *Brigitte Bardot and the Lolita Syndrome* (New York: Arno, 1972), 26.
59 Beauvoir, *The Second Sex*, 398.
60 Marina Blagojević, "Muški identiteti i nasilje na Balkanu," *Zeničke sveske: Časopis za društvenu fenomenologiju i kulturnu dijalogiku*, no. 17 (2013): 100.
61 Here, I draw attention to the atrocious statement by the Croatian President, Zoran Milanović, who claimed the following about sexual abuse: "When actresses who don't get out of bed for less than five million dollars complain about it, I don't really see it as something I should be interested in. When this is done by women who are employees, officials, mothers or younger colleagues at the Academy, that's a problem." See: "Petrinja: Milanović o optužbama za seksualno zlostavljanje na fakultetima," YouTube video, HINA multimedija, 2021, https://www.youtube.com/watch?v=AFgWkodTvIA.
62 Unfortunately, at the time of writing, not a single center had opened. In addition to the usual financial reasons, the cause should also be seen in the COVID-19 pandemic, which further slowed numerous political and social processes.
63 Here I draw attention to the topic of political mobilization, covered in Chapter 11 of this volume by Elaine Stavro ("Why Thoughtfulness Matters: Black Lives Matter and Elsewhere"), and her take on Simone de Beauvoir's understanding of women's participation in political activism.

References

Amnesty International. "Criminalization and Prosecution of Rape in Bosnia and Herzegovina: Submission to the UN Special Rapporteur on Violence against Women, Its Causes and Consequences." Accessed March 2022. https://www.amnesty.org/en/wp-content/uploads/2021/05/EUR6324572020ENGLISH.pdf.
Beauvoir, Simone de. "Pour Djamila Boupacha." *Le Monde*, June 1, 1960. https://www.lemonde.fr/archives/article/1960/06/02/pour-djamila-boupacha_2092987_1819218.html.
Beauvoir, Simone de. *Brigitte Bardot and the Lolita Syndrome*. New York: Arno, 1972.
Beauvoir, Simone de. "Interview with Simone de Beauvoir: The Second Sex 25 Years Later," by John Gerassi. *Society*, Jan–Feb 1976. Accessed September 3, 2022. https://www.marxists.org/reference/subject/ethics/de-beauvoir/1976/interview.htm.
Beauvoir, Simone de. *Drugi Pol*. Translated by Zorica Milosavljević and Mirjana Vukmirović. Belgrade: Beogradski izdavačko-grafički zavod, 1982.
Beauvoir, Simone de. *The Second Sex*. Translated by Constance Borde and Sheila Malovany-Chevallier. New York: Vintage, 2011.
Beauvoir, Simone de. *Drugi Spol*. Translated by Šimat Mirna. Zagreb: Naklada Ljevak, 2016.
Bideleux, Robert, and Ian Jeffries. *The Balkans: A Post-Communist History*. London: Routledge, 2007.
Blagojević, Marina. "Muški identiteti i nasilje na Balkanu [Male Identities and Violence in the Balkans]." *Zeničke sveske: Časopis za društvenu fenomenologiju i kulturnu dijalogiku*, no. 17 (2013): 98–110.
Bosanac, Gordana. "Još jednom o nazivlju političkog iluzionizma: inauguralni paradoks [Once More about the Terminology of Political Illusionism: Inaugural

Paradox]." *Philosophical Investigations* 38, no. 1 (2018): 183–193. https://doi.org/10.21464/fi38114.

Čerkez, Vladimir. *Bosanski Petrovac u NOB: zbornik sjećanja* [Bosanski Petrovac in NLW: Collection of Memories], Volume 4. Bosanski Petrovac: Opštinski odbor SUBNOR-a, 1974.

Clark, Lorenne M, and Debra J. Lewis. *Rape: The Price of Coercive Sexuality*. Toronto: Women's Press, 1977.

Council of Europe. "The Council of Europe Convention on Preventing and Combating Violence against Women and Domestic Violence." May 5, 2011. https://rm.coe.int/168008482e.

Cviticanin, Dolores. "#NisiSama: The Constructive Role of Social Media in Supporting the Ex-Yugoslav #MeToo Movement." *International Public Policy Review*, February 27, 2021. https://ippr-journal.com/2021/02/27/nisisama-the-constructive-role-of-social-media-in-supporting-the-ex-yugoslav-metoo-movement/.

Dakić, Dušan. "Silovanje Bez Prinude? [Rape without Coercion?]" *Otvorena vrata pravosuđa*, January 17, 2022. https://www.otvorenavratapravosudja.rs/teme/krivicno-pravo/silovanje-bez-prinude.

Dautry, Marion. "'You Are Not Alone': Balkan Women Seize #Metoo Moment." *France* 24, January 27, 2021. https://www.france24.com/en/live-news/20210127-you-are-not-alone-balkan-women-seize-metoo-moment.

Despot, Blaženka. *Žensko pitanje i socijalističko samoupravljanje* [Women's Question and Socialist Self-Management]. Zagreb: Cekade, 1987.

Domović, Želimir, Šime Anić, and Nikola Klaić. "Prostituirati se." In *Rječnik stranih riječi: tuđice, posuđenice, izrazi, kratice i fraze*, 1176. Zagreb: Sani-Plus, 2002.

Engels, Friedrich. *The Origin of the Family, Private Property and the State*. Chippendale, NSW: Resistance Books, 2004.

Estrada-Hollenbeck, Mica, and Todd F. Heatherton. "Avoiding and Alleviating Guilt through Prosocial Behavior." In *Guilt and Children*, edited by Jane Bybee, 215–231. San Diego: Academic Press, 1998.

Fischer, Ivan. "Serbian Rape Testimonies Spark Regional Women's Movements." *Brussels Morning Newspaper*, February 5, 2021. https://brusselsmorning.com/serbian-rape-testimonies-spark-regional-womens-movements/10463/.

Fricker, Miranda. *Epistemic Injustice: Power and the Ethics of Knowing*. Oxford: Oxford University Press, 2007.

Gottschall, Jonathan. "Explaining Wartime Rape." *Journal of Sex Research* 41, no. 2 (2004): 129–136. https://doi.org/10.1080/00224490409552221.

Jackson, Chris, and Brian A. Thomas-Peter. "Denial in Sex Offenders: Workers' Perceptions." *Criminal Behaviour and Mental Health* 4, no. 1 (1994): 21–32. https://doi.org/10.1002/cbm.1994.4.1.21.

Kennedy, H.G., and Donald H. Grubin. "Patterns of Denial in Sex Offenders." *Psychological Medicine* 22, no. 1 (1992): 191–196. https://doi.org/10.1017/s0033291700032840.

Kidd, Ian James, Jose Medina, and Gaile Pohlhaus, Jr. "Introduction to *The Routledge Handbook of Epistemic Injustice*." In *The Routledge Handbook of Epistemic Injustice*, edited by Ian James Kidd, José Medina, and Gaile Pohlhaus, Jr., 1–9. London: Routledge, 2019.

Klaić, Bratoljub. "Prostitucija." In *Rjecnik stranih rijeci A–Z*, 1102. Zagreb: Nakladni zavod Matice Hrvatske, 1986.

Levenson, Jill S. "'But I Didn't Do It!'" *Sexual Abuse* 23, no. 3 (2010): 346–364. https://doi.org/10.1177/1079063210382048.

Maskalan, Ana. "Place of Women's Rights in Supra-Nation-Building: Comparison of Socialist Yugoslavia and the European Union." *Croatian Political Science Review* 59, no. 2 (2022): 41–65.

Mastilović Jasnić, Ivana. "Poznata mlada glumica Milena Radulović: 'silovao me učitelj glume Miroslav Mika Aleksić kad sam imala 17 godina' [Famous Young Actress Milena Radulović: 'I Was Raped by My Acting Teacher Miroslav Mika Aleksić When I Was 17 Years Old']." *Blic.rs*, January 16, 2021. https://www.blic.rs/vesti/hronika/milena-radulovic-miroslav-mika-aleksic-optuzbe-silovanje-seksualno-zlostavljanje/5fj8cjv.

Mills, Charles W. "Ideology." In *The Routledge Handbook of Epistemic Injustice*, edited by Ian James Kidd, José Medina, and Gaile Pohlhaus, Jr., 100–111. London: Routledge, 2019.

Mlađenović, Lepa, Milena Milojević, and Mina Damjanović. "Balkan Women Uprising against Sexual Violence." *CSSP Civil Society Strengthening Platform*, February 1, 2021. https://cssplatform.org/balkan-women-uprising-against-sexual-violence.

OECD. "Social Institutions & Gender Index 2019: Montenegro." Accessed August 26, 2022. https://www.genderindex.org/wp-content/uploads/files/datasheets/2019/ME.pdf.

Pandey, Madhumita. "'My Mother Is A Goddess', 'I Am an Inmate Here': Male Prisoners' Attitudes Towards Women and Their Perceptions of Culpability from Delhi Prison." Doctoral thesis. Cambridge: Anglia Ruskin University, 2018. https://arro.anglia.ac.uk/id/eprint/704101/1/Pandey_2018.pdf.

Radulović, Đurđa. "How Facebook Became the New Feminist Battleground for #MeToo in the Western Balkans." *The Calvert Journal*, June 21, 2021. https://www.calvertjournal.com/features/show/12875/feminist-facebook-groups-fighting-change-memes-western-balkans.

Schmid, Stephanie L. "Date Rape/Acquaintance Rape." In *Encyclopaedia of Rape*, edited by Merril D. Smith, 54–56. Westport, CT: Greenwood, 2004.

Snyder, Cindy S., Wesley J. Gabbard, J. Dean May, and Nihada Zulcic. "On the Battleground of Women's Bodies." *Affilia* 21, no. 2 (2006): 184–195. https://doi.org/10.1177/0886109905286017.

Sofic Salihbegovic, Aida. "The Balkans Face Their #Metoo Moment." *Deutsche Welle*, February 7, 2021. https://www.dw.com/en/the-balkans-face-their-metoo-moment/a-56469884.

STA. "Slovenia Redefines Rape to Focus on Consent, Not Violence." *Total Slovenia News*, May 6, 2021. https://www.total-slovenia-news.com/politics/8233-slovenia-redefines-rape-to-focus-on-consent-not-violence.

Statistical Office of the Republic of Serbia. "Statistical Release: Average salaries and wages per employee, January 2021." April 26, 2021. https://publikacije.stat.gov.rs/G2021/HtmlE/G20211080.html.

Stojanović, Milica. "Renowned Serbian Acting Teacher Detained over Rape Claims." *Balkan Insight*, January 19, 2021. https://balkaninsight.com/2021/01/18/custody-urged-for-serbian-acting-teacher-accused-of-rape/.

Taylor, Dianna. "Humiliation as a Harm of Sexual Violence: Feminist versus Neoliberal Perspectives." *Hypatia* 33, no. 3 (2018): 434–450. https://doi.org/10.1111/hypa.12427.

Todorova, Maria. "The Balkans: From Discovery to Invention." *Slavic Review* 53, no. 2 (1994): 453–482. https://doi.org/10.2307/2501301.
Todorova, Maria. *Imagining the Balkans*. Oxford: Oxford University Press, 2009.
Trešnjo, Samira. "Nisam Tražila: Four Girls Who Fought against Gender-Based Violence." *Balkan Diskurs*, January 12, 2022. https://balkandiskurs.com/en/2022/01/12/nisam-trazila-initiative/.
Vasić, Vladana. "Krivična djela seksualnog nasilja u pravnom sistemu Bosne i Hercegovine [Criminal Acts of Sexual Violence in the Legal System of Bosnia and Herzegovina]." In *Krivična djela silovanja i ostalog seksualnog nasilja u Bosni i Hercegovini*, edited by Vesna Pirija. Sarajevo: Sarajevo Open Centre, 2017.
Velikonja, Mitja. "Lost in Transition." *East European Politics and Societies* 23, no. 4 (2009): 535–551. https://doi.org/10.1177/0888325409345140.
Vladisavljevic, Anja. "Croatia Toughens Penalties for Domestic and Sexual Violence." *Balkan Insight*, November 5, 2019. https://balkaninsight.com/2019/10/25/croatia-toughens-penalties-for-domestic-and-sexual-violence/.
Zablocki, Tamara, "Žene koje su otvorile Pandorinu kutiju [The Women Who Opened Pandora's Box]." *Urban Magazine*, September 2, 2021. https://www.urbanmagazin.ba/ispovijesti-prezivjelih-zene-koje-su-otvorile-pandorinu-kutiju/.

11
WHY THOUGHTFULNESS MATTERS
Black Lives Matter and Elsewhere

Elaine Stavro

In our world of growing inequalities, ongoing global strife, systemic racism, threat of pandemics, and climate change, the importance of collaboration across difference is more necessary than ever. Having turned away from electoral politics, representative institutions, and deliberative processes, radical democrats focus on the power of things, aesthetic experiences, amorphous affects, and human and non-human assemblages to catalyze popular protest. In doing so, I argue, they have diminished the significance of human conversations, good arguments, and conscious commitment as the mainstays of collective movements. Beauvoir's notion of embodied and situated subjectivity accommodates both feeling and thoughtfulness as well as recognizing the significance of a historical field in which one acts, providing a more fitting approach to protest politics. She thereby finds a middle ground that recognizes affect as a motivator without overestimating its powers. In this chapter I will briefly assess the shortcomings of two radical democratic thinkers—specifically Jodi Dean and Stefan Jonsson, both of whom have written on the democratic potential of crowds. I offer Beauvoir as an alternative. Dean's reliance on erotic crowd energy harnessed by a Communist Party and Jonsson's focus on aesthetic knowledge minimize the power of human understanding and the importance of conscious human commitment. Beauvoir's living body, which entwines reflection, sensation, and emotions, allows seamless movement between these registers of experience—thereby accommodating aesthetics and philosophy as well as history as resources for progressive coalitional politics. In the final section I turn to the politics of Black Lives Matter to underscore the significance of Beauvoir's attention to reflection, passion, and organization in political mobilization.

Simone de Beauvoir's Thinking: Respecting the Ontological and the Ontic

Ontologically, Beauvoir describes humans as "ecstatic, a "spontaneous upsurge," and "a thrust towards beings"—hence free.[1] More specifically she describes our original attachment to being not as the relationship of "wanting to be" but rather as "wanting to disclose being" (EA 12). From our embedded relations we launch ourselves in the world respecting the singular situations in which we find ourselves. Hence, we are not masterful individuals who are able to transcend our pre-reflective relations and transform ourselves (a fantasy associated with liberal thinkers); but nor are we effects of the empirical world, social structures, or social locations. Beauvoir believes we choose our affiliations but we can't choose the context of our choice, which impacts our choice. Beginning with our embeddedness (comprised of pre-reflective relations and our social-historical context), she urges us to loosen our ties to our specific situations through communication and collective action: in addition to verbal communication (strong arguments), pre-reflective experiences foster social interaction and collaboration. Although our situations are irreducibly singular, she says, "at the same time there is communication in this very separation." "The world exists for all of us and [...] allows us to agree upon what is green and what is red for example" (EA 199). So, despite her theory of singularity, Beauvoir avoids autonomous individuality.

Beauvoir does not believe the individual reflective subject can know the world, yet our singular situation envelops the entire world. "This does not mean that one knows it, but reflects it, typifies it and expresses it."[2] "By uprooting himself from the world, man makes himself present in the world and the world present in him" (EA 12). This act of synchronization or reversibility "goes some way to decentre the cognitive, potentially masterful, subject, given the significance of sensory experiences and pre-reflective embodied relations; certainty is not a goal, nor is reason ultimate register."[3] However, they are part of the process of becoming free.

There are ontological as well as ontic limits to the realization of freedom.[4] Ambiguity is an ontological fact; hence humans experience themselves as both subjects and objects, as transcendence and immanence, "as a pure internality against which no external power can take hold" as well as "a thing crushed by the dark weight of other things" (EA 7). We are all exposed to this paradoxical and dual reality, which problematizes the power of reason and our agentic capacity. Nevertheless, we live our ambiguity differently. We are not equally constrained. Beauvoir would agree with Judith Butler, who has drawn our attention to the fact that the precarious, the poor, refugees, those dependent upon social services are more vulnerable than those who are not.[5] Lori Marso also captures Beauvoir's respect for ontic differences, as she writes that "some are disproportionately vulnerable, marked as other, doomed to immanence and not transcendence."[6] Minorities are influenced by the intransigent forces of oppression, objectification, and systemic violence, yet these relations are not permanent.

Another impediment to freedom is human complicity. People are prone to flee their freedom, preferring to believe that they are determined by their class or social circumstances; hence collective action is necessary to combat their bad faith. But we are warned by Beauvoir not to lose ourselves in social/political movements, for that would involve denying our ambiguity and human frailties. So, unlike those radical democrats who prioritize the effects of impersonal affect and aesthetic experiences, Beauvoir relies upon embodied affect as well as embedded will, which qualifies their project of freedom.

Protest Politics According to Jodi Dean and Simone de Beauvoir

In *Crowds and Party*, Jodi Dean believes the energy of the crowd must be harnessed by a Communist Party to support revolutionary change. Inspired by Lacan, Dean celebrates 'lack,' which she identifies with an unconscious amorphous desire for change. Strong affective bonds and shared love objects produce a contagious energy that constitutes and sustains the protesting crowd. This erotic energy is infectious: affectively experienced, discharged, and cathected on the collective body. In so far as it is impersonal, it comes from being in a crowd; and when one leaves the crowd, Dean argues, it dissipates—hence the party is needed to sustain it. She describes the crowd as a de-subjective experience,[7] a "negation of individuality,"[8] and celebrates the positive collective desires that emerge as an antidote to the robust individualism of liberal capitalism.

Dean relies upon her experience in the Occupy movement in New York City's Zuccotti Park to support her position: that the individual, and specifically our reflective capacity, is a threat to collective action. Describing the collective will to occupy the park as mounting, she reiterates their chant: "We can take this park."[9] But someone intervened, calling attention to the need for autonomous choice. As soon as people began to reflect upon their decision, Dean says, the mood of the crowd was destroyed. Becoming individuals again, their radical energy dissipated. So, while the contagious feelings of a crowd may foster collective action and cultivate a mood of optimism, this does not last. When everyone packs up and goes home, Dean argues, this positive energy disappears; for this reason a party must be there to hold and preserve their energy, and reflection is to be avoided.[10]

While Dean is critical of autonomous individuality, Beauvoir's thinking of singularity that presumes a non-individualist praxiological theory of the self eludes her critique. We are constituted relationally, with others and things, yet we are singular. Freedom is not freedom from others; nor does it involve selfless behaviour. In fact, in acting freely, Beauvoir believes, we must appreciate our pre-reflective being as well as contribute to the flourishing of others. This is implicit in her maxim, "in willing oneself free, one wills the freedom of all" (EA 73). This takes us beyond the individual to the furtherance of collective freedom. This does not require the negation of the self, as it does for Dean, but a unique self that bears others in mind whose agency is influenced by affective experiences as well as reflective ones. This decentered, responsive, and thoughtful self is better equipped to deal with the negotiation needed in collaborative politics.

Instead of relying upon Lacan's theory of desire, Beauvoir's theory of affect, or visceral feeling (in as much as she has one), is inspired by the young Hegel. Beauvoir respects that we are incomplete, restless, always moving outside ourselves; and, while this precludes determinism, it is not universally seen as having positive or liberating effects. Nor is this restless movement necessarily an erotic desire for change, as Dean presumes. For Beauvoir sexuality is only one aspect of being: working the soil, playfully creating things, joining a social movement are not expressions of sexuality.[11] There are various aspects of being by which humans choose themselves.

Dean sees affect as an autonomous impersonal experience that comes from outside and constitutes egalitarian feelings. Beauvoir is more interested in the embodied subject whose entrainment of affects and emotions depends both upon their sedimented free projects and the conditions in which freedom finds itself. Since our situations are singular, we cannot assume we similarly experience affects, or that affective crowd experiences are necessarily progressive. One must consider the context—the conditions in which freedom finds itself. While Dean is optimistic that a Communist Party will hold or harness these autonomous affects, Beauvoir's experience of the Communist Party of France (PCF) led her to be skeptical of their liberating effects. In her novel *The Blood of Others* [1945], she was concerned with the personal transformation that underpins the process of politicization.[12] She narrates Hélène and Jean's circumstances and their arduous journey. Their participation in the Resistance movement was a consequence of reconfiguring their relationships to others over time. Impersonal events may have been catalysts in their transformation, but would be insufficient to sustain a long-term commitment.

Unlike the radical democrats who see affect as world-building and place reason, emotion, and affects on different registers, Beauvoir's body subject presumes their entwinement. Hélène's experience in *The Blood of Others* is illustrative of this fact. She is invited to dinner with Mr. Bergman, a German businessman who is going to offer her a job. She cycles to the dinner with enthusiasm and indulges in the pleasures of a meal. But her enjoyment is disturbed by her conversation. She naively tries to enlist Mr. Bergman to help free her friends (Yvonne and Marcel) from Nazi camps, but he refuses. At this point, she stops eating and realizes their differences are insurmountable. In the end reflection trumps affect: "She was no longer hungry. She watched the bespectacled officers gorging themselves on rich French food [...]. Marcel had been a week without eating anything at all [...]. Why am I here?" (BOO 211–212).

Marcel's liberty, and security for Yvonne; [...] the life of [...] [the] engineer, who was shot this morning. The young woman had moved away. There was an icy silence [...]. All at once a thousand daggers stabbed her heart: "I exist, and I have lost Jean forever." [...]. "I do not think I shall be able to leave for Berlin," she said.

(BOO 214)

Through conversation Hélène realizes she cannot go to Germany: she is French, and the Nazis are depriving the French people of food and freedom. Her enthusiasm for life motivated her to join Mr. Bergmann for dinner, yet her friendship and realization of the effects of the Occupation lead her to leave prematurely and join the Resistance. Her judgment was both visceral and thoughtful.

While Dean focuses upon the world-building power of affect, Beauvoir sees affect and emotion as promiscuous, capable of inspiring selfish or progressive actions. At the outset of *The Blood of Others*, Hélène is lively; however her liveliness manifested itself in impetuous and narcissistic acts. Rather than cultivating democratic sensibilities and solidarity with others, as radical democrats assume, her liveliness furthered insensitivity and selfishness. At the outset of the novel we witness Hélène using others and endangering herself. She notices a beautiful bike and desires it; she convinces Jean to retrieve it for her, without telling him it is not hers. Her desire leads to deceiving and endangering others (BOO 45). She is portrayed as desperate to be loved, all too ready to lose herself in a man. She flits from one sexual encounter to another and ends up pregnant. Since her lover is fundamentally unknown to her, she endures a dangerous/illegal abortion. So, while liveliness can be world-building, it inspired Hélène's dangerous acts and carried negative emotions such as fear, anger, and envy. We must be able to distinguish between affects that are world-building and those that contribute to selfish, destructive, or othering behaviour.

Beauvoir's attention to affect and emotion is more complicated: negative emotions such as anger can prompt positive sentiments (e.g. compassion) that have generous political consequences. Beauvoir's reflections on the Algerian war confirm this. Disgust and anger prompted her to join a committee to ensure that Djamila Boupacha, the Algerian woman who had been raped by French soldiers, got a fair trial.

"I'm French." The words scalded my throat like the admission of a hideous deformity. For millions of men and women, old men and children, I was just one of the people who were torturing them, burning them, machine gunning them, slashing their throats, starving them; I deserved their hatred, because I could still sleep, write, enjoy a walk or a book.[13]

She continues: "I am an accomplice of the privileged classes and compromised by this connexion; that is the reason why living through the Algerian war was like experiencing a personal tragedy."[14]

For Beauvoir, feelings are social as well as personal—we cannot assume that humans are similarly affected by the war or crowd experiences. In returning to Dean's example, the reminder "decide for yourself" prompted different responses: some individuals were unwilling to break the law and decided not "to take the park"[15] while others were emboldened and angered by their withdrawal. I see this moment rather differently from Dean. In committing oneself to breaking the law, one must decide for oneself. It is not a sovereign individual who is choosing, but a relational and historically situated self. One may have been inspired by collective effervescence and a sense that one was able to achieve something in common; but one must be willing to commit to a protest movement and acts of civil disobedience. Rather than bemoan the lost opportunity, the diminishing of radical energy, as Dean does, Beauvoir would think this moment invites the need for personal reappraisal. The crowd is not a de-subjective experience, but a place where the collective and individual are in tension. The invitation to reflect doesn't necessarily mean the collective will is broken; but it does ensure that commitment, when it is forthcoming, is backed up by thoughtful choice.

In *The Blood of Others*, Jean, one of the leaders of the Resistance, had to make a difficult decision. In a painful discussion with his mother he had to defend the organization's tactics, which involved shedding the blood of French civilians: "But those men didn't want to die, no one asked them about it.' Her voice chokes. 'They've no right, it is murder.'" (BOO 224). Jean felt guilty and responsible for the lives lost, yet, in the end, he persisted in this course of action. He hated to sacrifice the lives of French civilians; but, for the future of a free, de-Nazified France, he took the risk and accepted responsibility for their deaths. Again, this underlines the significance of conversation, or thoughtful reflection, in collective action. In addition, it draws attention to the inevitability of conflict in politics: progressive change will inevitably entail disagreement and harm, yet the risk must be assessed to see if its promises outweigh the perils.

Dean has gone too far in relying upon the affective domain and not acknowledging the importance of persuasion arising from good arguments and reliable information. In *The Second Sex* [1949] Beauvoir compiles a strong case exposing the 'Othering' of women in different times and places. Not only were women seen as sexual objects, and as inferior to men, but they were also marginalized in public spaces and excluded from professional life. Beauvoir believed their feelings would steer women to feminism, but that convincing arguments were also required to challenge patriarchal common sense. So, unlike the radical democrats who focus on feelings and amorphous forces, Beauvoir recuperates the power of individuals to make choices and commit to collective actions. Emotion or affects motivate commitment, but thoughtfulness also has a role to play. Altered circumstances may involve the reappraisal of one's visceral judgment. Beauvoir's defense of Boupacha was motivated by strong feelings; but, after the latter's release from prison Beauvoir did not support her desire to return to France for risk of offending the new liberation forces in Algeria (FNL). Here the broader political good, the emancipatory potential of the FNL, trumped Beauvoir's concern with Boupacha's well-being. So, while strong affects and emotions inspired Beauvoir's work on behalf of Boupacha, good judgment and progressive political organizations have a vital role to play in coalitional politics. Beauvoir banked on the potential of the FLN to liberate the Algerian people, and supported them rather than Boupacha's personal desires—though in the end the FLN turned out not to be the liberating force it aspired to be.[16]

Jodi Dean and the Communist Party

Dean believes that a radical party is required to harness contagious affects to guide and inspire the movement. The Occupy movement in New York failed to translate protest into progressive change because it was leaderless and depended upon consensus, which proved impossible. Dean proposes a Communist Party to sustain and build upon this radical energy. However, experience of the Chinese Communist Party, the French Communist Party (PCF), or vanguard parties historically have hardly been exemplary. In fact, Beauvoir's critique of the Communist Party is worth reviewing.

As a member of the *Temps modernes* collective, Beauvoir did not support the PCF as they were consolidating their power rather than empowering the proletariat. Marx had not envisioned the need for a party; but Lenin argued it was necessary to develop the proletariat to assume their role as liberators since the USSR was populated by peasants. Lenin insisted that the party would be temporary. The French Communist Party supported this idea. Yet the French were not peasants; nor was there any evidence that the PCF was developing the proletariat to assume their power. In fact, the PCF's obedience to the USSR and its hierarchical structures and authoritarian practices inhibited its democratic potential. While Beauvoir was not optimistic that the PCF was instantiating the democratic principles of equality and liberty, the strength of support it garnered made her wary of repudiating Marxism *tout court*.

Returning to the power of collective action and the individual, Beauvoir believes that without an individual willing their freedom, revolution would be impossible: "The very notion of action would lose all meaning if history were a mechanical unrolling in which man appears only as a passive conductor of outside forces" (EA 20). Here we see Beauvoir reflecting on the problems within Marxism and offering suggestions. If "to admit to the ontological possibility of choice is already to betray the Cause" (EA 22), then how is commitment to the revolution possible? Further, she says, "autonomy is not the privilege or defect of the bourgeoisie," for every judgment is a "political choice"; and "an ethical choice: it is a wager as well as a decision: one bets on the chances and risks of the measure under consideration [...] and in so doing one sets up values" (EA 149). Again, the historical and dialectical materialists who assume one's choice is "objectively" or historically determined are acting in bad faith, ignoring ambiguity as well as the role of individual choice and judgment. In acting, one makes a calculated assessment as how to best realize one's values (EA 109). Before one acts, one must assess the situation: since one can never know with certainty the effects of one's action, one's choice always involves a wager. Nevertheless, for Beauvoir, one can and must choose a course of action and accept responsibility for its effects, even if they were unanticipated. Here Beauvoir approaches the problem of Communist Party practices: their belief in structural contradiction or historical teleology led to the excessive use of force and violence, which culminated in the camps and show trials. For these reasons, Beauvoir did not join the French Communist Party, and Dean should take seriously her concerns. Instead of banking on the party to direct change and create psychic spaces, Beauvoir would support protestors who, through passionate and thoughtful commitment and collective action, join and mold democratic movements. These could then collaborate with other progressive groups.

Beauvoir's critique of the PCF is directed at Marxist Leninists rather than Marx himself. Hence this is not an anti-revolutionary position, but a critique of certain forms of Marxism. While Marx begins with the abject condition of humans and works on the negative without a blueprint, some Marxists presume a finished socialist state (EA 8). Here Beauvoir compares "Christianity and Marxism" (EA 51): both promise redemption at the end of life; both believe in "supernatural imperatives" (EA 8), and hence their actions are justified by an absolute end, be it communism or heaven. When Beauvoir explores the dire implications of presuming "a complete history" (EA 41), she turns to Lenin and his theory of objective necessity. She quotes him as saying: "I call any action useful to the party moral action; I call it immoral if it is harmful to the party" (EA 22). The idea that the party is essential to realizing the revolution, and whatever it deems necessary is justifiable, has led to subverting the democratic ideals of the revolution.

Beauvoir's theory of singularity and respect for historical contingency would counter these abuses of power. In *The Second Sex* she describes 'democratic socialism' as "abolish[ing] classes but not individuals" (67). She believed we cannot rely on history to resolve itself and yield freedom; but, in taking our bearing in history and collaborating with others, she believes individuals are able to further not only their personal freedom but also the freedom of all. Returning to the young Marx, and challenging Hegel's dialectic, Beauvoir describes the dialectic as a conversion not "a negation of the negation" or an *aufgehoben* that produces a positive (EA 15). Instead of sublating all that is positive and shedding the negative, there must be temporal continuity that furthers interdependent projects.

The individual being is an amalgam of free projects over time, and hence coheres. It is not simply an effect of class relations, discursive practices, or impersonal affects; it has been created in its engagement with forces outside itself, and yet takes these on in a specific way—hence is both a singular and social being. Instead of relying on the resolution of the dualisms into a higher synthesis, which minimizes the agency of the individual, Beauvoir assumes a dialectical conversion which respects the negative and that which cannot be sublated, hence "[a] conquest of this kind [of freedom] is never finished" (EA 157). We must situate ourselves in the forces available to further the possibility of success, rather than assume objective history will pave the way to freedom. Yet, given contingency (history is incomplete), there is always the risk of failure but also success.

Beauvoir's thinking of incompleteness has an ontological basis. Psychic lack or incompleteness must be accepted, and this involves reconciling ourselves with our ambiguity, vulnerability, mortality, and melancholia. In so far as one is living, one is incomplete—there is always a lack in one's being, until death (EA 12).

Despite recognizing incompleteness and ontological lack, Beauvoir was an activist who believed that collective action could change history. Through communication our understanding is broadened and collaboration more likely to yield positive results; nevertheless collective action is always tenuous and riddled with risk and failure. This is not a reason to give up on the idea of revolutionary socialism, but does challenge its contemporary forms.

Rethinking the Aesthetic: Jonsson and Beauvoir

Let me turn to the radical democrats' focus on the aesthetic sphere. Aesthetics is not used in the conventional sense to refer to the exclusive beauty of a text, an image, or a piece of high art, but rather as an understanding acquired through sensory perception and imagination. The work of Stefan Jonsson is my reference point, though his interpretation is hardly unique. He relies on a strong distinction between representational epistemology and aesthetic knowing: the former strives for an accurate picture of the world, whereas the latter is disruptive of the status quo. The former seeks to explain phenomena presuming logic and an impartial perspective, and establishes causality, whereas the aesthetic epistemology presumes amorphous, visceral, and perceptual experiences. The former epistemological approach relies on conversations that generate thoughtfulness, and the latter focuses on perceptual and sensory experiences, which are believed to enhance human agency. While the representational presumes coherent and reliable knowledge is possible and desirable, the aesthetic challenges these assumptions. However, for Beauvoir, commitment to a political movement involves taking one's bearing in history. This involves reflection as well as inspiration, assessing the situation, understanding the forces at play as well as being inspired to struggle for change. These features are evident in her portrayal of Hélène and Jean in *The Blood of Others* as well as in her own activism around the Algerian Civil War. Sensory, perceptual, and affective experiences motivated action, but sustained commitment was the product of thoughtful reflection and conscious choice as well.

Jonsson argues that the representational sphere is incapable of understanding emergent political struggles. In fact, the lived experience of protest, solidarity, contiguous bodies, and emancipatory desires can only be approached through sensory experiences mediated by the aesthetic.[17] Without denying the significance of strong feelings underpinning protests, thoughtfulness should not be glossed over. Disagreements arise, and activists must try to persuade as well as inspire. In *The Blood of Others*, although Jean did not persuade his mother to support the Resistance movement's tactics, he was convinced it was the right thing to do. His risk was based upon his evaluation of the situation. If his thinking was based upon the feelings that arose between him and his mother, he might not have pursued their strategy and the Resistance would not have been successful.

Interestingly, Jonsson acknowledges the power of phenomenology to explore lived experience; however, he says, that its subject-centered rationalist orientation and its inability to capture the collective experience of protest and revolt disqualify it.[18] He describes the aesthetic experience "as a piercing event which releases the popular surplus of materiality, affect, and 'flesh,' as something that gets under the skin or can be known only by exposing one's mind and body to it."[19] Before I try to make sense of this passage, I contend that Beauvoir's critical phenomenology is neither rationalist nor incapable of accommodating intense affects or material relations. Beauvoir's fiction presumes people are affected by perceptional and sensory experiences, but she uses words, associations, and metaphors to express these feelings. Hence she does not rely on the release of "the popular surplus of materiality, affect, and 'flesh.'" Attention to the aesthetic as "a piercing event"—that is, an episodic event that exceeds words—is troubling. At best it may trigger solidarity and compassion in the moment; but one must not overstate its capacity to fuel and sustain radical political movements or further collaboration with other movements.

While Jonsson believes literature, testimonials, and poems all fall within an aesthetic epistemology, Beauvoir focuses on the novel, which is both aesthetic and philosophic. Narrating the lives of women in dire situations, Beauvoir believed literature and later film had emancipatory potential. Her novels fostered dissonance between ontology and social reality, freedom and the lived experiences of otherness—thereby encouraging free and ethical action.[20] Dean and Jonsson may be correct that discharge of affect cannot be captured in words, yet Beauvoir resists seeing these experiences as mute since an idea, a desire, a fantasy underpins their expression. For Beauvoir these affects are a form of social communication; their meaning and sense can be approached relying on metaphor and description. While Dean and Jonsson rely on autonomous impersonal affects, Beauvoir's interest lies in embodied and situated affect, so she describes the specificity of individual feelings, situated subjectivity, and their struggles for freedom.

In *The Blood of Others*, we see how visceral experiences—the smell of the bleeding body, the spectacle of an elaborate dinner, the vision of a child wrenched from its mother's arms—prompt compassion and solidarity. Witnessing these experiences culminated in Hélène joining the Resistance. Beauvoir fictionalizes them, as we see above; but I'm also reminded of the importance of Hélène's conversations and her thoughtfulness. Clare Hemmings uses the term 'affective solidarity' to convey how feelings and reflections on those feelings facilitate emancipatory feminist politics.[21] Reflection does not need to be conceived as rule-following of which the goal is truth or a correct picture. Rather, feeling and thinking help one orient oneself towards change. Doing what feels appropriate to the situation, as well as discerning the best way to realize one's values, involves affects as well as reason.

Although Beauvoir was often seen as a realist novelist, she expressly says literature is not about recording the real, but establishing communication with others by starting from the singularity of one's own experiences and going beyond it.[22] The 'metaphysical novel' explores the complexity of lived experiences, elaborating the singularity of life as well as the possibility of sharing lived experiences.[23] The novel captures pre-reflective communication as well as thoughts, but also connects characters to specific social, political, and economic circumstances. As such, aesthetic experiences can further human connections and embolden political coalitions, complementing rather than subverting discerning action.

The power of the aesthetic realm is not to be over-estimated: the novel does not displace philosophy, but rather supplements it. Beauvoir used the novel as well as *The Second Sex* to expose the demeaned and exploited condition of women, believing she could both inspire and persuasively convince women to pursue their liberation. Along with Sartre and Marx, she endorses creative, playful actions that are not reducible to instrumental logic. Nevertheless, the success of her radical politics was thanks to collaboration with grassroots struggles and political activism securing the trust of those with whom she collaborated. So, to summarize, while an aesthetic experience may be intense, it is entangled in emotion and ideas, and hopefully it furthers understanding and orients political collaboration. However, since radical democrats focus upon disruptive impersonal experiences that are episodic, they are unlikely to sustain attachment to collective and collaborative action over the long haul. In contrast to the anti- or post-humanists who focus upon impersonal or undirected affects, I have shown how important it is to take one's bearing in history. This entails an assessment of and attachment to a progressive movement; it also involves personal transformation which is altering one's relations to others, not simply de-subjective or impersonal aesthetic experiences.

Coalitional Politics Today: Black Lives Matter

In this final section, I am going to bring to bear Beauvoir's insights on a successful coalitional movement—Black Lives Matter (BLM). As Beauvoir accommodated empirical facts, I too will rely on them. Two insights will be addressed: the role of emotion, thinking, and organization in political mobilization; and the problem of relying on parties and hierarchies. Both confirm the salience of Beauvoir's insights.

Thinking from embodied subjectivity, Beauvoir recognizes the power of feelings as well as reason in mobilizing radical movements, given our embodiment or situatedness, macro forces (sedimented power relations) and technology impact human agency, and the potential for successful coalitions. BLM relies heavily on new social media, which distinguishes its protest movement from those in the first decade of this century. The original organizers used Tumblr and Twitter to post and circulate acts of abuse and violence, as well as accomplishments that were not reported in the mainstream press. Since many young people rely on social media (and specifically their cell phones), they were able not only to organize protests without a strong organizational basis, but also to document police acts of violence and upload them within minutes. Social media has also been instrumental in convicting police as well as persuading people of systemic racism, thus contributing to the movement's popular support.

Beauvoir's activism has drawn our attention to the role of raising consciousness as well as passion in cultivating solidarity. Witnessing the indifference of police officer Derek Chauvin with his knee pressed to George Floyd's neck for more than nine minutes was terrifying. Equally disturbing was the indifference of other police officers who failed to intervene to protect

Floyd while he was bleeding and suffering. Witnessing this event on TV or social media culminated in a huge rise in support for BLM: within two days it had recruited as much support as it had in the previous two years.[24] Data from online survey research firm Civiqs showed that a majority of American voters supported the movement by a 28-point margin, a dramatic increase from a 17-point margin before the most recent wave of protests began, and that the largest group of protestors were white men.[25] Protests throughout the USA were unparalleled in scope and depth, and stimulated world-wide demonstrations occasioning reflection on systemic racism and police abuse.

Other affective (aesthetic) events buttressed support. For example the dismantling of sculptures was a contagious performance that was uploaded and traveled between the USA, the UK, Belgium, and Canada, with demonstrators actively involved in removing/defacing statues that celebrated colonizers. Campaigns to dismantle these memorials were already underway, but witnessing Floyd's murder on May 25, 2020 was a tipping point, moving people to collectively dismantle them. Demonstrations were not only inspired by the killing but were also influenced by sound arguments and powerful stories. For some time, accounts of the enduring legacy of slavery, research into structural inequalities, and stories of Black artists documenting racism have been available on mainstream and alternate media. BLM contributed to publicizing these stories and disclosing suppressed facts to help persuade people to revise their understanding of America's economic development, acknowledging the role slavery played in its capital accumulation.

Although there was a marked rise in support following George Floyd's death, shifts in popular attitudes took place over seven years. In 2016, when American football player Colin Kaepernick took the knee during the US national anthem in protest at racism, he was dismissed by the National Football League (NFL) and subject to considerable criticism. Many of his teammates were worried that they would be fired or benched if they followed suit. In 2016, 52 percent of respondents surveyed supported Kaepernick, but in 2020 this figure had increased to 76 percent.[26] A poll in that year by Monmouth University (New Jersey) found 76 percent of Americans considered racism and discrimination a big problem (up 26 points from 2015). Most believed there was systemic racism against Black people, 57 percent felt their anger was fully justified, and 20 percent partially agreed.[27]

Yet, following the shooting of Jacob Blake in August 2020, Civiqs noted a drop in overall support for BLM from 52 percent on May 27 to 47 percent, and on March 12, 2021 a notable increase in opposition, from 29 percent to 40 percent.[28] How does one explain this? Months of daily telecasts of violent protests, civil disruption, and property damage in places like Portland, Oregon, and elsewhere contributed to a general atmosphere of fear and anxiety.[29] These feelings were harnessed during Donald Trump's election campaign, where he daily railed against the chaos and anarchy that would ensue with Joe Biden's presidency.

This is also consistent with Beauvoir's reflections; although she saw emotion as a powerful motivator, it was not necessarily progressive. In her novels she recognized how women can lose themselves in the lives of their male lovers and fail to develop their own talents, so emotion is promiscuous. While affective experiences like the murder of George Floyd triggered compassion and solidarity, compassion can give way to fear and resentment, and promote othering and intolerant behaviour. One of BLM's action points was 'Defund the Police'—they were intent upon diverting 5 percent of police budgets to social services. This became a plank in Trump's campaign to boost fear. While there was much support for this amongst Democrats in 2020, it was no longer popular 18 months later, attesting to how visceral judgments get re-evaluated as situations change. In the New York mayoral election (fall of 2021) only two of seven Democratic candidates supported Defund the Police and, in the end, a former police sergeant was elected who called for better and more policing. Feelings of fear were not groundless: 2021 had seen a huge increase in homicides and violent crime in New York City. In 2020, 23 million guns were purchased in the USA. Many protestors who had been moved by the murder of Floyd were clearly troubled by the civil unrest, disruption, and crime that ensued in US streets. As Beauvoir suggests, both anger and compassion motivate people, but political commitment presumes temporal continuity. One's past must lead to present support for change and collaboration with the other's project. Belief in the goals and tactics of the movement must be reappraised if the situation changes. Hence both emotion and reflection play a vital role in activism.

Successful protests arise out of systemic inequality and racism, but the praxis of the exploited and oppressed is vital to change. Beauvoir's words are apt: "The very notion of action would lose all meaning if history were a mechanical unrolling in which man appears only as a passive conductor of outside forces" (EA 20). Beauvoir's concern over parties and leadership led her to support responsible and committed individuals who would craft democratic movements rather than relying upon leaders who would direct from above. Black Lives Matter was a grassroots movement founded by three queer women in the wake of teenager Trayvon Martin's death in Florida in 2012 and the failure to convict George Zimmerman of first-degree murder. The organization's founders wanted to reinvigorate a civil rights movement that was not led by a "black straight preacher." They wanted to be inclusive, and encouraged popular participation. Committed to horizontalism, or what they called a leaderful rather than leaderless movement, they believed anyone from the community should be able to speak and be heard.

BLM was not unified by a party but grew out of resistance against multiple racist practices (in policing, education, housing, poverty, etc.) and involved collaborations with multiple organizations. Although gender concerns were at the forefront of its founders' mission, they deferred to the urgent need to mobilize around racist policing and incarceration in the wake of a police murder of another unarmed teen, Michael Brown, in the suburbs of St. Louis in 2014. Racial identity is a unifying feature of BLM, as was gender identity in the feminist movements that Beauvoir supported in the 1960s; yet both managed to successfully collaborate with progressive movements. Protest groups such as Antifa and gun control groups supported BLM. Their success in collaboration is evident in their recruitment of white supporters. However this was not without controversy: many members welcomed alliance and coalitional politics, while others felt white protestors in Portland detracted from their struggle and rallied around identity.

To circle back to my initial concern: collaboration across difference is a challenge. Black Lives Matter faces tensions with other movements as well as within its own movement. BLM is unified by the goal of subverting systemic racism; but there are different tactics, concerns, and interests that direct such movements. There are tensions between reformers and revolutionaries: those who want to work within the system to challenge some of the impediments Black people face versus those who want to upend capitalism; those who are committed to coalitional strategies versus those who are committed to identity; those who endorse symbolic tactics versus those who seek concrete changes in policy and procedures. Like Beauvoir, BLM recognizes both cultural and socio-economic or material barriers to equality. Respect and visibility are required (more Black actors, professionals, entrepreneurs, etc.), but tackling systemic racism that involves police reform as well as systemic poverty is more difficult to achieve. So far, BLM has been successful in managing differences in tactics and concerns within the movement. This has possibly been facilitated by their de-centralized and democratic structure, though success is not guaranteed. Beauvoir's words around political movements are worth remembering: acknowledging ambiguity, incompleteness, and failure does not undermine the prospects of radical change, but it does qualify what one can expect. Affective events—like the witnessing of George Floyd's murder, footballers taking the knee, or statues being toppled—all contributed to the movement, yet this is not sufficient to sustain commitment in the long run. Thoughtfulness and persuasive arguments are vital, as are strong organizations to sustain the cultural and policy changes required to realize aspirations. We are reminded of the absence of organizations in the Occupy movement and the ensuing dispersion of their energy.

Notes

1 Simone de Beauvoir, *Ethics of Ambiguity*, trans. Bernard Frechtman (New York: Citadel, 1948), 14; hereafter cited as EA in the text.
2 Simone de Beauvoir, *The Useless Mouth and Other Literary Works*, ed. Margaret A. Simons and Marybeth Timmerman (Urbana: University of Illinois Press, 2011), 199.

3 Elaine Stavro, *Emancipatory Thinking: Simone de Beauvoir and Contemporary Political Thought* (Montreal: McGill-Queen's University Press, 2018), 194.
4 Ontology is concerned with what all entities in the widest sense share—their essences, whereas ontic refers to empirical or historical/geographical manifestations of existence.
5 Judith Butler, *Notes Towards a Performative Theory of Assembly* (Cambridge, MA: Harvard University Press, 2015), 16.
6 Lori Jo Marso, *Politics with Beauvoir: Freedom in the Encounter* (Durham, NC: Duke University Press, 2017), 3.
7 Jodi Dean, *Crowds and Party* (London: Verso, 2016), 178.
8 Ibid., 120.
9 Ibid., 3.
10 In *Crowds and Party* Dean sees the party as a "psychic space" (181), an antidote to "autonomous individuality" (4), and the affectlessness and narcissism of neoliberalism. But let's remember that the party is also the place where decisions are coordinated, and mid- and long-term goals set. Thus, procedures of debate ought to be put in place to accept different opinions and tolerate criticism. Dean overplays the importance of cultivating and sustaining affective bonds, displacing the importance of reflective capacities and ironing out inclusive procedures.
11 Simone de Beauvoir, *The Second Sex*, trans. Constance Borde and Sheila Malovany-Chevallier (New York: Vintage, 2011), 56.
12 Simone de Beauvoir, *The Blood of Others*, trans. Yvonne Moyse and Roger Senhouse (Harmondsworth, UK: Penguin, 1966); hereafter referred to in-text as BOO.
13 Simone de Beauvoir, *The Force of Circumstance*, trans. Richard Howard (New York: Paragon House, 1992), 384.
14 Ibid., 652.
15 Dean, *Crowds and Party*, 3.
16 Stavro, *Emancipatory Thinking*, 267–315.
17 Stefan Jonsson, "The Art of Protest: Understanding and Misunderstanding Monstrous Events," *Theory & Event* 24, no. 2 (2021): 520–521.
18 Ibid., 514.
19 Ibid., 523.
20 Beauvoir's 'realist' novel—which emphasized plot, narrative, character development, and authorial voice—departed from the trends in French literary and cultural practices of the 1950s and 1960s. The *Nouveau Roman*, the French New Wave in cinema, and the *Tel Quel* literary group spurned these traditional literary forms.
21 Clare Hemmings, "Affective Solidarity: Feminist Reflexivity and Political Transformation," *Feminist Theory* 13, no. 2 (2012): 147–161.
22 Simone de Beauvoir, *All Said and Done*, trans. Patrick O'Brien (New York: Paragon House, 1993), 130.
23 Simone de Beauvoir, "Literature and Metaphysics," in *Philosophical Writings*, ed. Margaret A. Simons and Marybeth Timmerman (Urbana: University of Illinois Press, 2006), 261–268. This attention to the concrete and specific is evident not only in Beauvoir's approach to literature but also in her philosophic statements. In *The Second Sex*, she is explicit: "When I use the word 'woman' or 'feminine' I obviously refer to no archetype, to no immutable essence: 'in the present state of education and customs' must be understood to follow most of my affirmations" (279).
24 Nate Cohn and Kevin Quealy, "How Public Opinion Has Moved on Black Lives Matter," *New York Times*, June 10, 2020. https://www.nytimes.com/interactive/2020/06/10/upshot/black-lives-matter-attitudes.html.

25 Civiqs, "Do You Support or Oppose the Black Lives Matter Movement?" https://civiqs.com/results/black_lives_matter?annotations=true&uncertainty=true&zoomIn=true.
26 Tom Schad, "Nearly Four Years after Colin Kaepernick First Took a Knee, NFL Tides Are Turning on Protests during the National Anthem," *USA Today*, June 12, 2020. https://www.usatoday.com/story/sports/nfl/2020/06/12/nfl-protest-kneeling-national-anthem-colin-kaepernick-social-justice/5341565002/.
27 Monmouth University Polling Institute, "Protestors' Anger Justified Even If Actions May Not Be," June 2, 2020. https://www.monmouth.edu/polling-institute/reports/monmouthpoll_us_060220/.
28 Blake was shot in Kenosha, Wisconsin by a local police officer during a domestic dispute. This led to several nights of intense protests in Kenosha in which white vigilantes shot two protestors.
29 Thomas Fuller, "How One of America's Whitest Cities Became the Center of B.L.M. Protests," *New York Times*, July 24, 2020. https://www.nytimes.com/2020/07/24/us/portland-oregon-protests-white-race.html.

References

Beauvoir, Simone de. *Ethics of Ambiguity*. Translated by Bernard Frechtman. New York: Citadel, 1948.
Beauvoir, Simone de. *The Blood of Others*. Translated by Yvonne Moyse and Roger Senhouse. Harmondsworth: Penguin, 1966.
Beauvoir, Simone de. *The Force of Circumstance*. Translated by Richard Howard. New York: Paragon House, 1992.
Beauvoir, Simone de. *All Said and Done*. Translated by Patrick O'Brien. New York: Paragon House, 1993.
Beauvoir, Simone de. "Literature and Metaphysics." In *Philosophical Writings*, edited by Margaret A. Simons and Marybeth Timmerman, 261–268. Urbana: University of Illinois Press, 2006.
Beauvoir, Simone de. *The Second Sex*. Translated by Constance Borde and Sheila Malovany-Chevallier. New York: Vintage, 2011.
Beauvoir, Simone de. *The Useless Mouth and Other Literary Works*. Edited by Margaret A. Simons and Marybeth Timmerman. Urbana: University of Illinois Press, 2011.
Butler, Judith. *Notes Towards a Performative Theory of Assembly*. Cambridge, MA: Harvard University Press, 2015.
Civiqs, "Do You Support or Oppose the Black Lives Matter Movement?" https://civiqs.com/results/black_lives_matter?annotations=true&uncertainty=true&zoomIn=true.
Cohn, Nate, and Kevin Quealy. "How Public Opinion Has Moved on Black Lives Matter." *New York Times*, June 10, 2020. https://www.nytimes.com/interactive/2020/06/10/upshot/black-lives-matter-attitudes.html.
Dean, Jodi. *Crowds and Party*. London: Verso, 2016.
Grant, Laurens (director) and Jesse Williams (producer). *Stay Woke: The Black Lives Matter Documentary*. (2016) https://www.youtube.com/watch?v=eIoYtKOqxeU.
Hemmings, Clare. "Affective Solidarity: Feminist Reflexivity and Political Transformation." *Feminist Theory* 13, no. 2 (2012): 147–161.
Jonsson, Stefan. "The Art of Protest: Understanding and Misunderstanding Monstrous Events." *Theory & Event* 24, no. 2 (2021): 511–536.

Monmouth University Polling Institute. "Protestors' Anger Justified Even If Actions May Not Be." June 2, 2020. https://www.monmouth.edu/polling-institute/reports/monmouthpoll_us_060220/.

Marso, Lori Jo. *Politics with Beauvoir: Freedom in the Encounter*. Durham, NC: Duke University Press, 2017.

Schad, Tom. "Nearly Four Years after Colin Kaepernick First Took a Knee, NFL Tides Are Turning on Protests during the National Anthem." *USA Today*, June 12, 2020. https://www.usatoday.com/story/sports/nfl/2020/06/12/nfl-protest-kneeling-national-anthem-colin-kaepernick-social-justice/5341565002/.

Stavro, Elaine. *Emancipatory Thinking: Simone de Beauvoir and Contemporary Political Thought*. Montreal: McGill-Queen's University Press, 2018.

INDEX

abortion 153–155, 156; Yugoslavia and US 192–193
Adebayo, A. 157
aesthetic sphere 219–222
affect 15; individual vs collective 214–217, 221; and myth: political mobilization 13–15
Ahmed, S. 93, 101–102
Algeria 169; war rape victim 121, 198, 215–216, 217
Altman, M. 52
ambiguity 212–213; *see also* Black Feminist perspective on ambiguity
ancient civilizations and myths 49, 51, 58
Anderson, P. S. 51, 52
Andreas-Salomé, L. 138
anonymity and epistemic justice: Balkan rape victims 195–197
"apprenticeship of freedom" 118, 119–120
"apprenticeship in violence" 172
Arendt, H. 3, 17
Arp, K. 112–113, 117–118, 119

bad faith *see* old age (authenticity vs bad faith)
Balkan women and rape ("I didn't ask for it") 186–187; anonymity and epistemic justice 195–197; backlash and Balkan masculinity 197–200; guilt and otherness 187–91; resistance and resignation 191–194

Bardot (BB) and modern France 67–70, 198–199; as national myth 74–81; rewriting the Eternal Feminine myth 70–74
Bauer, N. 35
becoming a woman 56–57, 127, 128, 171–172, 188
Belle, K. 20
Benjamin, W. 16
Bennett, B. 155
Bergoffen, D. 141
Bernasconi, R. 117
birth control/contraception 153, 156
Black colonized women's rights and freedom 111, 116–121; existential ethics vs philosophy of freedom 112–113, 117; Martinique 114–116, 117, 120–121
Black Feminist perspective on ambiguity 91–94; 2020 events 97–99; ambiguity as useful tool 104–106; Beauvoirian ambiguity 99–101; early influence of Beauvoir 95–96; growing with Beauvoir 96–97; mapping ambiguities 103–104; positionality of author 94; use/ usefulness as concept and criteria 93, 101–103
Black Lives Matter (BLM) movement 98–99, 222–225
Blagojević, M. 199–200
Blake, J. 223–224

The Blood of Others (novel) 214–215, 216, 220–221
Bosanac, G. 193
Bottici, C. 14, 51, 56–57
Boupacha, D. 121, 198, 215, 217
boys: "apprenticeship in violence" 172
Braidotti, R. 51, 53
brand/branding of Bardot (BB) 74, 77, 78–79
Brown, M. 225
burqinis 69
Butler, J. 16, 169, 170, 212

Card, C. 173, 174–175
celebrity culture 72–73, 74
Chancel, J. 75–76, 81–82
choice *see* expectant anxiety/pregnancy; freedom
Churchill, W. 138
Cicero 150
Cixous, H. 51
class and Bardot (BB) phenomenon 72
class struggle and sex struggle 193–194
Cohen-Shabot, S. 141
collectivism *see* individualism/singularity vs collectivism
colonialism 168–170: *see also* Algeria; Black colonized women's rights and freedom; *see also* Martinique
Communist Party (CPF) 213, 214, 217–219
complicity: of Balkan rape victims 197; as impediment to freedom 213; old age stereotypes 139
contemporary political theory 13; lived experience 18–21; political mobilization 13–15; resistance strategies 16–18
contraception/birth control 153, 156
Cornell, D. 52–53
counter-violence 175–178; and institutional reform 16–18; *Promising Young Woman* (film) 178–181
COVID-19 pandemic 97–98, 99
critical phenomenology 93–94
'culture of praxis' 102

Daly, M. 51
de Gaulle, C. 75, 82
Dean, J. 213–214, 215, 216, 217, 218, 221
death in childbirth 148, 156
deep myths *see* myths
Despot, B. 193

Devi, S. P. 177–178
dialectical conversion 219
disability and illness in old age 134, 137–138, 141–142
Dotson, K. 102
Duncan, I. 156
Duras, M. 80

education and employment: Martinique 120–121; Yugoslavia 194
embodiment: male and female 152; pregnant 148–150
emotions *see* affect
entitlement, as problem of incel ambivalence 34, 39, 43
epistemic justice and anonymity: Balkan rape victims 195–197
eroticism *see* sexuality/eroticism
Eternal Feminine myth and Bardot (BB) 70–74
existentialism: Black 101; myth of Woman 60–61; and progressive-poststructuralism 51–52; vs philosophy of freedom 112–113, 117
expectant anxiety/pregnancy 147–148, 151–158; ethical, political, and medical ends 158–159; phenomenologies of pregnant embodiment 148–150; *Second Sex* 150–151; translations of anxiety 148, 151–152

Facebook: "I didn't ask for it" movement 187–188, 191–192, 195, 196, 197–198, 200–201
Fanon, F. 168–170
feminine body 59–60
Femininity, patriarchal concept of 54, 58–60
feminists of color: critique of lived experience 19–20; *see also* Black colonized women's rights and freedom
Flaubert, G. 137
Floyd, G. 98, 222–223, 224
Foucault, M. 2–3, 15, 18–19
France *see* Bardot (BB) and modern France
freedom: and history 218–219; limits to 212–213; myth of 61–62; and oppression 168; of self and others 112–113, 116–118, 214; *see also* Black colonized women's rights and

freedom; old age (authenticity
vs bad faith)
Freud, S. 138
Fricker, M. 195–196
Fullilove, B. 100–101

gender, normative, as oppressive system 170–173
gender equality: class struggle and sex struggle 193–194; France 71; France and US, compared 68
gender-neutrality 52–53, 71–72
gendered power relations 190–191
Gordon, L. 101
guilt and otherness: Balkans rape victims 187–191
Gulabi Gang, India 177–178

Habermas, J. 14
habit and old age 133
Halimi, G. 121
Haraway, D. 51, 52, 53
Hecht, G. 82–83
Hegel, G.W.F. 112, 189, 214, 219
Heinämaa, S. 151, 153
hermeneutical injustice 196
Hill Collins, P. 20
history and freedom 217–219
Hoang, S. 157
hooks, b. 95, 96
Hugo, V. 137–138
hypochondria and old age 134

identity of 'colonized person' 169–170
illness and disability in old age 134, 137–138, 141–142
impoverishment and bad faith in old age 132–135
incel violence 31–32; dream of sovereignty 39–42; problem of ambivalence 32–34; sovereign subjects and Woman as Other 34–39; unbecoming sovereign 42–43
India: Gulabi Gang 177–178
individualism/singularity vs collectivism 212, 213–219, 221; freedom of self and others 112–113, 116–117, 214
infanticide 149, 154
infertility 157
institutional reform 17
institutional and structural violence 168–175
internalization and self-constitution 173

International Simone de Beauvoir Society: Conference (2016) 96; President 97
Intersectionality 13, 20; ambiguity 96–97
Irigaray, L. 52

Japan: *mizuko kuyō* memorial and Jizō statues for unborn children 154–155
Jonsson, S. 219–221
Joseph, R. 105

Kaepernick, C. 223
Kant, I. 112
Keum, T-Y. 49–50, 53, 54, 56
Kierkegaard, S. 151–152
Kristeva, J. 149
Kruks, S. 19, 100

Lacan, J. 213, 214
Le Doeuff, M. 51–52
Le Pen, M. 69
Leiris, M. 59
Lenin, V. 217, 218
Lennon, K. and Wilde, A. 141
Lévi-Strauss, 189
Levy, R. 74
literary and deep myths *see* myths
lived experience 18–21; and ambiguity 99–100, 103–104, 105, 112; and "being-in-the-world" 128; and political action of women 115–116; pregnancy 150, 153–158
Lolita syndrome 71
Lorde, A. 93, 95, 102
Lugones, M. 94, 104, 105
Lundquist, C. 149, 150, 156, 158

MacKinnon, C. 173–174, 175
Manne, K. 33
marital rape, Yugoslavia 194
Marso, L. J. 113, 212–213
Martin, T. 224
Martinique 114–116, 117, 120, 121
Marx/Marxism 112, 217, 218, 219, 222; analytical approach 13, 17, 18
Mason, H. V. 98
"Me Too" and Balkans women's movements 186, 187, 191, 195, 200–201
men/masculinity: Balkan 199–200; Black American, police murders of 98–99, 222–225; and female sexual maturation 171–172; old age 131, 132,

134–135, 136–138, 140; ontology and epistemology 190; perpetrators of sexual violence 188, 195, 196, 199, 201; *see also* Other, Woman as; patriarchy
mental illness and motherhood 148, 158
Michelangelo 137
Mills, C.W. 197
miscarriage 153, 154, 156
moral vs ontological freedom 116–120
morality, existential 60–61
motherhood: and family role, Yugoslavia 192–193, 194, 199; *see also* expectant anxiety/pregnancy
The Mothers (novel) 155
myths 14–15, 48, 50; contemporary literary and deep myths 49–50; literary myths and patriarchal oppression 53–58; myth-affirming feminist tradition 51–53; Woman as deep myth 58–62; *see also* Bardot (BB) and modern France

Nardal, P. 111, 114–117, 119, 120–121
Nature: men as sovereign subjects and Women as Other 36–37, 38–39, 42, 43
nonviolence 16–17, 18
Nussbaum, M. 139

objectification: and entitlement: problem of incel ambivalence 32–34, 39, 43; self-objectification in old age 133–134
Occupy movement 213, 225
old age (authenticity vs bad faith) 127–128; "active" old age 135–138; "desert" world 132–135, 140; freedom and rethinking "the project" 141–142; from "within" and "without" 128–131; neither/nor antithesis 138–141; relationship with time 151
ontological and the ontic, respect for 212–213
ontological vs moral freedom 116–120
ontology and epistemology, masculine 190
oppression: systemic 168–173; Western and non-Western women 118–120
Ostriker, A. 51
Other: old as 130; Woman as 34–39, 40–43, 54–55, 120, 127, 188–190, 217–218

Parshley, H. M. 148
passivity 173, 189, 199; in old age 130, 135, 151; in pregnancy 150

patriarchy: concept of Femininity 54, 58–60; myths and oppression 53–58; rape culture 190–201; *see also* men/masculinity; Other, Woman as
'personal is political' 102
phenomenology: aesthetic sphere 220–221; and ambiguity *see* Black feminist perspective; feminine body 59–60; pregnant embodiment 148–150; *see also* lived experience
philosophy: critique of 100; and 'culture of praxis' 102
police murders of Black American men 98–99, 222–225
political mobilization: affect and myth 13–15; *see also* protest politics
possessions in old age 133–134
praxis 102, 129–130
pregnancy *see* expectant anxiety
poststructuralism 51–52
Promising Young Woman (film) 178–181
protest politics 213–217; *see also* political mobilization
puberty 171

racism: and right-wing politics, France 69, 80–81, 82; *see also* Black Lives Matter (BLM) movement
Radulović, M. 188–189, 191, 196, 198
rape *see* Balkan women and rape ("I didn't ask for it"); sexual violence
reciprocal recognition 129–130
rejected/denied pregnancies 149
religion: "Christianity and Marxism" 218; French Muslim women 69; memorial and statues for unborn children, Japan 154–155; pregnancy 155–156, 157; social duty of women 120
Renoir, P-A. 137–138
resistance to violence 16–18; and resignation 191–194
retirement 129–130, 132–133
rights 17, 18; abortion 192–193; voting 114–116, 117; *see also* Black colonized women's rights and freedom
Rihoit, C. 76, 77, 80, 81–82
Rodger, E. 31, 32, 33, 34, 39–43
Rousseau, J-J. 130–131
Russell, B. 136

Sartre, J-P. 18, 58, 116–117, 131, 151–152, 222

Scott, J. 19
Scott Littleton, C. 53
self: and others, freedom of 112–113, 116–118, 214; pregnancy and childbirth 157–158
self-assertion 119–120, 121
self-constitution 173
self-defence 177
self-harm 173
self-objectification 133–134
September 11 terrorist attacks 173–175
seriousness 62–63, 128
sexual humiliation 189–190
sexual intercourse 172; and rape, Balkan law 191
sexual violence: childhood to adolescent transitions 170–173; and counter-violence 177–181; and terrorism 173–175; *see also* Balkan women and rape ("I didn't ask for it")
sexuality/eroticism 68–69, 71, 73, 78–80, 95; in old age 130; and other types of being 214
Sharpley-Whiting, T. D. 114–115, 120
Shaw, G.B. 136
singularity *see* individualism/singularity vs collectivism
social and biological old age 128–131
social class *see* class
social construction of experience 19
social duty 116, 120
social media: Black Lives Matter (BLM) movement 222; *see also* Facebook
socialism: Yugoslavia 192–194; *see also* Communist Party (CPF)
Sorbonne 95, 111, 120
Spock, B. 136
St-Tropez 79
'Stacy' meme 34, 42, 43
statues/memorials: dismantling of 223; for unborn children, Japan 154–155
subject and object ambiguity 101
Swift, J. 136

Taylor, D. 189–190
teenage pregnancy 155
terrorism and sexual violence 173–175
testimonial injustice 196
"third-person" stance 19

thoughtfulness 211; aesthetic sphere 219–222; Black Lives Matter (BLM) movement 222–225; Communist Party (PCF) 213, 214, 217–219; protest politics 213–217; respect for ontological and ontic 212–213
time: and anxiety 152; and old age 130–131; "temporal structures" 151, 153
Tito, J. B. 192, 193
toolkit approach vs totalizing theory 2–3
Trump, D. 224

unrealizability of old age 129
US: abortion right 192–193; *The Mothers* (novel) 155; reception of Bardot (BB) 68, 74, 77; September 11 terrorist attacks 173–175
use/usefulness as concept and criteria 93, 101–103

Vadim, R. 68, 76, 77, 199
Verdi, G. 137
victim-blaming: Balkan rape victims 195–197
Vincendeau, G. 73–74, 80
violence: structural and institutional 168–175; *see also* Balkan women and rape ("I didn't ask for it"); counter-violence; incel violence; sexual violence
voting rights 114–116, 117

Wallace, Jr., W. 98–9
war rapes: Algeria 121, 198, 215–216; Balkans 197
Weiss, G. et al. 93
Western and non-Western women 118–120
Whitman, W. 138
Women's Anti-fascist Front (WAF), Yugoslavia 192–193
Women's Liberation Movement (MLF) 176–177
Wood, C. 196
World Health Organization 99, 158

Young, I. M. 148–149, 150, 152, 156

Zajko, V. and Leonard, M. 51
Zemmour, E. 82